AMERICAN
ARBITRATION ASSOCIATION

HANDBOOK ON CONSTRUCTION ARBITRATION AND ADR

EXECUTIVE EDITORS:

Thomas E. Carbonneau
Orlando Distinguished Professor of Law
Penn State University

Philip J. McConnaughay
Dean & Donald J. Farage Professor of Law
Penn State University

ASSISTANT EDITOR:

Crystal L. Stryker
Penn State University

Questions About This Publication

For assistance with shipments, billing or other customer service matters, please call our Customer Services Department at:

1-631-350-2100

To obtain a copy of this book, call our Sales Department:

1-631-351-5430
Fax: 1-631-351-5712

Toll Free Order Line:
1-800-887-4064 (United States & Canada)

See our web page about this book:
http://www.arbitrationlaw.com

COPYRIGHT © 2007
by JurisNet, LLC

All Rights Reserved
Printed in the United States of America
ISBN-13: 978-1-929446-44-5
ISBN-10: 1-929446-44-6

JurisNet, LLC
71 New Street
Huntington, New York 11743
USA
www.arbitrationlaw.com

INTRODUCTION

It is with both pride and pleasure that the Penn State University Dickinson School of Law and the Institute of Dispute Resolution present the AAA HANDBOOKS on arbitration and ADR. The HANDBOOKS contain recent important publications on the subject matter of each HANDBOOK written by authors who are recognized specialists in that area. Often the authors have both national and international reputations in the area. The contributions cover a wide array of topics that are of substantial interest in the field and provide analytically thorough, professional, and practical answers to problems that have emerged in the field.

The articles were selected from an extensive body of writings and, in the main, represent world class assessments of arbitration and practice. All the major facets of the field are addressed. The articles provide the reader with comprehensive and accurate information, lucid evaluations, and an indication of future developments. They not only acquaint, but also ground the reader in the field.

The American Arbitration Association, Juris Publishing, Inc., and Penn State welcome the opportunity to provide readers with a body of knowledge and interpretation that will allow them to take an active and effective part in arbitration and ADR. Arbitration and ADR are rapidly emerging as the new vehicles for legality and fairness in the social order—both domestically and internationally.

—Thomas E. Carbonneau
Orlando Distinguished Professor of Law
Penn State University

TABLE OF CONTENTS

Introduction iii

Chapter One: ADR in the Construction Industry 1

    I. **The Broadened Scope of ADR in Construction Disputes** 1

        Alternative Dispute Resolution in the Construction Industry
        By James P. Groton

    II. **American Institute of Architects (AIA) Expands the Use of ADR** 19

        Construction ADR at Its Best: The New AIA A-201 Document
        By Howard G. Goldberg

    III. **Using Hybrid ADR Techniques in Construction Disputes** 25

        "Hybrid ADR" in the Construction Industry
        By James H. Keil

    IV. **The Duty to Disclose** 39

        Neutral Corner—The Duty to Disclose
        By Neil Carmichael

    V. **Postponement Requests** 41

        Neutral Corner—Dealing with Postponement Requests
        By Neil Carmichael

    VI. **Using a Neutral Architect** 43

        Dispute Resolution Using a Neutral Architect
        By Jack Kemp

Chapter Two: Managing Risk and Avoiding Disputes 51

    I. **Identify and Manage Project Risk to Contain Claims** 51

        The Key to Claims-Free Projects— Identifying and Managing Construction Project Risk
        By Ava J. Abramowitz

II. Preventing Contract Disputes 65
Strategies to Prevent Construction Contract Disputes
By Luc Picard

III. Industry Guidelines for Avoiding and Resolving Construction Disputes 71
ASA/AGC/ASC Joint Guideline on the Avoidance and Resolution of Construction Disputes
ASA/AGC/ASC

IV. Tailoring Design-Build Agreements to Avoid and Resolve Conflicts 75
Avoiding Disputes in the Design-Build Environment
By Michael C. Loulakis

V. Waivers of Consequential Damages 83
Negotiating Consequential Damages Waivers
By Charles M. Sink

Chapter Three: Dispute Resolution Boards 87

I. New AAA Protocol for Dispute Resolution Boards 87
A New Look at DRBs—AAA Offers New DRB Roster and Protocol
By Robert J. Smith & Robert A. Rubin

II. Using Dispute Resolution Boards for Real Time Solutions 95
Dispute Review Boards: Resolving Construction Disputes in Real Time
By Robert J. Smith

III. Experience with Advisory Dispute Review Boards 103
Expanding the DRB's Role—The Boston Central Artery Tunnel Project's Experience with Advisory Dispute Review Boards
By Brison S. Shipley

TABLE OF CONTENTS

Chapter Four: Partnering 111

  I. The Importance of Trust in the Partnering Process 111

    I Don't Trust You, But Why Don't You Trust Me? Recognizing the Fragility of Trust and Its Importance in the Partnering Process
    By Jeffrey S. Busch & Nicole Hantusch

  II. AAA Task Force Guide to Partnering 129

    Building Success for the 21st Century: A Guide to Partnering in the Construction Industry
    Report of the Dispute Avoidance and Resolution Task Force of the American Arbitration Association

  III. The Benefits of Partnering 139

    The Benefits of Partnering
    By James H. Keil

  IV. Using Partnering to Manage Construction Disputes 147

    Partnering and the Management of Construction Disputes
    By Steve Pinnell

  V. Effective Partnering 157

    Practical Tips for Effective Partnering
    By Bruce Johnsen

  VI. "Beware of Partnering" 161

    Team Players-Not "Partners"! "Partnering" Does Not Create "Partners"
    By Robert S. Peckar

  VII. The Limitations of Partnering 165

    The Truth about Partnering—Limitations and Solutions
    By Allen L. Overcash

Chapter Five: Arbitration 171

I. Drafting Arbitration Clauses 171
Dangers in Drafting the Arbitration Clause
By Stanley P. Sklar

II. Effective Construction Arbitration Advocacy 175
*Tips on Advocacy in Arbitration Before
an Industry Arbitrator*
By Jorge R. Cibran

III. Selecting an Arbitrator 179
Unilateral Selection of the Arbitrator
By Robert J. MacPherson & Sarah B. Biser

IV. Avoiding Litigation over Arbitrability 183
Removing Roadblocks to Arbitration
By Paul M. Lurie

V. Guidelines to Writing Explanatory Awards 187
The ABCs of Writing a "Reasoned Award"
By James R. Holbrook

VI. Jurisdictional Labor Disputes and Subcontracting 195
*Between the Devil and the Deep Blue Sea—
Subcontracting and Jurisdictional
Labor Disputes*
By Gregory R. Begg

Chapter Six: Mediation 199

I. Successful Mediation 199
Recipe for Success in Construction Mediation
By John P. Madden

II. Tips for Better Mediation from the AAA 215
Mediator Wisdom from the Experts
By James Acret

III. Using Procedure for Effective Mediation 221
*The Importance of Process Design to a
Successful Mediation*
By Paul M. Lurie

TABLE OF CONTENTS

    IV. Effective Advocacy in Mediation 225
        Some Guidelines for Effective Advocacy in Mediation
        By Howard D. Venzie, Jr.

    V. Litigators and Mediation 231
        Should Trial Counsel Represent the Client
        in Mediation?
        By Robert Korn

    VI. Experts and Mediation 235
        The Expert's Role in Construction Mediation
        By Richard Lamb

    VII. Closure Issues 239
        Closure Issues in Construction Mediation
        By Howard D. Venzie, Jr.

    VIII. Mediators Not Giving Participants
        What They Want 247
        Construction Attorneys' Mediation Preferences
        Surveyed—Is There a Gap between Supply
        and Demand?
        By Dean B. Thomson

    IX. Mediator Confidentiality and Court Testimony 255
        Danger Looms for Mediation—Mediators
        Likely to Testify under UMA Draft
        By Mark Appel

Chapter Seven: Large and Complex Case Management 259

    I. Managing the Preliminary Hearing under Rule L-4 259
        Management of the Preliminary Hearing
        under Construction Rule L-4 for Large,
        Complex Cases
        By Anthony E. Battelle

    II. Large-Case Management Techniques for Arbitrators 271
        Now Is the Time to Control the Big Case
        By Allen L. Overcash

III. Selecting a Mediator for a Complex Dispute 277
Choosing the Right Mediator for a Complex Construction Dispute
By Joseph C. Malpasuto

IV. Effective Mediation Techniques for Complex Cases 281
Effective Mediation Techniques in Complex Multiparty Synthetic Stucco Cases
By C. Allen Gibson, Jr.

Chapter Eight: International Construction Dispute Resolution 287

I. Strengths and Weaknesses of the U.S. And English Systems 287
Comparing Dispute Review Boards and Adjudication
By James P. Groton, Robert A. Rubin & Bettina Quintas

II. Dispute Resolution Advisors in Hong Kong 293
The Dispute Resolution Advisor as an ADR Method in Hong Kong Construction Disputes
By John W.K. Luk & W.T. Wong

III. Construction Arbitration in The Netherlands 299
Arbitration in the Building Industry in The Netherlands
By Etienne van Bladel

Index 311

Note on Sources 321

CHAPTER ONE

ADR IN THE CONSTRUCTION INDUSTRY

I. The Broadened Scope of ADR in Construction Disputes

Alternative Dispute Resolution in the Construction Industry[†]

by James P. Groton*

The term "ADR" has moved far beyond its original use as referring to arbitration and mediation, the traditional dispute resolution "alternatives" to the formal judicial process. Within the last several years the scope of ADR has broadened to cover a vast array of techniques that have been developed not only to resolve existing disputes, but also to control, minimize and even prevent disputes. These techniques can be used selectively in a variety of ways to fit a multitude of relationships and business situations, particularly in the construction industry. Beyond the mere resolution of disputes, these ADR systems actually change attitudes and behavior so that further disputes are prevented or their impact minimized.

The Construction Industry Institute (CII) has concluded that "the U.S. construction industry is ill," and has complained that "litigation related to design and construction continues to increase." *Engineering-News Record*, the weekly magazine of the construction industry, has editorially lamented "the awful litigious nature of this industry." The Business Roundtable has concluded that the U.S. construction industry is one of the country's least efficient industries, and blames much of this inefficiency on the "adversarial dance" between the parties to the

---

[†] This article has been excerpted and reprinted with permission from the chapter entitled *The Progressive or 'Stepped' Approach to ADR: Designing Systems to Prevent, Control, and Resolve Disputes*, by James P. Groton. It appears in the CONSTRUCTION RESOLUTION FORMBOOK, (copyright 1997 John Wiley and Sons, Inc.).

* The author is a retired senior partner of Sutherland, Asbill & Brennan. His principal areas of law practice involved ADR, problem solving and litigation, especially in the construction industry. He is a long-time panelist and a member of the board of directors of the American Arbitration Association and is a past recipient of the Whitney North Seymour Medal for outstanding contributions to the responsible use of ADR.

construction project, which creates "a constant state of confrontation." It is ironic that the one industry in the country that more than all others depends on coordination, cooperation and teamwork among multiple participants should be the country's most adversarial industry.

This adversarial attitude is reflected in antagonistic relationships, "win-lose" attitudes and general dissension. Construction disputes and claims have become more common. Lawyers are more involved in disputes and claims. The dispute process is more legalized. There is a tendency to postpone the resolution of many disputes, especially those disputes involving money, until after construction is complete. Unresolved problems that hold up payments create uncertainty as to the outcome and engender even more adversarial relationships, which cause delays and disruptions to the project. These delays and disruptions adversely affect not only the project completion time, they cause added costs to the project participants, which in turn breed new claims and disputes in an ever-increasing "spiral of conflict." Massive project-end arbitrations and court cases have become common. The strains in relationships while all these problems accumulate have affected the way projects are constructed. The transaction costs of all of these disputes have increased geometrically. The costs to the industry in fees paid to lawyers, claims consultants and expert witnesses, and in the lost time of the parties themselves are incalculable.[1]

Construction Contributions to ADR

As a reaction to this ever-increasing spiral of conflict, a quiet revolution has been developing within the industry to find ways of dealing with the prevailing climate of litigiousness. Beginning several years ago, The Business Roundtable and the Construction Industry Institute began to investigate the basic root causes of construction problems and pioneered research of the "construction cost influence curve," the sources and causes of construction disputes, "best" construction practices, the disputes potential index to predict the likelihood of disputes on a project, realistic risk allocation, and the use of incentives and long-term partnering to foster cooperative relationships. The U.S. Army Corps of Engineers has been using mediation and mini-trials to resolve some massive disputes and has

---

[1] Adapted with permission from materials that the author contributed to PREVENTING AND RESOLVING CONSTRUCTION DISPUTES (CPR 1991). ©1991. CPR INSTITUTE FOR DISPUTE RESOLUTION. All rights reserved.

instituted successful project-specific partnering. Civil engineers, contractors and some results-oriented public owners have invented dispute review boards to resolve disputes at the jobsite level in major tunneling and civil projects; others in the construction industry have expanded that technique to cover industrial and commercial buildings as well. Innovative neutrals have developed variations and improvements on the mediation process. Summary advisory arbitrations have been employed to resolve major disputes.

The emphasis in most of the newly developed devices has been on moving ADR "upstream," closer to the sources of disputes; restoring concepts of reasonable dealing and teamwork into the conduct of construction projects; preventing or at least minimizing problems; fostering mutual problem solving; encouraging the earliest possible resolution of problems; and assisting the disputing parties to reach a joint resolution of their dispute during the course of construction so that valuable business relationships can be preserved. Now that these individual new private dispute resolution techniques have been developed for the construction industry and have been proved to be successful, they are beginning to be combined into systems that can prevent, control and screen all disputes, so that it is possible to have a construction project where no disputes are left unresolved at the completion of construction.

Development of ADR Systems

Although a variety of dispute prevention, control and resolution techniques have been developed for use specifically on construction projects, and at different stages in the evolution of disputes, the tendency has been to use these techniques on an ad hoc basis. Experience has shown that no single dispute resolution technique, regardless of how good it is, can be used for all disputes, or for different stages of the same dispute. The causes of disputes come from so many different sources and are so complex that there is no "one size fits all" technique for dispute resolution. At the same time, the spiral of conflict, which can cause a simple problem to develop into a difference of opinion, then a disagreement, then a dispute, and ultimately conflict, makes it impossible to use a single dispute resolution technique to deal with all successive stages in the development of a dispute. As simple problems develop into conflicts, there is an escalation in project costs, in levels of hostility between the parties, in the amount of time it takes to achieve ultimate resolution of the conflict, and in the transaction costs to the parties of resolving the conflict.

To deal with the complexities and escalations involved in the dispute process, it is helpful to consider three concepts or approaches to the intelligent management and control of both projects and disputes.

Cost influence curve. The first of these useful concepts is the cost influence curve developed as the result of CII research. This idea presents two fundamental project management concepts. First, the earlier and greater the emphasis on good project planning and design, the greater will be the payoff in cost savings during the later stages of the project. Conversely, the later in the project that critical decisions and changes are made, the greater is the cost of those decisions and changes. This idea, which is a more sophisticated extension of the traditional carpenter's adage "measure twice, saw once," is one of the most fundamental rules of good construction management and practice.

Management of disputes. The concept of the CII cost influence curve can also be applied to the handling of disputes. Just as construction projects have a life cycle, so do individual disputes, developing from simple problems into conflict in the ever-ascending spiral of conflict, unless they are properly managed and controlled. Applying the cost influence curve to disputes, it is axiomatic that the greater the emphasis on good dispute prevention and management planning during the earliest stages in the project or in the life of a dispute, the greater will be the payoff in cost savings and successful dispute resolution during the later stages of the project or of the individual dispute. Conversely, the later in the project or in the life of an individual dispute that attention is given to good dispute management, the greater is the cost, escalation in adversarial relationships, and the time it takes to resolve the dispute.

Dispute resolution systems. The best way to deal with disputes during the evolution of a construction project or the life of an individual dispute is not through the ad hoc application of individual dispute resolution techniques, but rather through a preplanned and well-managed "system" of dispute prevention, control and early resolution techniques. During recent years, the ADR community has developed and begun to implement the process of "ADR systems design." This is simply a process of analyzing the likelihood of a particular relationship or project to have disputes; determining the project's dispute resolution needs; and then designing a succession of techniques, filters, screens, and "safety nets" employing a series of ADR techniques that are best calculated to deal with a succession of different types of problems, at different stages in the life of the project, so that they are prevented, managed, controlled and ultimately resolved at the earliest possible time. The design of a dispute resolution system is not directed at settling a particular dispute, but rather at changing the overall pattern of dispute resolution and ultimately changing for the better the attitudes and relationships of the parties.

Good ADR systems design anticipates the types of problems that are likely to arise in a relationship or on a project and applies appropriate dispute control and resolution techniques to different types of problems, and to different stages in the development of a dispute, so that serious conflict is avoided. In these systems, disputes are approached as "problems to be solved," not "battles to be won."[2]

Spectrum of Techniques[3]

Today's construction industry members can choose from a vast spectrum of private dispute avoidance and resolution possibilities, and new techniques are being invented each day by imaginative professionals and practitioners in this field. This spectrum can be best illustrated by the stair-step sequential model, which depicts the broad range of dispute resolution approaches, beginning with prevention and ending with litigation. The rising steps in the model reflect escalating levels of dispute resolution and increasing levels of hostility and costs to the participants. Just as a strong early emphasis on the quality of the planning, design and engineering of a project can pay great dividends during the high-spending procurement and construction phases, the earlier the parties use dispute prevention and resolution techniques the greater will be the dividends to the project and the parties.

The use of prevention techniques, the step at the bottom of this stairway, creates the maximum harmony and involves the least cost. Negotiation to resolve construction problems involves cooperative effort among the parties and is relatively cost-free. If negotiations fail, the

---

[2] For general information on design of dispute resolution systems, *see* J.M. Brett, et. al., *Managing Conflict: The Strategy of Dispute Systems Design* (Bus. Wk. Executive Briefing Service, 1994); WILLIAM L. URY, ET. AL., GETTING DISPUTES RESOLVED: DESIGNING SYSTEMS TO CUT THE COST OF CONFLICT (1988); CATHY A. COSTANTINO & CHRISTINA SICKLES MERCHANT, DESIGNING CONFLICT MANAGEMENT SYSTEMS (1996).

[3] Adapted from James P. Groton, *Prompt and Constructive Resolution of Disputes in* CONSTRUCTION PROJECT FORMBOOK, Ch. 16 (Robert F. Cushman ed., 1994).

parties need to be assisted by a neutral. The standing neutral concept is a natural adjunct to the construction phase of a project, solves problems at the source, and is relatively inexpensive because problems are addressed relatively informally and while facts are fresh.

It is important to note at this point that if problems are not resolved by the time this level is reached, the costs of dispute resolution will escalate rapidly. If disputes cannot be disposed of at the source by the people directly involved in the project, or by the neutral advisors who have been keeping up with the project, then it becomes necessary to turn to outside consultants and lawyers who do not have first-hand familiarity with the project, to help with resolution. These people need to be educated about the history of the project; facts are not fresh; project personnel have dispersed; memories have become dim; recollections are conflicting; and the only reliable records are the thousands of documents that have been generated on the project. It therefore becomes necessary to reconstruct the project in a hearing room, based on documents and such other information as can be made available at the time, usually using outside consultants. These activities can be very expensive, and in many cases their costs eat up the profits of all of the parties involved in this exercise regardless of the outcome of this late dispute resolution process. The point in the dispute resolution continuum where resolution has to be turned over to outsiders has been identified by the Construction Industry Institute as the "Continental Divide" of dispute resolution: the point beyond which the spiral of conflict, cost, hostility and time needed for resolution begin to escalate so dramatically that the costs of resolution become essentially wasteful.

Moving up the stairway, mediations and mini-trials generally occur after a problem has become fully developed into a dispute. These processes generally require more preparation by the parties, and are more likely to require the services of lawyers. If problems are not consensually resolved through such procedures, the only remaining step is to turn the problem over to a third party for binding decision. This typically is a giant step, involving formal identification of opposing positions and issues and considerable preparation by the parties, typically with the assistance of lawyers, consultants, and expert witnesses, in an arbitration proceeding, a trial before a private judge, or the public and even more expensive step of litigation.

Following are examples of some techniques that can be incorporated into project documents and procedures to prevent, control, screen and resolve disputes.

Partnering

Partnering is a team-building effort in which the parties establish cooperative working relationships through a mutually developed, formal strategy of commitment and communication. It can be used for long-term relationships or on a project-specific basis. When used on a project-specific basis, partnering is usually instituted at the beginning of the construction process after the contractor has been selected, by holding a retreat among all project personnel who have leadership and management responsibilities. The participants, assisted by an independent facilitator, become acquainted with and understand each other's project objectives and expectations, recognize common aims, initiate open communications, and establish non-adversarial processes for resolving potential problems. Project-specific partnering, pioneered by the Army Corps of Engineers, shows great promise for improving cooperation and teamwork and helping to create a "healthy" project. Here is an example of a partnering specification adapted from an Arizona Department of Transportation project.

Sample Partnering Specification

A. Covenant of Good Faith and Fair Dealing

This contract imposes an obligation of good faith and fair dealing in its performance and enforcement.

The Contractor and the Owner, with a positive commitment to honesty and integrity, agree to the following mutual duties:

   a. Each will function within the laws and statutes applicable to their duties and responsibilities;
   b. Each will assist in the other's performance;
   c. Each will avoid hindering the other's performance;
   d. Each will proceed to fulfill its obligations diligently;
   e. Each will cooperate in the common endeavor of the contract.

B. Voluntary Partnering

The Owner intends to encourage the foundation of a cohesive partnering relationship with the Contractor and its principal subcontractors and suppliers. This relationship will be structured to draw on the strengths of each organization to identify and achieve reciprocal goals. The objectives are effective and efficient contract performance and completion within budget, on schedule, and in accordance with drawings and specifications.

This partnering relationship will be bilateral in makeup, and participation will be totally voluntary. Any cost associated with effectuating this relationship will be agreed to by both parties and will be shared equally.

To implement this partnering initiative prior to starting of work, prior to the preconstruction conference the Contractor's management personnel and the Owner's District Engineer will initiate a partnering development seminar/team-building workshop. These individuals will make arrangements to determine attendees at the workshop, agenda of the workshop, duration, and location. Persons required to be in attendance will be the Owner's Construction Supervisor and key project personnel; the Contractor's on-site project manager; and key project supervision personnel of both the prime and principal subcontractors and suppliers. The project design engineers, FHWA and key local government personnel will also be invited to attend as necessary. The contractors and the Owner will also be required to have Regional/District and Corporate/State level managers on the project team.

Follow-up workshops may be held periodically throughout the duration of the contract as agreed by the Contractor and the Owner.

The establishment of a partnering charter on a project will not change the legal relationship of the parties to the contract nor relieve either party from any of the terms of the contract.

Negotiation

Negotiation is a time-honored method of resolving disputes that arise during construction. However, there are many different techniques of negotiation. The most successful direct negotiation techniques are those in which the negotiators conduct their discussions on the basis of the respective interests of the parties, rather than the traditional approach of focusing on the positions of the parties. The following is a contract clause committing the parties to good faith negotiation:

Sample Good-Faith Negotiation Specification

The parties will attempt in good faith to resolve promptly any controversy or claim arising out of or relating to this agreement by negotiation between representatives of the parties who have authority to settle the controversy.

Step negotiation procedures are structured negotiations that can be used to break a standoff. Under this technique, if the jobsite representatives of different organizations are not able to resolve a problem at their level, their immediate superiors, who are not as closely identified with the problem, are asked to confer and try to resolve the problem. If they fail, the problem will be passed on to higher management in both organizations. Because of an intermediate manager's interest in keeping messy problems from bothering higher management and in demonstrating to higher management the manager's ability to solve problems, there is a built-in incentive to resolve disputes before they have to go to a higher level. The following language will implement this process:

Sample Step Negotiation Specification

If a controversy or claim should arise, the parties will attempt in good faith to resolve any controversy or claim arising out of or relating to this agreement promptly by step negotiations between managers and executives of the parties who have authority to settle the controversy.

If the controversy or claim cannot be resolved promptly by the most senior project site representatives of the parties, then the project managers for each party will meet at least once and will attempt to resolve the matter. Either project manager may request the other to meet within seven days, at a mutually agreed time and place.

If the matter has not been resolved within ten days of their first meeting, the project managers shall promptly prepare and exchange memoranda stating the issues in dispute and their position[s], summarizing the negotiations which have taken place and attaching relevant documents, and shall refer the matter to senior executives, who shall have authority to settle the dispute. The senior executives will promptly meet for negotiations to attempt to settle the dispute.

If the matter has not been resolved within ten days from the referral of the dispute to senior executives, either party may refer the dispute to another dispute resolution procedure.

Dispute Review Board

The dispute review board (DRB), a technique developed originally on large tunneling and civil projects, is a group of trusted experts, chosen by the parties at the commencement of a project, who will monitor the progress of the project and be available to render advisory decisions on short notice concerning any disputes the parties are not able to resolve themselves. The decisions are non-binding, but experience has shown that these panel decisions have generally been accepted by both parties without any attempt to seek relief from any other tribunal. This result is enhanced when there is a contract requirement that in the event of any subsequent arbitration or litigation, the DRB's decisions will be admissible in evidence. When used in accordance with the guidelines developed by the Underground Technology Research Council (UTRC), this technique has been remarkably successful in resolving disputes without arbitration or litigation.

Four critical elements are essential to the success of the dispute review board:

1. Early formation of the DRB;
2. Continuous DRB involvement;
3. Prompt action on any submitted disputes; and
4. Mutual selection and confidence in DRB members.

The best or classic example of the dispute review board technique is exemplified by the Dispute Review Board Specifications and Three-Party Agreement authored by the Technical Committee on Contracting Practices of the Underground Technology Research Council.[4]

An AAA publication, *Construction Industry Dispute Review Board Procedures of the American Arbitration Association*, proposes a somewhat less formal procedure for establishing and operating a dispute review board. These procedures attempt to follow the essential characteristics of the UTRC model that have proved to be successful. The chief difference between the AAA procedures and the UTRC procedures is that the AAA offers assistance to the parties in the selection of DRB members and provides administrative support to the

---

[4] For a checklist and analysis of the 22 characteristics that are essential to meet the UTRC model, *see* Michael C. Vorster, *Dispute Prevention and Resolution: Alternative Dispute Resolution in Construction with Emphasis on Dispute Review Boards*, Rep. to the Construction Industry Inst., Source Doc. No. 95, pp. 41-44 (1993).

DRB process. Under the AAA procedures, a simple agreement between the parties to institute a dispute review board "in accordance with the Dispute Review Board Procedures of the American Arbitration Association" incorporates by reference the AAA Dispute Review Board procedures. Language for implementing the AAA process follows:

Sample Agreement for AAA Dispute Review Board

The parties shall empanel a Dispute Review Board of three members in accordance with the Dispute Review Board Procedures of the American Arbitration Association. The Dispute Review Board, in close consultation with all interested parties, will assist and recommend the resolution of any disputes, claims and other controversies which may arise among the parties.

It is important to the success of a dispute review board that it follows the essential characteristics established by the UTRC model.[5] Also, the DRB provisions should be coordinated with other dispute resolution procedures required by the contract documents.

Standing Arbitration Panel

The standing or standby arbitration panel resembles the dispute review board in that an arbitrator or arbitration panel is selected and appointed at the beginning of the project for the purpose of becoming familiar with the project, to be available as needed throughout the construction period, and to act immediately to decide any disputes that the parties cannot resolve themselves. Its principal difference from the dispute review board concept is that the standing arbitrators make immediately binding decisions.

The existence of a pre-selected standing dispute review board or standing arbitrator or arbitrators already familiar with the project avoids many of the initial problems and delays that occur when selecting and appointing neutrals for a mini-trial or a conventional arbitration proceeding after a controversy has arisen. The ready availability of the panel, the speed with which it can render decisions and particularly the fact that this panel will hear every dispute that occurs during the history of the project all provide powerful incentives to the participants in the

---

[5] For an analysis of the preventive aspects of dispute review boards, *see* James P. Groton, *Dispute Review Boards: 'Backdoor Partnering,'* PROC. CONSTRUCTION LEADERSHIP CONF. (CEMC Seminars, 1993).

process to deal with each other and the panel in a timely and frank manner. Its use discourages game playing, dilatory tactics, and the taking of extreme and unsupportable positions. In practice, the nature of this process is such that the mere existence of the neutral always results in minimizing—and sometimes totally eliminating—the number of disputes to be presented to the neutral.

Even though some expense is involved in the process of selecting, appointing, and initially orienting the neutral, the costs are relatively minimal, even when the neutral is called on to resolve disputes. Compared to the legal costs and other expenses that are incurred in a mini-trial at the end of a construction project, or particularly compared to the expense of the typical project-end major arbitration proceeding, the costs of such a neutral are insignificant.

Mediation

Conventional mediation now plays an important role in construction industry dispute resolution. After a dispute has arisen, two or more parties involved in a dispute, through the assistance of an expert neutral, can be guided through negotiations toward a settlement of their mutual problems, promptly, and in a constructive way. More and more construction contracts today contain "combination" mediation-then-arbitration clauses, under which the parties agree to try mediation before submitting any dispute to arbitration. Following are forms for (1) negotiation, then mediation; (2) negotiation, then mediation, then arbitration; and (3) submission of an existing dispute to mediation:

Negotiation-Mediation

If a dispute arises out of or relates to this contract, or the breach thereof, and if the dispute cannot be settled through negotiation, the parties agree to try in good faith to settle the dispute by mediation under the Construction Industry Mediation Rules of the American Arbitration Association, before resorting to arbitration, litigation, or some other dispute resolution procedure.

Negotiation-Mediation-Arbitration

If a dispute arises out of or related to this contract, or the breach thereof, and if the dispute cannot be settled through negotiation, the parties agree to try in good faith to settle the dispute by mediation under the Construction Industry Mediation Rules of the American Arbitration Association, before resorting to arbitration. Thereafter, any remaining unresolved controversy or claim arising out of or relating to this contract, or the breach thereof, shall be settled by arbitration in accordance with the Construction Industry Arbitration Rules of the American Arbitration Association, and judgment upon the award rendered by the Arbitrator(s) may be entered in any court having jurisdiction.

Submission of an Existing Dispute to Mediation

The parties hereby submit the following dispute to mediation under the Construction Industry Mediation Rules of the American Arbitration Association: [describe dispute briefly].

Mini-trial

The mini-trial is being used increasingly to resolve construction disputes. It is a brief presentation of each side's "best case" arguments in the presence of principal executives of both parties, whose efforts to settle the dispute are usually facilitated by a neutral.

Following is a form for submission of an existing dispute for mini-trial:

Submission of an Existing Dispute to Mini-Trial

The parties hereby submit the following dispute to mini-trial under the [Mini-trial Procedures of the American Arbitration Association]: [describe dispute briefly].

Expert's Advisory Opinion

The advisory opinion technique consists of having an independent neutral expert meet with the parties both together and separately, obtain information from both parties, and then render a non-binding decision, evaluation or prediction as to the ultimate outcome of the dispute. Such a process usually brings a needed air of reality into the negotiations and frequently results in settlement.

Fact-Based Mediation

Fact-based mediation is a combination of an advisory opinion and mediation. It involves a confidential, impartial assessment of the factual data, probable outcome and possible future costs if the parties proceed to arbitration or litigation. After the parties have presented the mediator with the numerous facts, graphs, charts and documentation on the project, the mediator issues detailed reports to the parties assessing the facts and stating a recommended basis for settlement. However, the reports are different for each party with the exception of the bottom-line dollar recommendation. Armed with these assessments, parties can knowledgeably negotiate a settlement with the assistance of the mediator.

Advisory Arbitration

Non-binding advisory arbitration is another device that, although not conclusively resolving a dispute, can provide the parties with a realistic assessment that can lead to a consensual settlement of the matter. This type of arbitration is usually conducted with much less formality than a binding arbitration. Sometimes it consists merely of "best case" presentations of each party's case to the arbitrators. A sample form follows:

Submission of an Existing Dispute to Advisory Arbitration

The undersigned parties hereby submit the following dispute to non-binding advisory arbitration: [describe dispute briefly]. The arbitrators shall be selected under the Construction Industry Arbitration Rules of the American Arbitration Association, and the procedures shall be established by agreement between the parties and the arbitrators.

Sometimes, after all other attempts to resolve the matter voluntarily have failed, it becomes necessary for the parties to seek a binding adjudication. The two private choices are arbitration and private judging.

Arbitration

Although arbitration has been the forum of choice in the construction industry for over a century, it has experienced changes over the years in a number of different ways.

Beginning with the introduction of arbitration in the first AIA standard documents a century ago, arbitrations were conducted on an informal, ad hoc basis during the course of construction. Arbitration was used to resolve each individual dispute at the time it arose, whenever the architect's decision was not accepted by both parties. However, during the past couple of decades, arbitrations have tended to become more formal and structured, making it more difficult to arbitrate problems during construction. Accordingly, when problems cannot be resolved during construction, parties have increasingly been "reserving their rights" until all problems can be addressed at one time at the end of the project. The result has usually been an "omnibus" arbitration, covering a whole laundry list of disputes that have accumulated during the life of the project. The AAA recently reported that the number of arbitrations in which the claims exceed $1 million has doubled in the last five years.

The trend toward large complex arbitrations presents special problems to the parties, their counsel, arbitrators, and the AAA. Because these cases involve disputed issues that have been deferred for some time, positions become hardened, antagonisms increase, memories become dim, and facts grow stale. Discovery becomes a problem. The sheer size and volume of facts and paper and the complexity of issues create problems of case management and cost. The time for preparation becomes extended, and, unless the proceeding is tightly managed, the hearings drag on interminably, with frequent adjournments. The legal costs can become astronomical.

There have been two approaches to solving these problems. One approach has been to develop techniques that tend to avoid the necessity for such massive arbitrations, such as the prevention and early resolution techniques described previously. The other has been to focus on improvements to the arbitration process and the quality and training of arbitrators.

The AAA has accomplished much in recent years in developing improvements to arbitration procedures and techniques in complex cases, and in the identification of arbitrators who can handle such cases. Certain arbitrators have been specially trained in complex case management techniques to serve as chairs of arbitration panels in such cases.

AIA documents contain standard arbitration agreements that incorporate the American Arbitration Association Construction Industry Rules. If the parties wish to tailor their arbitration clause to meet special requirements of the parties or the project, they may wish to consider the following additions:

1. Adopting the AAA "Supplementary Procedures for Large, Complex Disputes" (which provide for appropriate pre-hearing document exchanges, discovery and depositions, if necessary).
2. The locale of the hearings.
3. Qualifications of the arbitrator(s).
4. Whether a reasoned award is required.
5. Whether the arbitrators are or are not empowered to award attorneys' fees or punitive damages.
6. The law to be applied.

This last point needs to be specifically considered with every arbitration agreement in the light of *Volt Information Sciences, Inc. v. Board of Trustees of Leland Stanford Junior University.*[6] In that case, the Supreme Court held that the Federal Arbitration Act, 9 U.S.C. §§ 1-16, (FAA), did not pre-empt the California Arbitration Act in an interstate dispute where the parties had agreed that their contract would be governed by California law. Accordingly, if the parties wish to assure that the FAA will apply to the arbitration proceeding, regardless of the law that they have specified to govern on substantive issues, the arbitration clause should provide that the arbitration will be conducted under the FAA.

The parties can provide for the arbitration of future disputes by inserting the following clause into their contracts:

Standard Pre-dispute Arbitration Clause

Any controversy or claim arising out of or relating to this contract, or the breach thereof, shall be settled by arbitration in accordance with the Construction Industry Arbitration Rules of the American Arbitration Association, and judgment upon the award rendered by the arbitrator(s) may be entered in any court having jurisdiction thereof. Regardless of

---

[6] *See* Allen J. Gross & Donald L. Comwell, *Drafting ADR Contract Provisions, in* ALTERNATIVE DISPUTE RESOLUTION IN THE CONSTRUCTION INDUSTRY (Robert F. Cushman, et. al. eds., 1991). This chapter discusses in detail a number of considerations involving the drafting of arbitration agreements and includes three sample clauses and alternative language.

any other choice of law provision in this contract, any arbitration shall be governed by the United States Arbitration Act, 9 U.S.C. §§ 1-16.

The parties can provide for the arbitration of an existing dispute by entering into the following Submission Agreement:

Submission of an Existing Dispute to Arbitration

We, the undersigned parties, hereby submit to arbitration under the Construction Industry Arbitration Rules of the American Arbitration Association the following controversy: [describe briefly]. We further agree that the above controversy be submitted to [one] [three] Arbitrator(s) selected from the Construction Industry Arbitration Panel of the American Arbitration Association. We further agree that we will faithfully observe this agreement and the Rules and that we will abide by and perform any award rendered by the Arbitrator(s) and that judgment on the award may be entered in any court having jurisdiction.

The drafter of an arbitration clause should be aware of the dangers of attempting to limit arbitration to specific kinds of disputes or to claims involving less than a specific sum. Such limitations can give rise to jurisdictional and arbitrability defenses, which can defeat the purpose of arbitration by generating parallel judicial proceedings.

Elements of an Effective Construction Dispute Resolution System

An effective construction dispute resolution system should take into account the following four basic principles.

Four Basic Principles

Consider the unique nature of the construction process. Construction is a dynamic and complex process that can confound even the most intricate management systems. It requires the coordinated effort of a temporarily assembled task force of many independent participants, each having a different specialty, and each expecting to make a profit. This complexity inevitably creates problems: no design can ever be perfect; construction is not an exact science; unanticipated events can always be expected. If problems are not resolved promptly, they can cause delays in the project, harm cooperative relationships, reduce efficiency, lead to claims and disputes, and ultimately, end in litigation.

Even when problems turn into disputes, litigation should not be the method used to resolve them. Some problems are inevitably going to grow into disputes, but they do not have to be resolved through litigation. Litigation is perhaps the bluntest instrument for resolving construction industry disputes. It is not well-suited for dealing with construction disputes because courts and juries do not have the expertise to understand construction problems, and the process is slow, inefficient and expensive. Regardless of the outcome, the cost of litigation frequently wipes out the potential profits of both parties. Litigation fosters a "win-lose" attitude, and it usually destroys any possibility of future mutually beneficial relationships between the parties.

If participants commit in advance to use dispute resolution techniques when problems arise, they create an atmosphere conducive to solving problems. Because a party to a dispute is often reluctant, when emotions are running high, to be the first to suggest that some method of dispute resolution be used other than litigation, participants in a construction project should commit themselves contractually in advance to explore non-adjudicative dispute resolution options before resorting to binding arbitration or litigation.

Many problem-prevention and litigation-avoidance approaches exist; these techniques are most effective when applied early in the project. Many alternative approaches are available during the course of a project for preventing and solving problems and avoiding litigation. These include, in order of project sequence, such devices as structuring project relationships in ways that prevent and avoid the most common sources of problems; establishing dispute resolution techniques that will resolve problems at the jobsite level; using mediation, mini-trials, advisory opinions or non-binding advisory arbitration when disputes arise; and as a last resort, using expert binding arbitration if other measures have failed. Generally, the earlier in the life of the project the parties begin to use dispute prevention and resolution techniques, the greater will be the benefit to the project.

II. American Institute of Architects (AIA) Expands the Use of ADR

Construction ADR at Its Best: The New AIA A-201 Document

*by Howard G. Goldberg**

When a standard form contract widely used in the construction industry undergoes revision (as with the A-201 in 1997), its influence can be enormous. And when one of the revisions expands the use of ADR, that industry can be expected to embrace that development.

More than any other industry, the construction industry has consistently led the way in adopting ADR solutions to disputes. For over thirty years it has been employing industry-wide standard form contracts, including the A-201 General Conditions of the Contract of Construction promulgated by the American Institute of Architects (AIA), which includes ADR mechanisms for resolving disputes between the owner and the contractor. The AIA's 1997 revision of A-201 (the first since 1987), which continues the AIA's long-standing support of ADR in its standard form contracts, came into widespread use in 1998.

This new edition not only incorporates the two traditional methods of ADR employed by the AIA for the past several decades—i.e., interim resolution by the project architect and then binding arbitration under the rules of the American Arbitration Association—it also adds an important step in between—mediation. This is expected to generate prompt and economical solutions to disputes that are satisfactory to both parties. The revised A-201 also contains changes in a number of areas in which construction disputes frequently arise, which should have the effect of heading off disputes. The key features of these provisions are described below.

---

* Mr. Goldberg is a principal with the Baltimore law firm of Goldberg, Pike & Besche, specializing in Construction Law. He received his J.D. from the University of Maryland School of Law. Mr. Goldberg is a Fellow of the Americans College of Construction Lawyers and is an honorary member of the AIA.

Submission to the Architect

As in prior editions of A-201, all claims by either the owner or the contractor must be submitted for an initial decision to the project architect within twenty-one days after the claim arises or the party asserting the claim first discovers the condition giving rise to the claim.

Why, some ask, is submission of the claim to the project architect the first step in the dispute resolution process? Doesn't the architect have a conflict of interest, since he or she is the owner's agent and the design work may be at issue? In making the value judgment that the project architect should play a role in the dispute resolution process, the AIA Documents Committee felt that any possible bias was outweighed by the architect's familiarity with both the construction documents and the intent underlying the design of the project, and by the architect's knowledge of the project and the course of construction. This feeling was reinforced by the fact that the architect's decision is neither final nor binding, since A-201 provides for additional steps in the dispute resolution process. Moreover, 1997 A-201 requires a party to wait only thirty days after filing the claim, regardless of whether the architect has rendered a decision, before bypassing this step completely.

The process following submission of a claim to the architect has been simplified. In addition to authorizing possible initial responses by the architect, including a request for additional information (now from either party) or a rejection or recommendation of the claim for approval, A-201 now permits the architect to opt out of the claims process because of insufficient expertise or because a conflict of interest precludes an appropriate decision. It also specifically authorizes the architect to request that the party against whom the claim is made respond to the claim with supporting evidence. It even allows the architect to seek advice or information from persons with special knowledge or expertise regarding the subject matter of the claim. This was considered desirable because of the possible complexity of the claim from a technical point of view. Now, instead of relying only on the architect's own knowledge and experience, the architect may consult outside experts in order to arrive at the best and fairest result.

The revised A-201 addresses the potential conflict between the claims provisions and mechanic's lien statutes. It makes it clear that a contractor who has the right to seek redress under a mechanic's lien statute may make the necessary filings to comply with the statute prior to resolution of the claim under A-201's three-step ADR process.

As under the 1987 edition, if a claim is asserted, the parties must continue contract performance. There are, however, two major exceptions to this rule in the 1997 edition. The first exception is if the owner fails to pay amounts certified by the architect to the contractor within the number of days required by the contract documents. The second deals with the occurrence of specific events giving rise to the contractor's right to suspend or terminate the contract.

Also continued from the 1987 edition, the contractor is compensated for changed conditions or allowed extensions of time for delays not due to the contractor's fault and not reasonably contemplated when the contract price and contract time were agreed upon by the parties. One new addition to the provision relating to "changed" physical conditions makes clear what was not explicit in the 1987 edition—that is, that the contractor will be allowed a time extension in addition to compensation.

One significant addition to the claims section is a mutual waiver by the owner and the contractor of consequential damages arising from a claimed breach of contract by the other. In order to avoid subsequent disputes over the meaning of the term "consequential damages," a list of items waived by each party is specifically included. On the owner's side these include the loss of rent, use, financing and future profits of other businesses. On the contractor's side, the waived items include home office overhead and the loss of financing (including bonding) and profits on other projects. While these lists are not exclusive, they do cover the majority of consequential damage claims.

Nothing in the waiver provision prevents the inclusion of a mutually agreeable provision specifying the consequential damages that will be recoverable in the event of a breach. Nor does it prevent the owner's use of a liquidated damages provision. The waiver provision expressly states: "Nothing contained in this subparagraph...shall be deemed to preclude an award of liquidated direct damages...."

Mediation and Arbitration

Five years before publication of 1997 A-201, the AIA Documents Committee met with representatives of the AAA to find out whether the AAA would be prepared to deal with the increased caseload in the event that mediation were to become a required dispute resolution process. The AAA said yes, so the AIA added a mediation step. Now, a party aggrieved by an architect's decision must submit the dispute to mediation under the AAA's mediation rules. Since both parties receive the benefit of the process, the costs of mediation are borne equally.

In order to avoid statute-of-limitations problems, the 1997 A-201 provides that demands for mediation and arbitration may be filed concurrently. If so, the mediation proceeds first. Just as in the case of submission of the claim to the project architect, the mediation process cannot be used by a party to delay resolution of the claim. Unless the parties agree otherwise, either one may abort the mediation process and move the dispute into the arbitration phase if it is not resolved within sixty days after submission to mediation.

If all else fails, the final step in the dispute resolution process is arbitration pursuant to the AAA's newly revamped construction arbitration rules. The arbitration provisions in the new A-201 closely track the provisions of the 1987 edition. All claims known to the party seeking arbitration and ripe for arbitration must be asserted at one time. The rules regarding consolidation and joinder—while widely debated during adoption of the 1997 edition—have been retained. The decision in arbitration is final and binding and is enforceable by a court of competent jurisdiction.

Avoiding Disputes

Job-site Safety. Safety concerns resulted in a change to the provision dealing with the contractor's responsibility for safety where the construction documents make specific provisions for the means and methods of construction. The 1997 edition of A-201 requires the contractor to independently evaluate its ability to perform the work in a safe manner using the specified methods. If the conclusion is that these methods are not safe, the contractor must advise the architect and owner. Only in (hopefully) rare circumstances where the owner instructs the contractor to proceed anyway will the owner be liable. Since the contractor is in the best position to determine whether the required methods of construction can be executed safely, requiring a second look at safety by the contractor should contribute substantially to job safety, and ultimately to a reduction in the number of disputes.

Substitutions. Disputes frequently have arisen because of substitutions that surprise the owner by their existence after the work is performed. Substitutions often occur during the shop drawing review process—when the architect, without the knowledge or prior consent of the owner, approves substitutions specifically proposed by the contractor. Now, A-201 puts all of the participants on notice that the architect's approval alone is not sufficient. Rather, substitutions must be made with approval of the owner and be documented by a change order.

Payment for Change Orders. Disputes also have arisen when the parties were unsure as to the method and frequency of payment for construction change directives. Owners sometimes assumed payment could be delayed until the entire changed work was completed and a change order memorializing the work and associated cost was issued. Contractors, who were expending funds on a current basis, felt payment should be made monthly. The AIA Documents Committee felt the equities on this issue were on the side of the contractors. Thus, the 1997 A-201 makes the formerly permissive provision allowing payment of amounts not in dispute for partially performed construction change directives mandatory. As to amounts in dispute, the architect is to make an interim determination of the amount to be paid on current applications for payment, subject to either party objecting by asserting a claim, which then would result in a formal architect's decision. Amounts determined and certified by the architect therefore must be paid by the owner.

Insurance. The AIA Documents Committee, in conjunction with CNA Insurance Co., has developed a new form of insurance for the construction industry in an attempt to reduce disputes regarding financial responsibility for job-site accidents. In states where workers' compensation laws do not provide immunity from civil suits to general contractors, owners and architects, this insurance protects them against vicarious liability claims by injured workers whose own employer, or some other employer, negligently caused the injury or loss.

Another benefit of this insurance is that it eliminates the inevitable cross-claims and third-party claims. It also reduces the transaction costs involved in having three lawyers, since the three primary parties are all insured within the same insurance policy. This insurance also eliminates much of the practical need for an indemnity provision, which in many cases may be unenforceable under local law.

Termination for Convenience. Previously, the owner involved in a deteriorating relationship with a contractor had only two choices: live with the situation or terminate the contractor. The termination caused a breach of contract unless legally sufficient cause existed for the termination. Now, another choice exists. The owner may terminate the contractor without having to face litigation, but it must pay the contractor not only for the work performed up to the termination date, but also its profit and overhead on the incomplete work. To allow a termination without this reimbursement would be unfair to the contractor, given its expenditure of resources on the project in the anticipation of recapturing overhead and profit. While this might not be a perfect solution when the owner-contractor relationship has deteriorated to the point where termination is the only realistic choice, it provides each party with an alternative that may convince them to negotiate a more satisfactory solution.

Conclusion

In addressing the construction industry's needs for the new century, the AIA Documents Committee felt that dispute avoidance and mediation should play a significant role in its cornerstone documents. Hopefully, those intentions will be fulfilled.

III. Using Hybrid ADR Techniques in Construction Disputes

"Hybrid ADR" in the Construction Industry

*by James H. Keil**

Many people in the 1980s thought "the construction industry [might] litigate itself out of existence," but the author says this is no longer the case due to the increased use of partnering. Based on the principle of hybrids, partnering combines several forms of ADR into a process that seeks to eliminate problems in the construction industry before they become disputes.

There are many forms of alternative dispute resolution that have developed over the years. For centuries, citizen tribunals have been used in various civilizations as parts of justice systems. These citizen tribunals rendered decisions in much the same way as arbitrators, judges, and juries do in the American justice system today.

Facilitation and mediation have come to be used as enhancements to communication and negotiation as opposed to arbitrary settlements by third parties, providing settlement options. Today, many of these processes are being combined into "hybrids" to be applied to specific situations in order to achieve specific goals.

RegNeg (negotiated rulemaking), for example, is a combination of facilitation, mediation, and negotiation that is being used in the public sector in the development of public policy. Hybrids, such as RegNeg, provide flexibility that helps to adjust to the ever-changing needs of society and its elements.

For the purpose of understanding hybrids within the general confines of ADR, let's look first at what has come to be known as "partnering." Partnering combines elements of several forms of ADR in an informal process. It first originated in the construction industry during the 1980s as a way of reducing the costs of lengthy and complex litigation and

---

* The author is an experienced mediator and arbitrator. He is a former policy-making official of Maine state government, having directed a 260-person bureau, and has been instrumental in leading the state of Maine into development of a total quality management (TQM) program. He is on the AAA's commercial mediation and arbitration panels and is a member of the AAA's Construction Advisory Council.

arbitration, by eliminating or minimizing issues that otherwise would become legal disputes.

Many people who worked in construction at that time were beginning to think that it might be possible for the construction industry to litigate itself out of existence. Long, protracted hearings, lengthy discovery proceedings, and entrenched positions were the norm rather than the exception on large, complex projects. In the end, settlements of such litigated cases were usually left to be worked out by people who may not even have been actively involved in the events leading to the initial claims, because the cases were taking so long to work their way through the system.

As a result of this trend, many of the riskier elements within the construction process were simply being ignored or overlooked. In some cases, good products or systems were discontinued, or otherwise written off because it was too difficult to predict how a judge or jury might decide a specific issue, and it was too difficult, therefore, to control the risk.

For example, it took only one significant tragedy involving lift-slab building systems that failed in Connecticut in the late 1980s, and the ensuing legal battles, to make many designers, contractors, and builders shy away from it, even though the concept held great promise. They feared it, not because the failure necessarily arose out of a permanently flawed design, but because the unpredictability of the risk made it too expensive to continue its use. The safer way to deal with it was simply to stop using it.

Partnering, which uses neutral facilitators to guide the communications processes between the multiple disciplines involved in a construction project, from the conceptual stage through design and construction, incorporates some of the principles of mediation and negotiation at certain times.

Even though the partnering process is not a legal process, the combination of facilitation, mediation, and negotiation is meant to improve communication and to provide a "platform" for the interdisciplinary management of project risk.

Rather than falling prey to the confusion that can be caused by the diversity of the participants, partnering makes use of that diversity among the disciplines required to construct buildings and other projects. Neutral facilitators, trained in and familiar with the industry's normal processes, lead discussions and help in clarifying and developing specific issues and identifying ways to better manage the risks.

Using group review and assessment, project participants have an improved opportunity to directly influence the construction processes adopted for their specific project. Done properly, they will review design specifications together and develop many of their own strategic plans for managing unique project risks, all the while building joint expectations for outcomes. Working on these expectations for outcomes is one of the most powerful tools within the partnering process, because it helps eliminate surprises, which are not typically conducive to construction excellence.

Interestingly, the concept of partnering has been formally endorsed by all major professional groups within the construction industry, including architects, design engineers, owners, and contractors, as well as federal and state governmental organizations and agencies. This is not an insignificant endorsement.

Partnering can be applied to many other areas of commerce outside the construction industry. Any complex contractual arrangements, whether part of a procurement system, joint venture, or reorganization of work forces, can make good use of neutral facilitators to enhance discussions and spend time first identifying, then evaluating and managing the risks to successful performance under the terms of the agreements.

Partnering can also help in reaching the proper balance between building codes and professional liability.

There can be no question that the most efficient and cost-effective design for any building is that which provides truly necessary, useful, and desired design standards, rather than one which overdesigns simply as a means to avoid perceived liability. That perception of liability arises from case law, the media, and problems demonstrated to have been associated with other projects. Unfortunately, such perceived liability sometimes shifts the balance too far in the direction of professional liability.

The interdisciplinary communication that can, and usually does, occur in partnering workshops, often helps those involved in the design of a project to have a better understanding of other elements that may impact a design choice. Outside of partnering workshops, engineers typically work within their own disciplines, and, even though an electrical engineer and mechanical engineer may both be designing elements in the same space within a building, they may not ever have a chance to discuss their choices face to face. Most often, they may not even need to, but occasionally this kind of communication will remedy situations that otherwise become potential legal disputes. The old saying "measure twice, cut once" applies.

Scope of work issues, which are proven to be the most common areas of legal disputes, can be clarified, in many cases, and simple, inexpensive corrections can be identified and utilized to eliminate later problems. Changing the fitting on a pipe while the trench is still open is much less costly than changing it after the trench has been back-filled, and a driveway paved over it. Although this may sound like an over-simplification, many of us have experienced it.

When projects become over-designed, or designed to accommodate the wrong values, the cost of the project goes up, its reliability may not, and owners are left financing an unnecessary over-improvement for years to come. An over-designed project, for example, might result in an extra 500 square feet being built into a project. There are many reasons, most having to do with poor communication, that this could, and does, happen. In any case, that 500 square feet could add more than $50,000 in total cost to the project, and it will be amortized over the length of the financing. That miscalculation will likely never be noticed by anyone. There will be no taxpayer revolts, no letters to the editor, but some other, perhaps even more worthwhile program will have to be cut to make up the deficit.

Partnering is a form of risk management, in which all of the various disciplines involved in a project work together in a non-adversarial workshop format to develop an interdisciplinary vision and to build a communications methodology that balances the strengths of the project team against its own weaknesses.

The key here is identifying the weaknesses of the project team. This is very difficult to accomplish, because most of us resist looking at our own weaknesses, especially in a public setting. It requires trust and the careful establishment of less threatening environments where free communication can take place. It needs continuous follow-up to gain the greatest cost-effectiveness. It is not enough to meet once in one workshop and expect things to change based on that one meeting alone. Changing the culture takes time and commitment and follow-up.

Most of the professionals involved in a construction project, whether engineers or architects, have only two basic things they can contribute to the construction process- time and talent. If they are required to be the lowest service provider, or must work within a fixed fee structure, they can either cut the time they spend on a project or reduce the extent of the talent they commit to the project. Neither choice is particularly good for the owner, in most circumstances.

There are two contractual relationships on any design-bid-build construction project, which is the most common contract delivery system used in the public sector. The owner enters into a contract with the architect/designer to develop the plans and specifications. The owner will then enter into another contract with the general contractor who has separate contracts with the subcontractors. (The contractors determine their costs from the plans and specifications developed by the architect/designer.)

The architect has no contract with any of the contractors, nor does the owner have a contract with any of the subcontractors, yet the actions of any of these individuals may have a decided impact on the other contractual relationships. Although this is a delicate and sometimes unwieldy balance, the system has worked well for many years.

Every action or "tweaking" of contract terms will have an impact somewhere else. Many of these impacts, despite good intentions, will come as a surprise to somebody. The notion of "tweaking" the process could be likened to trying to "evening up" the legs of a stool. Unless done very carefully, it is likely to produce a stool with no legs.

Other contract delivery systems, which are coming into greater use every year, and which would include (among many others) design-build, build-operate-transfer, and the use of construction managers, all have at least the same risks and perhaps more associated with them, and the same concerns over "tweaking" apply. Many of us in the industry feel that in these delivery systems, "tweaking" may actually be necessary, regardless of the additional risks.

In contract delivery systems other than design-bid-build, the "tweaking" becomes necessary more as a function of the changes in roles of the players than for any other reason. Architects and design engineers and contractors in these systems are sharing risks that would otherwise (under design-bid-build scenarios) be separate, and owners must accept submissions that are different from "the way we've always done it."

Despite the good intentions of senior level managers who commit their organizations to doing business the new way, many lower level employees find it extremely difficult, if not impossible to make decisions with less information on hand than they are used to. Making decisions with less or less specific information is precisely what they will be asked to do under most of these scenarios, since design-build often requires some designs to be completed while work is under way, rather than before work begins.

Outside of partnering, we often evaluate project costs primarily on a short-term basis, and in so doing may lose sight of the big picture. While paying a fee for a design professional's opinion on one individual project within a building (sizing a boiler, for example) may seem excessive to some, the real question is whether it makes sense to have a design professional's opinion on the whole building, including structural concerns, circuit loads, code and law compliance, and selection of construction materials. In the latter case, the percentage applied to design fees is minimal.

An undersized boiler is a "gift" that keeps on costing. The extra energy costs that go into an undersized boiler over a period of years might have financed a new ball field or an employee lounge, or saved a building from the devastation of a fire caused by space heaters used improperly.

Partnering workshops can sharpen the vision of project designers, and provide additional checks and balances on the ultimate design selected. The total cost of partnering is a tiny fraction of 1% of the total project cost, and almost infinitesimal when compared with the cost of litigating over the same issues.

It does not make good, long-term sense to argue with our doctor or dentist over price. Neither should we argue prices with the person responsible for assuring that the building we spend most of our waking hours in won't collapse around our ears. We should make value judgments based on the qualifications and strengths of the providers. Only when this is done, should we be ready to talk price.

Case Studies

The following are two partnering case studies. They provide clear examples of some of the things that can be gained through such an approach to any complicated contractually based agreement.

Case Study 1

Brownfield Redevelopment Project: James H. Keil Designed & Implemented Sessions

A suburban community with a long and complex history of dealing with a Superfund site (sites with known pollution that are managed by the federal government) moved forward in 1997 with a plan to redevelop the site under the Brownfield program of the federal EPA.

Included in the overall plan was a long list of governmental entities, contractors, neighborhood groups, regulatory agencies, trust funds, and private developers. The plan for redeveloping this site was brought to action by a series of meetings and understandings between the various participants.

A partnering session was scheduled in the fall to provide a risk management forum for participants to identify, evaluate, quantify, and manage risks to the various elements of the project.

By its very nature, a Brownfield redevelopment is subject to failure at a much more significant rate because of the numbers of entities involved, and because of the layering of multiple contracts, responsibilities, and agendas.

The project involved in this case study is subject to such a high potential failure rate. The state highway department entered into a contract with a contractor to build a major highway interchange, and the state's port authority entered into a contract with a contractor to build a major intermodal facility on a portion of the site. Both of these contracts followed separate contracts for the design of the facility and the interchange.

A third major contract link on the same site was established between a private developer whose intent was to build a shopping center on a portion of the site. This too followed a separate contract for the design of the center.

In addition to these contracts, a number of other contracts were in place to provide certain forms of remediation on portions of the site. All of the work is expected to take place concurrently.

The most important work of the partnering session involved risk identification by all of the disciplines involved in the work, followed by an open question-and-answer session with all concerned. That accomplished, the participants developed a better understanding of the communications network involved, both from the perspective of what exists, but more importantly, from the perspective of what was needed.

Interdisciplinary communication is, and continues to be, the most important goal of partnering, along with the opportunity it presents for participants to build more understanding of the goals and needs of those involved in the other contracts and how they impact each other.

This particular project represents a form of public/private sector partnership, even though participants did not all recognize it as such. As is always the case, participants were caught up in the dynamics of their own contract responsibilities.

In the process of examining the sequencing of separate contract links, it became apparent to all that if the interchange were delayed, the multimodal transportation facility construction would clearly run into difficulties and potential contract delays, and it would bring into question the private developer's ability to pay back its sizeable land investment and, indeed, its willingness to continue the project.

Computers and e-mail were utilized in order to help keep everyone informed of progress and problems, and regular meetings of key individuals on each contract link provides some further assurance. Agendas for these meetings are set by a process designed by project participants themselves and should assure that what needs to be discussed gets aired, and that time is not wasted.

Follow-up partnering sessions will be the key to the overall success of this project. If they are held regularly, the project has a greater chance of staying on track. If not, the initial gains made will suffer.

Case Study 2

NYCTA—ConEd Frequency Conversion Project: All sessions designed & implemented by James H. Keil

This project was initiated by Consolidated Edison's economically driven need to get out of the 25 Hz service business. Stemming from New York City's financial crisis in the mid-1970s, Con Edison developed a plan to terminate all 25 Hz service, but the plan was not implemented until 1998.

Making matters more complicated, the stubborn signal system still had some 25 Hz equipment that would not be replaced before the year 2000. This is a high-stakes contract between NYCT and Con Edison that includes $1 million per month in liquidated damages.

This project, quite literally, makes the transition from a power source that was developed in the early years of the 20th century, and will replace it with a power source suited for the beginning of the 21st century.

Recognizing the importance of all parties involved working together to accomplish this difficult goal, L.K. Comstock & Co., the successful installation contract bidder, and Cegelec Automation of Paris, France, the successful equipment manufacturer, agreed to support partnering of all three of these separate (but intertwined) contract links with NYCT.

The technical means by which the 25 Hz service is to be brought to an end is frequency conversion, and it will be done with two contracts.

Cegelec, in June of 1997, was awarded a $7.8 million contract to supply frequency converter packages to NYCT. On Dec. 2, 1997, L.K. Comstock & Co., was awarded a $10.4 million installation contract.

A kick-off meeting was held among all the players, immediately followed by a partnering workshop between representatives of ConEd, NYTC, Cegelec, and L.K. Comstock.

One of the most significant gains made in the partnering workshop was the pledge of ConEd to do its street work in parallel with Comstock's work, rather than sequentially which is the usual method. This pledge came as a direct result of the facilitated interdisciplinary communication among the parties that led all parties to pursue the best engineered solution, rather than simply evaluating positions based solely on contract provisions.

Cultural differences between the French company producing the conversion packages and the American companies involved in the installation were addressed more thoroughly and pledges were made among participants to provide extra assurances that vital information would be passed in a timely and reasonable fashion in order to assure overall project success.

Fourteen months into the project, follow-up sessions indicated that the need for adjustments in process was continuous, and that there is no substitute for face-to-face contact among the participants.

Mediation

Let us look next at mediation. Mediation of disputes almost always is of benefit to the parties. Because the process is confidential, notwithstanding other requirements of law, the parties can enter into mediation without jeopardizing their positions in subsequent legal actions. Agreement, in writing, should be reached among the parties before mediation commences, that nothing from the mediation will be used in any subsequent legal action. The average rate of settlement in several studies is in the 85%-plus category. Even when settlement is not reached, it is common to find that certain portions of a dispute or a claim may be removed by the parties, making subsequent litigation or arbitration faster and less costly. A major key to its success is the selection of the mediator.

Most important is that the parties to mediation should not, under any circumstances, leave the selection of the mediator solely up to their attorneys. The parties are expected to be actively involved in crafting the ultimate solution, and they also need to exercise their voices directly in the mediator selection process because the choice of mediator is of great importance.

The Fine Art of Mediation

Mediation really is an art, rather than a science, and a fine art at that. Successful mediators develop the necessary skills in many ways, and it is difficult to know precisely what qualities make a person a good mediator. Understanding this is important. And it is therefore important for parties to mediation to have an opportunity to meet and interview prospective mediators if they wish, and to ask whatever questions they deem necessary.

It is important that the mediator selected have the training and experience to create a fair and impartial process for the discussion of issues and know how to allow problem-solving efforts to take place. This sounds easy, but in practice, often is not—especially among strong adversarial parties. Trust is also important, and all parties must trust the mediator's skills and judgment.

The mediator selected should belong to one or more professional groups which require, as a condition of membership, compliance with published ethical standards. The American Arbitration Association, any number of local bar associations, or the Society of Professionals in Dispute Resolution (SPIDR) are representative of three such groups. These same ethical standards also provide support for the parties to any dispute, and a place to find answers to questions they may have. They have established and proven processes, and can provide names and qualifications of established mediators. Their case administrators can be helpful in providing a step-by-step process, and, for a fee, will even arrange a room in which to hold the hearings.

Good mediators do not have to be attorneys, and, in fact, many times should not be attorneys. They should have, however, intimate familiarity with our system of laws, along with direct experience in the specific business involved in the dispute.

In America, it is likely that 90% of all businesses in existence today will be sued at least once before they close their doors. A Rand Corporation Study done in 1985 showed that two thirds of the $35 billion spent annually on litigation went for legal fees and costs. Certainly anything that might reduce these expenses holds promise, especially since a civil lawsuit filed in America in 1995 takes an average of five to seven years, from the initiation of the action until the case is adjudicated.

Mediation is a method of settlement that is available to virtually anyone involved in any legal dispute, provided all other parties involved in that dispute also willingly agree to mediate.

What mediation is not is a third-party settlement process. In other words, mediation sets no one individual or group of individuals up as either judge or jury on the matters at hand as is the case with litigation or arbitration. Rather, a mediator is there solely to assist the parties and/or their attorneys in their own negotiations.

The power of mediation comes from the agreement of the parties. First, all parties must agree upon the selection of, and qualifications of the mediator. Second, the power of any settlement comes from the parties themselves; they must all agree on any settlement that derives from the mediation session.

If you are a business manager you will play an active role in the settlement of your own issues, and no settlement will be forced upon you that you do not wish to be part of. Your involvement will not be limited to sterile testimony under oath, as is the case in litigation or arbitration.

The mediator is able to facilitate discussions by controlling the process. Discussions may be open and involve all parties, working face to face, or they may be held separately, with each party talking with the mediator alone in caucus. In caucus, the mediator agrees to keep such discussions confidential, unless a party asks the mediator to share what is said with the other party or parties.

In any case, the entire mediation session is confidential (as opposed to arbitration or litigation, which are more likely to become part of a public record), and nothing from the mediation should be used in subsequent legal proceedings.

Arbitration

Arbitration differs from mediation in that it is a third-party settlement process that uses citizen panels of arbitrators instead of a judge or jury. Most people get to arbitration because a contract they have signed requires it for settling disputes. Labor contracts, construction contracts, and insurance contracts are but a few of the types of contracts that can include provisions for arbitration of disputes.

Since most arbitration hearings are binding on the parties, it is imperative that the parties have an active role in the selection of the arbitrator, or arbitrators, and, again, that the selection process not simply be left up to the attorneys. All too often, this process, which is intended to be faster, less expensive, and less formal than traditional courtroom litigation, is handled strictly by attorneys for the parties, almost as if it were a trial, with more stiff and stodgy proceedings than necessary, and much of the savings related to informality is therefore lost.

Done well, arbitration allows for considerably more interactions among the people involved than traditional courtroom justice. Again, large membership organizations, such as the AAA, have established and proven rules and procedures, and can provide a list of experienced neutrals who can serve as arbitrators.

The Mediation/Umpire Hybrid

One criticism of mediation is that it is non-binding, so if a settlement is not reached, parties must move to another process. While it is true that not reaching a settlement through mediation means that some other resolution process must then be used, the mediation process is very quick. Parties who don't reach settlement usually know this within a matter of hours, and can then move on to arbitration or litigation without delays.

Some state legislatures have blended some of the principles involved in both mediation and arbitration together. In Maine, the fire insurance industry has developed a hybrid form of mediation in which neutral mediators with significant background in the construction industry are used as dispute umpires.

In this model, the parties involved in a dispute over a claim must first agree on the qualifications of and selection of the umpire. Once the umpire has been selected, a hearing is held in which the umpire attempts to find areas of potential agreement between the two appraisal teams on a specific fire loss.

If the umpire sees any potential for settlement, such areas are discussed, and in that case, the umpire works as a mediator. If the umpire sees no potential for settlement through mediation, he then issues an award based on a review of the existing claims. Should either of the initial appraisers agree with the umpire's award, it becomes a binding settlement. In some states, this process is a required pre-condition to litigation.

Many in the dispute resolution industry feel that this process can be applied to other situations in other industries, as a contractual provision.

The Mediated Contract Negotiation Hybrid

Contract negotiation is a very crucial stage in any commercial venture. In the typical scenario, attorneys for the signatories handle negotiation of the contract, sometimes with direct input from the signatories, quite often without.

While there is obviously a great deal of variation in the negotiation of contracts, both in style and process, most attorneys will admit that they are often left wishing their clients had read the contracts more carefully. They wish their clients were willing to spend a few extra dollars to involve them earlier in the preparation of the contract so as to improve their understanding of the contract terms.

The result is that 95% or more of the effort going into contract negotiation is adversarial only. This emphasis on adversarial positions can lead parties into inequitable balances of risk. Most of us look for an "ironclad" position in our negotiations, but such a position is not always supported in subsequent litigation, and is supported even less in arbitration. Jury trials, as most have witnessed in the media in recent years, are not always predictable.

In many cases, we would be better served if we could more fully discuss and explore contract provisions before signature day. Neutrals (mediators) can play a valuable role in these negotiations. It is imperative that they be completely neutral, unbiased, extremely knowledgeable in the particular industries involved, and they should be compensated equally by all the parties.

Using the caucus in addition to plenary discussions, mediators can help to bring potentially contentious issues to the table for consideration, and may be able to do so in a less arguable fashion. Many times parties simply look the other way and ignore the riskier elements of contractual agreements. In the case of design or construction contracts, designers or contractors may be looking ahead to work coming out in future, and may be reluctant to broach certain issues for fear they will jeopardize their chances of getting that work. Or, they may fear being perceived as stiff, and unbending, rather than as prudent businessmen.

Owners, on the other hand, sometimes hold to impossible positions, thinking they are eliminating risk, or at least minimizing the owner's exposure. "No delay damages" claims (in which owners deny contractors the right to collect damages from them for delays, even if the delays are caused by the owner) are often included in contracts, even though some arbitrators have ruled in favor of contractors in actual cases. Sometimes owners hold steadfastly to this position, though what they really want is not protection from any such claims (where they truly may be the cause), but rather protection from frivolous delay claims. In construction, the two are not always the same.

Contractors may in fact be delayed for any number of reasons that are caused by the owner. Not being allowed access to a school building when promised is one such example. Despite best intentions, at times school years are not concluded on schedule. Snow or other weather delays may affect them, which creates unanticipated costs for the contractor.

Discussing this through mediators before contracts have been signed can result in contract provisions that more clearly deal with the real issues at hand. In construction, as in many other complex contractual businesses, there is plenty of potential for misunderstanding.

Attorneys for the parties in mediated contract negotiation still play an adversarial role as do the signatories or their delegates. The mediator, on the other hand, focuses on form and clarity as opposed to advantage. This is not unlike some European models, in which notaries play a similar role.

In typical negotiations, many issues are skirted simply because some people have difficulty dealing with, and shy away from, controversial exchanges. Experienced, successful mediators know that this is a common experience. They are trained to keep the parties focused on the issues, rather than the personalities.

Conclusion

The best forms of ADR may be those yet to be developed. As parties and their representatives use ADR, changes and modifications recommended by the participants will improve the process, as well as the end result.

Partnering, arbitration, mediation, facilitated negotiation, mediated contract negotiation, dispute umpiring all provide great process flexibility, and a variety of communications methods for disputants to deal with their own problems than traditional litigation does.

Since over 90% of all litigated cases settle some time prior to being heard by a judge or jury, all ADR seeks to accomplish is to bring these methods of resolution into the settlement discussions earlier.

IV. The Duty to Disclose

Neutral Corner—The Duty to Disclose

*by Neil Carmichael**

One of the most fertile grounds for challenging arbitration awards in court has been the failure of arbitrators to conscientiously disclose relationships with individuals or companies involved in cases to which they were assigned. Judicial challenges to awards based on disclosure failures are almost always avoidable. By following a few simple procedures, arbitrators can ensure that this does not happen to them.

Arbitrators must recognize that the duty to disclose any pertinent information relative to their appointment to a case rests first and foremost with them. Because of the arbitrator's extensive decision-making authority, and because of the limited judicial review of awards, it is extremely important that arbitrators disclose any past or present relationship with the parties or their counsel, direct or indirect, whether of a financial, professional, social or other nature.

The duty to disclose should be differentiated from the standards applied by the courts when deciding challenges to awards based on alleged arbitrator bias. An arbitrator should not fail to make a disclosure because of a belief that a court would not later determine the facts to be significant enough to upset an award. Any doubt as to whether information should be disclosed must be resolved in favor of full disclosure.

When making disclosure, specificity is essential. A comprehensive disclosure statement tells who, what, when, where and how. An arbitrator should decline an appointment when aware of a relationship which, to a reasonable person, would present an appearance of bias. An arbitrator should also ask, "Based on the relationship (past or present), can I be truly objective and render an impartial decision?"

---

* Mr. Carmichael is Vice President of U.S. and International Mediation Services, of the American Arbitration Association. He is a graduate of the University of North Carolina at Charlotte.

V. Postponement Requests

Neutral Corner—Dealing with Postponement Requests

*by Neil Carmichael**

Postponements are the primary cause of delay in construction arbitration cases and the chief frustration of arbitrators and parties. Arbitrators should do everything in their power to see that, once set, the hearings are conducted as originally scheduled, while keeping in mind that one of the few statutory grounds for vacating an arbitration award is "refusing to postpone the hearing upon sufficient cause shown." Federal Arbitration Act § 10(3).

Prior to April 1, 1996, arbitrators acting under the American Arbitration Association's Construction Industry Arbitration Rules had no option but to consent to postpone the hearing when all parties mutually agreed to do so. Over time, this restriction on the arbitrator's authority allowed parties to drag out arbitration proceedings over an extended period of time and contributed to the impression by some that arbitrations were taking too long.

Effective April 1, 1996, the AAA's Construction Industry Arbitration Rules were revised in numerous respects in order to expedite the process and meet the needs of the construction industry. Among the changes was an amendment of Rule 26, which gives arbitrators the authority to overrule a joint postponement request made by the parties. In exercising this new authority, however, arbitrators should be cautioned to use restraint and only deny joint postponement requests for good cause.

When considering a unilateral postponement request, arbitrators should ask the following questions:

- Does the reason for the request constitute what the arbitrator considers good cause?
- Is there a history of delay by one or more parties?
- Could the party have foreseen the problem and made alternative arrangements in order to proceed as scheduled?

---

* Mr. Carmichael is Vice President of U.S. and International Mediation Services, of the American Arbitration Association. He is a graduate of the University of North Carolina at Charlotte.

- Does the request relate to evidence or witnesses? While arbitrators should not second-guess a party's case, they should be reasonably sure that the witness or evidence is relevant and material to a party's presentation.
- Are there alternatives to a postponement? For example, if a witness is unavailable, could the order of witness presentation be changed? Or could the witness' testimony be taken by affidavit or deposition?

In determining whether to grant or deny a postponement request, the arbitrator should seek to balance the parties' expectations and their agreement to obtain a speedy, economical resolution of the dispute against their due process needs and concerns. In balancing these interests the arbitrator should find it helpful to ask both sides how they will be prejudiced if the postponement is granted, and if it is not.

VI. Using a Neutral Architect

Dispute Resolution Using a Neutral Architect

by Jack Kemp*

Merchant housing construction projects all too often result in post-occupancy distrust and acrimony on the part of the builder and the homeowner. This usually leads directly to a lengthy drawn-out legal process. Fortunately, builders and owners are beginning to recognize the futility and high cost of resolving disputes using the litigation process.

Numerous dispute avoidance, prevention and resolution methods exist that can save time, money and relationships. This article examines a variant of one of these methods that proved quite successful in resolving post-construction disputes in the merchant housing setting; it involves the use of a neutral architect in a manner similar to that of a standing neutral or dispute review board.

The difference between merchant housing and most other projects involving a standing neutral is that the neutral comes on board after the construction project has already been completed and occupying home owners have lodged complaints against the developer through their home owner association (HOA).

One reason for the frequently repeated pattern of litigating disputes arising out of merchant housing projects is that the traditional relationship between the builder and owner does not exist. The builder is usually a developer—often a large entity whose focus is on market share—who builds the project for future buyers—as opposed to a contractor or tradesman retained by the owner to construct the project. The buyers—the ultimate owners—are not the traditional client. They are not business entities, but rather are end users who come along later, when the project is completed or nearly completed, as individual homebuyers who form an HOA typically run by a lay governing board.

---

* Jack Kemp, a member of the American Institute of Architects, is director of architecture at Ian Mackinlay Architecture in San Francisco. He serves on the roster of neutrals of the American Arbitration Association. Mr. Kemp was the neutral architect on the project described in this article.

The design architect's role in these projects is also changed because of this nontraditional relationship. Unlike most projects in which the architect performs services for the owner, here the architect works for the developer. As a result, some of the architect's services, which are normally sensitive to the traditional owner, are often curtailed.

As problems in the construction of their units are discovered by homeowners, the developer and the HOA may each receive partial and often conflicting information and advice from within their respective organizations, or in the case of the HOA, from the property management company it uses. As the problems escalate into a dispute, the developer and the HOA move into a litigation mode, beginning an adversarial dance that often ends in costly legal proceedings.

A different approach was recently taken by an HOA and the developer of a 95-unit residential project built in northern California in 1994, which were immersed in seemingly intractable disputes. They agreed, jointly, to address their differences by use of a "neutral architect." How did this come about?

Background

The HOA notified the developer of a number of problems the homeowners were having with their units. These included such things as water intrusion, firewall and shear wall defects, sewer clean-outs, concrete cracks and the like. The developer expressed a desire to correct the problems to the homeowners' satisfaction and avoid the standard litigation track.

The HOA and the developer each employed their own architectural consultants to assess and test the nature of the individual homeowners' claims. Both sides participated in investigating these claims and produced reports reflecting differing and often conflicting results. Eventually a scope of work of repairs was agreed upon, despite the different positions of the parties' retained experts. Although the parties really wanted the process to work, the process started to unravel when the time came to determine whose architect was going to oversee the agreed scope of work. Each side distrusted the other's expert architect and neither wanted the other's architect on site. Thus, the concept of the neutral architect was proposed as an alternative.

The HOA and the developer accepted the proposal to seek the services of a neutral architect who had no connection with either party or their representatives. The role and function of the neutral architect was spelled out in an "owner-contractor" agreement between the HOA and the developer. This took several months to finalize in order to resolve conflicts of interests and other concerns. The neutral architect's selection was accomplished by the attorneys representing each party.

Upon selection, the neutral architect entered into an agreement with both parties to provide only the services described in the agreed-upon scope of work. The parties agreed, however, that the neutral architect would decide disputes arising from or connected with the scope of work and that he would mediate or arbitrate any other disputes arising between the parties whenever they might occur.

Construction documents describing the scope of work were provided to the neutral architect for comment prior to the start of repairs in order to determine whether the documents properly reflected the parties' agreement and appropriate industry standards. The neutral architect's comments were distributed to each party's architectural consultant for review and resolution of issues raised by these comments. After these issues were resolved, the remedial work proceeded using the developer's supervisors and subcontractors, all under the observation of the neutral architect.

The success of the process, which involved repairs in occupied homes, was largely dependent on a close working relationship between the developer's superintendent and the HOA representative, who arranged for access to the individual units based on a preplanned, phased schedule. Any disputes arising out of access to the units or delays to the developer were to be resolved by the neutral architect.

The primary goal of the neutral architect was to function as an intermediary between the homeowners and the developer in much the same way as a music conductor acts to render a symphony to an audience. The written score and lyric represent the scope of work. The orchestra and choir are the builders and subs. The task is to interpret the scope of work so that both the composer and the audience are satisfied with the results; at the same time making sure that the musicians are team players from beginning to end.

Neutral Architect's Tasks

The construction was scheduled in twelve groups of eight units at a time. Since the work included the interiors of all units, it was up to the homeowners' representative to schedule access to the units according to the builder's schedule. For the most part, this process went smoothly. However, disputes did arise with six homeowners, ranging from requests to alter the scope of work on their individual units to outright refusal to permit access to the builder or anyone else.

After attempts by the HOA representative to resolve these conflicts met impasse, it was up to the neutral architect to bring these individual disputes to closure. The neutral architect resolved some of these disputes by requiring "waiver letters" from the six homeowners, which relieved the developer of responsibility for required work in their particular units. These waiver letters, in effect, constituted an agreement between the developer and the HOA to modify their contract. When the one homeowner who denied access refused to sign a waiver letter, the neutral architect exempted the unit from the scope of work requirements, which relieved the developer of responsibility for repair work on that unit.

The neutral architect also became involved in resolving issues raised by the parties regarding the agreed scope of work. Because of the nature of potential construction defects, the original scope of work included several solutions that represented "worst case scenarios." For example, in the case of leaky pot shelves, the original scope of work required that all pot shelves be torn out and rebuilt. Presumably this repair scheme resulted from the fact that the original testing did not confirm the exact nature of the leaks.

During the first phase of the repair program, the developer proposed additional testing of the pot shelves to try to eliminate the need for a complete tear-out. The neutral architect agreed to undertake the testing. The results of these tests showed specific defects that would not require complete tear-out. The design architect was notified and, in turn, provided alternate details for correcting these defects. These were reviewed by the neutral architect and the homeowners' architect and eventually were approved. The new repair procedure was initiated throughout the rest of the project. It saved several months of work and several thousand dollars of unnecessary tear-out and repairs.

In another instance, special conditions were found in the attic construction that did not conform to assumptions of as-built conditions or fit the remedial repair details. The neutral architect submitted the found conditions to the developer's design architect to provide new details. Then he acted as an intermediary, seeking and ultimately obtaining approval of the proposed modifications from the homeowners' consulting architect. As a result, the attic work was reduced in scope, allowing the subcontractor to be out of the attics before the long hot summer, when the work was originally scheduled.

As might be expected, disputes arose between the developer and the homeowners during the repair work. In one dispute submitted to the neutral architect for resolution, the developer contended that a particular repair on a single house should be exempted from the work because it had already been repaired by another party during destructive testing. The home owner claimed that the destructive testing was due to construction defects built in by the developer. The neutral architect determined that since the work was not specifically exempted from the scope of work of repairs, it should be performed.

Even before they entered into the contract for construction, the parties were unable to agree on whether the developer would or could guarantee window leak repairs. In fact, window leaks were, in large part, a big mystery to both sides. Since occupancy of the project, a number of window leaks were reported and repaired; some successfully, some not. Thus, there was no consistent basis on which to establish a scope of work of repair program to address future leaks. The issue of how to treat window leaks was addressed in the following manner.

The parties agreed that for a period of eighteen months after the signing of the contract for construction, it would be up to the individual home owner to report any window leak to the developer's customer service office. The developer would then observe the leak and make repairs within a given time frame. If, after the repairs were made but prior to the sunset date, the home owner continued to experience leaks or had any other problems with the repairs, the neutral architect would be called in to examine the issues and determine a follow-up course of action that each side would be required to accept.

The remedial repair project was originally scheduled to be completed in a little over eight months. The project started on time and was completed three months ahead of schedule. This was, in part, due to the neutral architect's extensive observation schedule. This schedule called for detailed observations and recordings of the progress of the work on each unit. Based on the neutral architect's interpretations of the contract documents, his expectations became evident to the developer's team of supervisors and trades early in the project. They learned right away what was expected of them and they performed accordingly. Ultimately, when a unit was presented to the neutral architect for observation, there was almost never a rejection or call for additional work. The spirit of cooperation and progress pervaded the scene and cut significant time off the project.

Conclusion

The neutral architect process for post-occupancy merchant housing construction disputes described here resulted from a carefully crafted owner-contractor agreement and a separate neutral-architect agreement, which were conceived by attorneys highly experienced and knowledgeable in construction disputes. The process succeeded on many levels. The savings of time in construction and other scope of work details resulted in a considerable savings of funds originally budgeted by the developer to complete the repairs. In addition, disruption to the resident homeowners from construction operations to correct the problems in their units was cut by over 35% off the original schedule.

While these successes were mostly due to the excellent construction program provided by the developer and the full cooperation of the homeowners and the HOA, the presence and involvement of the neutral architect seemed to greatly facilitate and enhance the process. Possibly this was due to the fact that the neutral architect represented to the parties the ideals of impartiality and fair dealing. Not once were the terms and conditions of the neutral architect's engagement tested or found to be inadequate. Due to the foresight of the drafters, the process, in the end, met and exceeded everyone's goals at all levels.

Post-occupancy construction disputes make up a large proportion of construction litigation. More attention needs to be paid to developing non-litigious processes to resolve these disputes successfully. The success of the repair project described above suggests that post-occupancy construction disputes can successfully be handled using a non-traditional, non-litigious approach, such as the neutral architect. The services of a neutral architect can be obtained from the American Arbitration Association, whose panel of construction arbitrators and mediators includes many experienced, skilled architects.

In exploring whether the neutral architect can be productively employed, it is important to understand the goals of the parties to disputes and appreciate whether there is a middle ground shared by the opposing sides. For example, when homeowners purchase newly built, state-of-the-art homes, they expect a certain level of quality. At the same time, the developer, whose business is to build and sell homes, wants to provide quality as a means to ensure a larger market share. These are clearly comparable goals. Rather than look at the extremes in an environment of advocacy, it is necessary to look at the convergence of goals as a starting point in the process of resolving disputes that arise.

It may be mere speculation to suggest that the neutral-architect concept may have application earlier in the post-construction scenario described above. Nevertheless, it might be worth considering whether advantages might accrue from the parties using a single neutral architect at the inception of a dispute, in lieu of the traditional advocate architects. Might the neutral-architect approach used at an earlier stage reduce distrust and acrimony and foster an atmosphere of trust and cooperation? Might time and money be saved?

The modern architect is no longer the "master builder," but is an active team participant in the construction process. The role of the architect in the resolution of construction disputes has long been recognized in the American Institute of Architects standard form construction documents, which make the design architect the initial arbiter of disputes between the owner and the general contractor. The success of the neutral architect in resolving disputes in the merchant housing project described here suggests that an experienced neutral architect can play a more active and expanded dispute resolution role.

CHAPTER TWO

MANAGING RISK AND AVOIDING DISPUTES

I.   Identify and Manage Project Risk to Contain Claims

The Key to Claims-Free Projects—
Identifying and Managing Construction Project Risk

by Ava J. Abramowitz*

Containing claims and their costs looms ever larger in the minds of those concerned with profitability and repeat business. In the construction field, the major construction industry groups selected mediation as litigation has become more costly.[1]

While everyone expects litigators to suffer some loss of business as a result of the move to mediation, there are two other probable unanticipated results. The first will be a drop in reported cases, as fewer disputants shoot it out in court. This will make legal counseling harder. After all, who can be certain of what courts will say when they lack opportunities to speak? The second will be the rise of the

---

* The author is a mediator in private practice in Chevy Chase, Maryland. Formerly an assistant U.S. attorney for the District of Columbia, deputy general counsel of the American Institute of Architects, and a vice president of Victor O. Schinnerer & Co., she is also a founding fellow of the American College of Construction Lawyers. Ms. Abramowitz is a graduate of Brandeis University and the George Washington University National Law Center. She is the author of NEGOTIATION ARCHITECT'S ESSENTIALS OF CONTRACT NEGOTIATION (John Wiley & Sons, 2002). This article was adopted from a paper presented before the ABA Forum on the Construction Industry.

[1] *See, e.g.,* AMERICAN INSTITUTE OF ARCHITECTS B151, ABBREVIATED OWNER-ARCHITECT AGREEMENT, ART. 7.1 (1997 ed.); ENGINEERS JOINT CONTRACT DOCUMENTS COMMITTEE 1910-1, OWNER-ENGINEER STANDARD AGREEMENT, EXH. H, 6.09A (1996 ed.); ASSOCIATED GENERAL CONTRACTORS DOC. NO. 200, OWNER-CONTRACTOR AGREEMENT AND GENERAL CONDITIONS, Sec. 12.2 (1997 ed.); and DESIGN BUILD INSTITUTE OF AMERICA DOC. 535, STANDARD FORM OF GENERAL CONDITIONS OF CONTRACT OWNER AND DESIGN-BUILDER, Sec. 10.2.4 (1998 ed.). The American Arbitration Association is the sole ADR provider expressly mentioned in all of the standard documents.

"full-service counselor" who focuses as much on preventing claims as on resolving them.

This article explores some of the key factors involved in claims prevention and how construction parties and counsel can use this information to succeed by better managing project risk. While the article focuses on construction data, its findings are universal. With analysis and strategic thinking, businesses can prevent claims, maintain client relations and profit in the process.

Ask yourself, "When does a construction project start to go bad?" You may think it's sometime after the contract is implemented, perhaps after the parties try to ignore a dispute that has arisen or attempt to resolve it without the benefit of counsel. But research suggests that construction projects get into trouble much earlier, well before litigators are retained to deal with the problem. In fact, the project may already be in trouble even by the time the lawyers begin contract negotiations.

This insight came to light as the result of a 1995 study, commissioned by CNA Insurance Companies and Victor O. Schinnerer & Co., which attempted to determine what precipitates construction claims.[2] The results of this study indicate that, while many factors can precipitate or prevent claims, a combination of several factors, when "aligned" by the construction owner and the other participants in the project at the front end of project development, can ward off claims.

Background of the Study

In 1993, CNA and Schinnerer, the underwriter of CNA's errors and omissions programs for architects and engineers (A/E), retained David Haviland, professor of architecture at Rensselaer Polytechnic Institute, to see if insureds under CNA's A/E program had special insights into the

---

[2] David Haviland, *Managing Your Project: Structuring the Project Team*, Vol. XXV, No. 2, GUIDELINES FOR IMPROVING PRAC. (Victor O. Schinnerer & Co., Apr. 1995); *Managing Your Project: Providing Professional Services*, Vol. XXV, No. 4, GUIDELINES FOR IMPROVING PRAC. (Victor O. Schinnerer & Co., Sept. 1995); *Managing Your Project: Claims Factors—Listening to Experience*, Vol. XXVI, No. 2, GUIDELINES FOR IMPROVING PRAC. (Victor O. Schinnerer & Co. Mar. 1996). This three-part paper, which contained a description of the methodologies, analyses and findings, looked at the raw data collected during the course of the study. The author thanks Schinnerer and Haviland for allowing her to plumb this data. However, the analyses and conclusions here are the author's alone, as are any mistakes.

causes of claims.[3] Data for the study came from Schinnerer, which opened up nearly forty years of insurance applications and claims files. Haviland stratified this database in order to come up with a core group that would receive an 18-page questionnaire examining management practices and claims experience.

To select the core group, Haviland identified 1,000 policyholders continuously insured with Schinnerer from 1981 through 1991—a rather rough and tumble economic period. He preliminarily divided that group into three subgroups: architects, engineers, and combined A/E firms. Then he further stratified them by the size of the firm (small, medium-small, medium-large, and large), and by the firm's claims experience (high, medium, or low loss, or no loss as compared to similar firms of that type and size).

Out of the 1,800 firms, Haviland selected seventy-two A/E firms to complete the questionnaire. The questionnaire asked the respondents to identify which of ninety-nine management practices they engaged in during the 10-year study period. Among the practices it covered were "various project delivery approaches, criteria for the selection of the architect, engineer and contractor, types of services provided, types of form agreements used, construction contracting practices, compensation methods and their adequacy, responsibilities for establishing project parameters, client characteristics and practices, selection of and practices employed by project staff and consultants, and approaches to planning, marketing, and risk management."[4]

In addition, the questionnaire asked, with respect to each of 138 factors whether, in the respondent's opinion and experience, the factor prevented or ameliorated claims or started or aggravated claims, or both.[5]

The answers to these questions would allow Haviland to assess the impact of the insureds' management practices and business opportunities, as reported in their insurance applications, on claims production.

---

[3] Haviland, *Managing Your Project: Structuring the Project Team*, supra n. 2, at p. 4.

[4] Under the CNA/Schinnerer policy a claim is "a demand for money or services" as a result of the insured's alleged wrongdoing. Hence, an angry phone call from an owner demanding that the A/E "come over now and fix it" is a claim. A lawsuit is not necessary to trigger the policy.

[5] The factors were selected based on the conventional wisdom that certain activities reduce the probability of conflict or the seriousness of claims, e.g., having a signed contract, limiting liability, invoking pre-claims assistance, continuing education and the like. In addition, certain hypotheses were tested, e.g., was high turnover seen as a producer of claims? Were recessions? Boom periods?

Findings

The study found that 25% of the seventy-two firms were free of claims over the 10-year period.[6] The report concluded that no one factor or practice warded off or caused claims. "Rather, a number came into play, many at the very outset of the project, when the owner and key players assemble the team." Haviland identified forty factors, twenty "claims preventers" and twenty "claims starters."

But a clearer picture emerges when the top twenty claims preventers (or ameliorators) are juxtaposed against the top twenty claims starters (or aggravators) and analyzed for commonalties. A number of factors are present in all of the claims-free insureds. These factors reflect an alignment of the project participants as to their objectives and ability to work effectively together at the outset of the project, before the contract is negotiated, which allows the project to be completed without any claims.

These are the factors that make up "front-end alignment:"

- The owner chooses experienced, capable participants.
- The owner chooses committed participants who work well together.
- The owner allocates the risks and responsibilities to the party most capable of handling them, and does not seek to retain all the benefits and none of the risks. Further, the owner provides each party with the authority and economic means to handle their assigned risks and responsibilities well.
- The owner makes necessary decisions promptly and is open to resolving disputes as soon as they arise.

While significant, these findings must be interpreted in context. First, the respondent group, while representative, is a small sampling of a large profession. Second, the data is not comprehensive. Third, the findings have not been blind-tested. Nonetheless, they teach an important lesson: Before any contract is negotiated, the owner and its counsel should open discussions with the other participants about the project and engage in advance planning to manage project risk.

---

[6] CNA/Schinnerer's data shows that claims have hovered at 22 claims per 100 insured firms for the last six years.

Below is a discussion of some of the factors found to be important to project success.

The Role of Experience

If one factor reverberates throughout the study, having experienced parties is a core predicate to project success. Experience is as necessary for the owner and its key staff as it is for the architect, the engineer, contractor and subcontractor. To be blunt, inexperienced people tend to cause problems because they usually have unrealistic expectations and make unreasonable demands. The more power inexperienced parties have in the project's hegemony, the more problems they can cause.

What kind of experience is indicated? A certain level of competence is assumed. Beyond that, the parties must be familiar with both the project type and the project delivery system (e.g., "design-bid-build" or "design-build"). Without this expertise, they will be handicapped in foreseeing problems and take remedial steps.

Additionally, the parties must be comfortable with the contract and its division of labor. They must be able to work effectively, both individually and as a team. The research suggests that when the parties have previously worked together effectively, the project benefits. This may be because they know what to expect of each other and have developed a level of trust. Parties are less prone to finger pointing when they have had proven working relationships that they wish to maintain.

Does this mean that inexperienced parties need not apply? Of course not. But they must recognize their inexperience as a limitation and take measures to remedy their lack of real experience. For example, they can form strategic alliances with more experienced persons, or bring in consultants. They must also be open to the advice and insights of others. Counsel to an inexperienced owner, A/E firm, contractor or subcontractor can help here by devising a strategy with the client to fill the experience void.

One strategy counsel might suggest to enhance the project's success is "partnering." This is an interactive method by which all the parties to the design and construction processes get together with a partnering facilitator in order to "strategize" ways to reduce risk, open channels of communications, agree on the steps to be taken to resolve disputes, and maximize the attainment of the participant's individual and collective goals and project success. Partnering works best when performed before any contracts are signed and all the partnering documents reflect a commitment to the partnering process and its goals.

The Owner's Role

If the claims-free A/E firms had anything in common, it was the ability to make an intelligent choice about the owner they wished to work with. While each participant in a construction project has the power to make or break the project, the owner plays a unique role since it selects the design and construction teams that will work on the project and it is the owner's expectations that are to be satisfied.

The design professionals who participated in the study observed that successful owners shared these attributes:

- They were experienced with the project type and delivery process.
- They were clear in their goals, objectives, project parameters and restraints.
- They were willing to compensate the A/E firm appropriately for the scope of work to be done.
- They were flexible in their approaches to the various issues that arose.
- They made decisions firmly and on time.
- They were open to resolving disputes immediately.

In other words, the owner was an active contributor to the success of the project.

These owner-attributes warrant attention at a time when so many owners are asking their lawyers for contracts that give them rights without responsibilities and rewards without risks. The study makes clear that this one-sided approach to the project endangers its chances of success. It is the owner's project, yes, but the owner has to be a proactive participant in project formation and implementation.

This means the owner must take on certain responsibilities. It must determine the scope, quality, time-frame, budget, and the objectives of the project. After all, no other participant in the construction process is in a position to know the owner's objectives.

The owner also must make timely decisions to keep the project on track, and must give the other participants sufficient support and guidance to permit them to meet their responsibilities. That support invariably means paying an appropriate fee for the work as much as it means positive feedback. The study indicated that the nature of the owner's feedback can influence the project. It seems that negative feedback (e.g., anger and adversarial posturing) does little to contribute to keeping the project on schedule.[7]

The owner's counsel should advise the passive owner or the owner who is prone to adversarial posturing that it receives the ultimate rewards of the construction project. Maximizing those rewards over the long run requires the owner to step up to bat in the design and construction innings with an openness and flexibility that encourages problems to surface and get resolved quickly.

Stability of the Firm

Six of the top forty factors that A/E firms identified with claims prevention relate to stability. The firms ranked a high turnover rate of the professional staff as the number nine aggravator of claims.

The more stable a firm's leadership and staff, the less likely claims will occur. This follows logically if we assume that experience and a commitment to the project are two key claims preventers. While the study looked only at the A/E firms' experience, the issue of stability would seem to have equal application to the other construction participants. Similarly, the stability of firm finances is also a factor in claims prevention. The tightness of money may stretch a firm more than any project can afford. The extra mile most owners want the A/E firm or the contractor to walk may just not be walkable, economically speaking.

An attorney who becomes aware that the client's professional staff is turning over at an increasing rate should raise the issue immediately and explain how firm instability might affect the project. Counsel and client should brainstorm potential options to manage those risks until a viable solution is found and implemented.

---

[7] "Study participants were asked to indicate the frequency with which their clients were assertive and positive, assertive and adversarial, or passive. Firms with more adversarial clients had more claims, but not higher losses from claims." Haviland, *Managing Your Project: Providing Professional Services*, *supra* n. 2, at p. 2.

Similarly, whenever a construction party's conduct is increasing the risk of claims or disputes, counsel should bring that conduct to the client's attention. There is no reason not to do so. In design and construction, one party's challenge can all too easily become another party's catastrophe. Stable firms, self-aware and in constant communication with each other can more quickly identify and manage risk.

Other Factors

The data shows that five factors are more important claims preventers than the specific type of delivery approach selected. The first factor is experience with the particular project delivery approach selected. As stated earlier, experienced people succeed more often than not, if only because they can anticipate and address problems faster and better than one who is new to the situation. Thus, the owner's counsel should think twice before proposing unique delivery systems with which few are familiar.

The second factor is allowing the A/E firm to be involved in the selection of the contractor, or the construction manager (CM), if there is to be one. Since construction contract documents are never complete, construction will go more smoothly if the contractor (or CM) can work effectively with the designer to bring the construction documents to life. That is why so many claims-free firms volunteer a list of good contractors (or CMs) from which the owner may invite bids. Some of these firms charge a lower fee for construction contact administration services when the contractor (or CM) is selected from the "recommended" list.

Using qualifications to select the contractor, rather than bid price alone, is the third factor. The data suggests that contractors selected on the basis of qualifications perform better. The federal government is beginning to recognize the value of qualifications in the contractor selection process.[8] The U.S. Army Corps of Engineers, for example, is increasingly using a "best value" approach to contractor selection. The Corps decides what contractor skills and qualifications are necessary, assigns a weight to each of the qualifications, and makes its selection

---

[8] "For the firms participating in the study, selection based principally on price or fee produced more claims and, to a lesser extent, higher losses from these claims." *Id.*

accordingly.[9] Immediate cost is invariably a measure, but it no longer needs to be the controlling one.

A related factor is whether the project involved a CM. The data shows that the presence of a CM increased the number of claims for the studied firms and, albeit to a lesser extent, losses from those claims. This is not an anti-CM statement. In many projects, having a CM can make all the difference. However, in many projects CMs are brought in too late to have their ideas and expertise incorporated into the A/E's thinking. Often all the CM can do is "undo" the design that was bid on, under the guise of "value engineering."[10]

Even when the CM is brought into the project early, it is yet another party with its own ideas and objectives for the project. This adds one more risk that needs to be managed.

The fifth and final factor is having adequate time to perform the job. Undue speed can cause problems. There is nothing inherently wrong with "fast tracking" a project. But fast tracking, without the careful detailing of an agreed program and scope of work can be dangerous. Designs implemented at one stage may prove to be insufficient at a later stage. This is especially true if the parties' understanding of the project changes over time.

Implementable Contracts

A review of the forty issues identified as claims starters or preventers reveals that 85% of them can be discovered before the project begins, and more than half of these can be addressed in the negotiating process. It follows that, to enhance the potential for a claims-free project, each of these issues should be resolved before counsel even puts pen to paper to draft the construction contract. Once these issues are resolved, counsel can incorporate their resolution into the contracts. This will ensure that the contracts are implementable and provide clear, coordinated, consistent and realistic predictions of what will happen, whether all goes well or not.[11]

---

[9] Several organizations, including AGC and AIA, have produced suggested contractor qualification criteria. Owners interested in maintaining a safe site may want to ask all bidders to reveal their "workers' compensation modification factor."

[10] Value engineering, by and large, is a misnomer, having little to do with engineering and even less with value. The later in the process it is introduced, the more likely, according to CNA/Schinnerer data, it will cause a claim.

[11] The AIA underscored this aspect of contracts in the section *Working with Owner-*

This is easier to say than do. We lawyers are trained and ethically required to zealously protect our client's parochial interests. Front-end alignment, however, requires we do that by looking out first for their projects. This may mean that at the outset of a project, counsel to construction parties should behave less like adversarial lawyers and more like business counselors, turning their attention away from contract language toward the construction process and the division of labor. That way project risks and responsibilities can be assigned to the party most capable of managing them, and the activities and fees of all can be orchestrated for coordinated success.

The study also recognizes the inherent dangers in letting difficult issues lie. Hence, the emphasis on decision-making up front and dispute resolution later. Counsel should help the client recognize early when a dispute is in the offing, as disputes stand a better chance of being resolved when they are approached quietly and quickly. To the extent that litigation is in the offing, counsel should keep an eye clearly on the interests of the project and less on legal positions. This should lead counsel to prepare the client for mediation.

The Role of Full A/E Services

The data indicates that A/E firms place great importance on providing full construction contract administration (CCA) services. They see this as a significant claims-preventer.

The reason for this is obvious. An A/E with CCA responsibilities, if on site at the appropriate moments, will be in a position to help catch and rectify mistakes, answer questions, interpret drawings and facilitate the construction process. Moreover, since some design work is best left to the field, that work can be completed by the A/E, consistent with the overall project. Under most standard documents, the A/E with CCA responsibilities is the only person on site serving as the express agent of the owner charged with looking out for the project's best interests.

With today's bundling and unbundling of A/E services, it is possible to have more than one A/E firm providing services. The owner's counsel should make sure that some A/E firm is providing CCA services to the project. If not, the owner should be advised of the impact of this

---

Developed Contracts in THE ARCHITECT'S HANDBOOK OF PROFESSIONAL PRACTICE, 514-518 (12th ed. AIA Press 1994).

arrangement so that it will not have unrealistic expectations concerning the A/E's role.

Steps for Lawyers

Not only construction parties need to learn the techniques of front-end alignment. Construction lawyers need to learn them too. Lawyers should help clients meet their strategic goals and objectives. This may be an antidote to the nascent "commoditization" of the legal profession.

The steps to becoming an effective front-end counselor are as follows:

- Educate yourself about design, construction and building economics. The more you know about how projects are conceived and built, the more you can help your client and foresee problems that might arise during the project.
- Get involved in the project early. This is easier said than done. Clients are acutely aware of legal fees, and an offer of earlier service can all too easily be misinterpreted.
- As soon as possible, introduce your client to the concept of front-end alignment and its value to the success of the project. The first time some parties consider some of the major claims preventers is the day they start reading the proposed contract. That's too late. They must understand the need to align the project before the contract drafting stage.
- Encourage your client to take the lead in the negotiation process. The top 20 claims preventers tell you why this is a good idea. During the contract negotiation process such issues as site responsibilities, risk/reward allocation, construction contract administration, scope of work, schedule and budget, dispute resolution, and other key issues could be brought to closure. Most of these are not legal issues. Yet, each of them must be decided before the contract is signed. Let your client address them early.
- Increase your client's experience base. The fact that experience contributes so strongly to claims prevention is a strong incentive for your client to boost its experience quotient. Ask your clients if they would like your assistance in helping them increase their experience through continuing education. You could arrange

seminars on negotiating contracts, front-end alignment, pre-project planning, and claims prevention. For many clients, recognizing the indicia of a problem when the world is whirling around them is hard. Harder still is accepting that there is a problem that can't be wished away. Teaching the warning signs of a potential claims situation should sensitize your clients to pick up signals they might otherwise ignore.
- Stop thinking of the contract as the primary, if not the sole, method of handling risk. Even the best lawyers cannot insulate their clients from risk. Nor should they try to do so. In general, people who take on reasonable risks and manage them well make money. People who try to avoid reasonable risks don't. Most clients want to make money. So the next time you jump for your favorite "hold-harmless" clause, ask your client, "Is this a reasonable risk for you, and, if not, how should it be handled so it is a reasonable risk for someone, maybe even you, to take?"
- In the same vein, stop thinking about litigation every time your client feels threatened. Think conciliation whenever possible. Conciliation and mediation should be the first choice.

There is one more step we lawyers can take to prevent claims in our profession and in the industries in which we practice law. We can encourage more studies on the causes and preventers of claims. As more is known, focusing on front-end alignment skills can only contribute to our clients' successes.

The 40 Factors

These are the forty factors architects and engineers identified as the top claims preventers and starters. Pre-project factors are highlighted with an asterisk (*). These can be addressed and managed before a contract is signed.

MANAGING RISK AND AVOIDING DISPUTES

	TOP 20 CLAIMS PREVENTERS	Prevention Value Highest=5	TOP 20 CLAIMS STARTERS	Starter Value Highest=5
1	Site responsibilities are clear and coordinated.	4.32	Site responsibilities are not clear and coordinated.	4.10
2	Firm turns down projects with uncompensated risks.	4.27	Client differences are not resolved immediately.	3.90
3	Construction administration services are in the contract.	4.26	Construction schedule, budget, are not tied to scope.	3.85
4	Project staff in the firm are experienced.	4.21	Client's project representative is inexperienced.	3.74
5	Firm has substantial experience with project type.	4.21	Firm accepts projects with uncompensated risks.	3.74
6	Scope, schedule, and budget are determined at the outset.	4.20	Infrequent site observations are made.	3.63
7	Firm's PM is experienced in managing projects.	4.11	Client has difficulty making decisions.	3.60
8	Client differences are resolved immediately.	4.10	Key issues are resolved after agreement signed.	3.56
9	Firm's values and orientation are stable over time.	4.08	Firm has high professional staff turnover rate.	3.53
10	Client's project representative is experienced.	4.07	Consultant project staff are not very experienced.	3.52
11	Systematic review of construction documents is undertaken.	4.06	Firm's PM is inexperienced in managing projects.	3.50

12	Firm has past experience with the client.	4.03	Construction contract admin. services are not in contract.	3.48
13	Key issues are resolved before agreement is signed.	4.02	Project agreements are not well coordinated.	3.46
14	Project staff have experience with project type.	4.02	The project is fast-tracked.	3.41
15	Staff are assigned to the project on a continuous basis.	3.98	The construction budget is inflexible.	3.40
16	Firm's PM has experience with the project type.	3.97	There is a high volume of change orders.	3.39
17	Firm's leadership/ownership is stable over time.	3.97	The construction schedule is inflexible.	3.39
18	Construction schedule, budget are appropriate to scope.	3.95	Client decisions are not systematically documented.	3.35
19	The client makes decisions firmly and on time.	3.95	Consultant's PM is not very experienced.	3.35
20	Systematic materials/product investigation.	3.95	The client is a committee.	3.31

II. Preventing Contract Disputes

Strategies to Prevent Construction Contract Disputes

*by Luc Picard**

Contract disputes arise on almost every large construction project. These disputes can be a costly drain on the parties' time and money. Think of all the people, apart from the lawyers, who become involved when a dispute erupts. Designers, engineers, site personnel, project managers, upper management, surveyors and expert witnesses all might be called upon to dedicate days or even weeks of full time work to research, compile and analyze information for the upcoming legal battle. Whether the dispute will be tried in court or settled in a less adversarial alternative dispute resolution (ADR) proceeding, it will have exhausted a lot of resources, both internally and externally.

The amount of money spent on resolving disputes can make the difference between a profitable project and a losing one. Certainly much of that money could be saved if the number of disputes were reduced, and if those that arose were resolved through ADR. This article offers suggestions to general contractors on how to take a proactive approach to preventing contract disputes through negotiation and drafting of construction contract documents.

Why Contract Disputes Arise

A well-written construction contract usually contains terms and conditions addressing the most foreseeable situations but cannot cover all possible issues that may arise during the life of a project. Thus, when unforeseen problems arise, as they inevitably do, the contract may not provide an answer.

Even when the contract addresses a particular issue, a dispute may arise because the contract lacks clear direction on how to resolve the

---

* The author is a senior contract claims manager under contract to a Fortune 500 company in the power generation industry. He is a member of the *Ordre des Ingenieurs du Quebec.*

matter. The contract provision may be vague or subject to different interpretations. Issues pertaining to contract language abound on international projects, where the parties often come from different cultures, or have different beliefs, values, needs and education. Translated contract documents may also produce problems since the translation could be incorrect, ambiguous or influenced by cultural nuances. It also may be interpreted differently than the original text.

Steps can be taken before and during contract negotiation to lay the groundwork to prevent disputes.

Prepare a Preliminary Project Evaluation

The owner will usually approach several contractors to bid on a project or circulate a request for proposal (RFP). The contractor generally responds with a formal bid or proposal. The prudent contractor decides whether to respond to the RFP by first preparing a "preliminary project evaluation" (PPE) that assesses and weighs all the risks involved with the undertaking.

The PPE considers the scope and feasibility of the project. Is the schedule reasonable? What impact might the location have on the project? Are there any labor concerns or subcontracting restrictions? Any problematic weather conditions? Are currency exchange rates likely to pose a problem? Are there any political risks? Does the contractor have the necessary experience to complete the project successfully? If not, what are the costs of obtaining the necessary experience? What are the capital needs of the project from the contractor's point of view? Does the contractor have the resources to meet that need? Can the contractor meet the owner's expectation and expect to make a profit?

To measure the expected reward against the full range of risks associated with the project, the contractor must imagine all the possible "what if" scenarios that could arise. For example, what would happen if local building codes were to change, or if a threatened labor strike were to push construction into a season when weather conditions would make construction more difficult?

If the contractor ultimately submits a proposal or bid and is awarded the contract, each risk identified in the PPE should be addressed and appropriately allocated in the contract.

Use Teams

During the proposal or bid-preparation process, it is important for all of the engineers who are working on the technical specifications to meet regularly with their commercial team to discuss and clarify each aspect of the project, including any related documents that need to be prepared. In addition, all staff members working on the commercial, financial, engineering and legal aspects of the proposal should work together as a team. They should meet regularly or hold conference calls to report to each other on the progress of the proposal and review each other's work.

It is advisable to form a committee of experts in sales, finance, law and engineering to proofread the proposal or bid. The committee should consist of people who are not directly involved in developing the proposal or bid. Taking this step can identify critical errors and omissions that could save the contractor from making very costly mistakes.

The contractor's upper management should review and approve the proposal or bid package before sending it to the owner. I recommend that an internal review board, composed of senior management staff, read, comment on and approve the final proposal or bid package.

Avoid Low Margin Bids

Contractors should beware of submitting a bid or proposal with a narrow profit margin. The belief that a thin margin can be made up with change orders for extra work is misplaced. Extra work orders rarely compensate the contractor for low profitability. Moreover, a contractor who regularly submits change-order requests for extra work risks alienating the owner. The owner may simply refuse the request or even require the contractor to perform the extra work without allowing any price change. In the end, a project bid or proposal with a thin margin greatly increases the odds that disputes will arise over change orders.

Take Time for Drafting

After the project is awarded, the parties often rush to finish drafting the contract. This should be avoided. The parties should meet as often as necessary to question, clarify and resolve all issues concerning the scope of work, deliverables, performance schedule, division of responsibilities, allocation of risk, and any other matters of concern. Pitfalls and problems can be identified by asking probing questions. What is the owner expecting? What is the contractor promising? What does the draft contract say? Does it reflect what the owner and contractor intend to agree upon? Does it accurately reflect who is required to do what and when? What kinds of guarantees are being given? Are they appropriate? What are the consequences for failing to meet contract milestones or missing contract deadlines?

Disputes can be minimized by taking the time to ensure that the contract is complete, accurate and consistent. It helps to prepare a list of all the project responsibilities, including those of subcontractors and third-party suppliers, listing next to each the actions that need to be taken, when they are required to be made, and who will be responsible for them. This list can be compared to the contract to determine if the goals of accuracy, completeness and consistency have been achieved.

Many construction contract disputes arise because there is a gap between, or an overlap in, the scope of work of the prime contractor and subcontractors. To reduce the potential for disputes, all contract requirements, obligations, deliverables, guarantees and milestones should be assigned to the appropriate subcontractors and suppliers. Carefully delegating and coordinating the responsibilities of the prime contractor and the subcontractors will help avoid having contract responsibilities slip through the cracks.

Don't Assume

A contractor should never speculate or assume anything. For example, never assume that the owner will approve change orders for extra work. The owner may believe that a prudent, diligent contractor should have foreseen the need for the work.

It is not advisable to reopen a contract after it is signed, even though it is possible to do so, because the owner generally will ask for greater concessions from the contractor. The owner may even feel deceived by a contractor who seeks to reopen a contract or be relieved of contract obligations. Such a loss of credibility is not in the contractor's interest since a disgruntled owner will be more likely to find areas of dispute.

The contractor is better off understanding the obligations imposed by a contract and saying "no" before the contract is signed to those obligations that seem unattainable, unrealistic or beyond the contractor's control. This will help the contractor avoid being placed in a default situation at a later date.

A Fair Agreement in Plain English

A fair contract is less likely to generate disputes. A contract that clearly favors one party over another can sabotage the project. The disadvantaged party is likely to feel frustration and resentment, emotions that are not conducive to completing a project without claims.

An agreement that is clear and easy to understand is also less likely to generate problems. Adjectives and adverbs like "very" and "reasonable" are subject to interpretation and can lead to misunderstandings. The expression "good engineering practice" also can be interpreted in different ways.

The drafter should opt for quantitative words, rather than qualitative ones, and use tested language that has worked well in prior contracts. This does not mean that generic provisions and "boilerplate" terms may be used with impunity. Such provisions should be used with care since they may not be appropriate to the particular project. It is important for the contract to be tailored to the specific needs of the project.

Include an ADR Clause

Although the goal is to avoid all disputes, this may not be possible. Because the project must continue even when the parties disagree, the contract should prescribe methods of dispute resolution that the parties can use if they are unable to resolve their differences amicably themselves.

I recommend that parties include an ADR clause providing for mediation first, followed by arbitration if the parties do not reach a settlement in mediation. These processes are more efficient and less costly than litigation. They are also more private and allow the parties to enter into confidentiality agreements. The parties would be well advised to adopt the widely accepted mediation and arbitration rules of an experienced ADR organization, such as the American Arbitration Association (AAA) to govern their ADR proceedings.

I also suggest that the parties consider supplementing their contract with an agreement to use early dispute resolution techniques, such as the dispute review board (DRB). The AAA recently issued guide specifications for the use of DRBs, along with a model contract.

A Smooth Transition

Disputes also may arise after responsibility for the project is transferred from the commercial team (which negotiated the contract) to the "execution" team (which is responsible for completing the project under the leadership of the project manager). The project manager generally played no role in drafting the contract documents and thus may perceive the contract requirements differently from the sales people who did the negotiating. Different perceptions can sometimes lead to negative attitudes that can poison the atmosphere when things do go wrong on the project.

The risk of these disputes can be reduced by providing a smooth transition between the commercial team and the execution team. It helps to have a project "kick-off" meeting at which the two teams can discuss any ambiguous contract terms, conditions and requirements. Individuals who were involved in the contract negotiation also should be available, when necessary, as a resource to the execution team to clarify the meaning of ambiguous contract language.

During the execution of a project, the parties should be alert to early warnings of potential disputes. An example of such a "red flag" is a progress report that indicates variances between the actual work and the contract requirements.

Potential disputes should not be accumulated for a global settlement at the end of a project. It is vital to address and resolve them as they arise. When it is not possible to defuse an emerging dispute despite efforts at communication and collaboration, the parties should resolve their dispute in accordance with the ADR provisions in the contract.

Conclusion

Taking a proactive approach during the process of preparing the proposal and negotiating and drafting the contract documents should help reduce the number of disputes on construction projects. Keeping an inventory of success stories, lessons learned, and the strategies that worked on the project will make experience a useful teacher. This will help future execution teams identify the most common pitfalls and causes of construction disputes, as well as the "best practices" that can be implemented in future contracts.

III. Industry Guidelines for Avoiding and Resolving Construction Disputes

ASA/AGC/ASC Joint Guideline on the Avoidance and Resolution of Construction Disputes

The American Subcontractors Association (ASA), the Associated General Contractors of America (AGC) and the Associated Specialty Contractors (ASC) have adopted the Guideline on the Avoidance and Resolution of Construction Disputes. The full text of this guideline is printed below.*

The construction industry is complex and so are most building construction projects. In the process, inevitable differences arise concerning project scope definition, delays, accelerations, obstructions, and changed conditions. All the while, the process of building must go forward with a minimum of disruptions.

Resorting to lawsuits can be costly and time consuming. Also, judges and juries generally lack an understanding of the construction process. The net result is that all too often only lawyers, consultants and expert witnesses benefit from lengthy court actions.

Dispute Avoidance

The Associated General Contractors of America, the American Subcontractors Association, and the Associated Specialty Contractors support programs to minimize disputes through equitable allocation of risks in contracts and fostering cooperation among members of the construction team throughout the building process. That may be accomplished through teamwork programs such as Partnering. It involves a post-award program that includes several days of meetings among owner, design professional, construction manager, and major specialty contractor representatives working together to identify potential problems and to develop practical solutions.

AGC, ASA and ASC support the principle that the vast majority of construction disputes are susceptible to settlement through the give-and-take process by decision makers of construction team members without

---

* Reprinted with permission from THE SUBCONTRACTOR, Feb./March 2000.

resort to formal third-party intervention. The associations further urge minimizing the role of lawyers in as much as construction problems usually relate more to fact and customary industry practice rather than emphasis on legal issues.

Because of the desirability of settling disputes quickly and inexpensively, AGC, ASA and ASC jointly endorse the use of contract language calling for the parties to endeavor to settle disputes through direct discussions before using other forms of dispute resolution, such as a dispute review board, advisory arbitration (nonbinding), a mini-trial, binding arbitration, or resort to a judicial tribunal.

Some construction contract documents require referral of claims initially to the architect prior to use of mediation, alternate dispute resolution or litigation. The associations oppose this practice for claims between contractors and subcontractors as being an impediment to quick, economical dispute resolution.

Nonbinding Alternative Dispute Resolution (ADR) Methods

The most frequently used method of nonbinding alternative dispute resolution (ADR) is mediation. Mediation consists of one or more impartial parties advising and consulting with those involved in a dispute. The mediator cannot impose a settlement but rather guides the parties toward their own settlement. Mediation is available to the parties by mutual agreement even though a contract may specify arbitration. Moreover, in many jurisdictions courts will require mediation before a lawsuit can proceed. AGC, ASA and ASC support contract language requiring the parties to use mediation prior to other ADR methods or litigation.

Another nonbinding ADR method available for use is the mini-trial. It is not a trial in the usual sense of an adversarial judicial proceeding. Instead, it is a relatively structured process whereby management representatives of the parties to a dispute operate within mutually agreed upon time limits to conduct informal conferences and hold nonbinding, confidential discussions. It is normal for attorneys to prepare positions for the parties. The basic idea is to have the principals of firms see the relative strengths and weaknesses of their cases and to serve as a basis for negotiations among them to resolve the dispute.

Dispute resolution and counseling panels, often referred to as dispute review boards, are other nonbinding ADR services. These involve use of panel members who ordinarily are technical experts chosen in advance to address disputes as they arise on a project. The aim is to act quickly on moderately-sized disputes before confrontational attitudes harden. Panel decisions entered as evidence in arbitration or litigation, by agreement of the parties, can be accepted as final and binding.

A similar method, the project neutral, employs a single construction professional to serve as a dispute forum for the project. This method often is used for relatively small projects, while a full panel is often used on larger projects. Still other ADR techniques are: (1) step negotiations involving the passing of disputes to successively higher levels of management until resolved; (2) referral of technical questions to project architects for initial decisions; (3) advisory rulings by neutral experts; (4) nonbinding advisory arbitration; and (5) fact-based mediation whereby a mediator suggests a settlement amount and then assists in negotiation.

Arbitration

Unlike most other ADR methods, arbitration is final and binding. Decisions are subject to challenge only on narrow grounds such as prejudice or bad faith. Arbitration is used widely in the construction industry, and the practice is encouraged by provisions in standard documents calling for arbitration in accordance with the Construction Industry Arbitration Rules of the American Arbitration Association.

Arbitration may involve one or three arbitrators jointly chosen by the parties. The process normally is simpler than litigation and has the major advantage of cases being heard by persons experienced in the construction industry. AGC, ASA and ASC recognize the desirability of using the flexibility of arbitration by tailoring rules to fit specific cases but deplore the growing excessive use of legalistic approaches that unnecessarily slow the settlement process and increase costs to the parties.

Conclusion

AGC, ASA and ASC support initial efforts to settle disputes through direct negotiations. If it becomes necessary to use neutral third parties to assist in the resolution process, AGC, ASA and ASC encourage consideration first of the use of mediation or other nonbinding ADR methods because of speed and cost considerations. Finally, where parties to a dispute want final and binding resolution, the associations support arbitration using qualified, properly trained persons as arbitrators and utilizing expedited and equitable procedures to the extent practical.

IV. Tailoring Design-Build Agreements to Avoid and Resolve Conflicts

Avoiding Disputes in the Design-Build Environment

by Michael C. Loulakis*

Many owners turn to the design-build delivery system because they want to avoid disputes.[†] The standard form design-build contracts for owners and design-builders published by the Design Build Institute of America, a Washington, D.C.-based trade organization that promotes design-build delivery systems, contain dispute resolution provisions that call for both binding and nonbinding dispute resolution methods when disputes arise.

The advantages of these dispute resolution processes are discussed below. But as this article also demonstrates, through creative contracting and administration of both the prime design-build contract and the contracts between the design-builder and its team members, the parties can minimize and perhaps avoid disputes altogether.

What Is Design-Build?

In a design-build project, the design-builder is contractually responsible for completing both the design and construction of the project—regardless of how many subcontractors (including architects and engineers) it will rely upon to carry out these tasks. Thus, all architectural, engineering and construction services are covered in a single agreement between the owner and the design-builder.

In the traditional project delivery system, the owner bears the risk of gaps in the contract documents. The owner impliedly warrants the

---

* Mr. Loulakis is a senior shareholder in the Vienna, Va., office of Wickwire Gavin, P.C., where he has practiced construction law for more than 20 years. He received a B.S. in Civil Engineering from Tufts University and a J.D. from Boston University School of Law. His publications include *Design-Build for the Water and Wastewater Industry,* CONSTRUCTION BRIEFINGS (West 2003, co-author).

† Adapted from chapter 10 of DESIGN-BUILD CONTRACTING CLAIMS (Barry B. Branble & Joseph D. West, eds. Aspen Law & Business © 1999). Reprinted with permission. Copies of DESIGN-BUILD CONTRACTING CLAIMS may be ordered from Aspen Law & Business.

sufficiency of the design to the contractor and if there are defects in the design, the contractor may be entitled to additional sums from the owner. Since the owner probably cannot recover these sums from the architect/engineer because the A/E's liability is governed by a negligence standard of care, it must absorb this loss.

By contrast, in the design-build system, gaps in the contract are the responsibility of the design-builder, which is deemed to provide an implied warranty of the sufficiency of the documents to the trade subcontractors working on the project. Making the design-builder responsible for these gaps removes a major area of potential dispute between the owner and the design-builder. However, there are numerous other fertile areas where potential conflict could arise.

Dispute Resolution

Despite the parties' best efforts to avoid conflict, disputes can and will arise on construction projects. Disputes are generally resolved in one of two ways—through binding or nonbinding processes.

A binding dispute resolution process is one in which a neutral third party, such as a judge, jury or arbitrator, makes a decision that is final and binding on the parties. The two traditional types of binding dispute resolution are arbitration and litigation. Arbitration is a consensual method for resolving disputes, with the consent coming either in the form of an executory agreement to arbitrate (as when the parties agree in their contract to arbitrate all disputes) or an agreement to arbitrate after the dispute has arisen.

Because arbitration occurs by agreement, the parties are free to adopt or modify the rules of an ADR provider, such as the American Arbitration Association, or craft their own arbitration rules. For example, the parties may determine the number of arbitrators who will decide the dispute, the extent, if any, of discovery, the time and location of the hearing, and whether other related disputes can be consolidated with the dispute at hand.

Litigation, on the other hand, does not require an agreement by the parties. It is the dispute mechanism of last resort. Procedures for litigation are prescribed by applicable state and federal statutes and regulations, with the parties having little control over the process once it begins. As a result, once litigation commences, the parties may be faced with motions, discovery requests and scheduling orders that will pace the overall process, which is usually quite lengthy and prone to delay. It should be noted that some issues—such as the waiver of a jury trial and the forum for the proceedings—can be established by contract.

Nonbinding dispute resolution processes, by contrast, involve methods that encourage the parties to resolve their own disputes, typically by using a neutral to assist in the process. Nonbinding processes that are popular with some construction parties include "stepped" negotiations at the job site, dispute review boards (DRBs), and mediation. These all provide for the involvement of the parties' top decision-makers in informal, structured-settlement proceedings, with a third-party neutral helping them reach a fair and equitable settlement. Some processes, like mediation, offer the opportunity for a creative solution and involve the parties in fashioning the settlement, while the DRB offers objective case evaluation. One technique that has proven effective in decreasing conflict on a project is partnering. This involves educating the stakeholders on the project about the value of communication and developing a commitment to teamwork and to reducing conflict on the job site.

The DBIA model agreements, both the Standard Form of Preliminary Agreement Between the Owner and the Design-Builder (Document 520), and the General Conditions of Contract Between the Owner and the Design-Builder (Document 535) provide for "stepped" ADR processes. The Preliminary Agreement calls for mediation, but if the mediation does not resolve the dispute, the next step is arbitration. Both arbitration and mediation are conducted under the AAA Construction Industry Dispute Resolution Procedures.

The General Conditions contain an additional step. It provides first for "stepped negotiations," a process in which discussions take place at the field level between the parties' representatives. If these discussions fail to resolve the dispute, the next step is for the senior representatives of the parties to meet to try to settle the matter. If that fails, then the dispute proceeds to mediation, and if necessary to arbitration under the AAA Construction Industry Arbitration Rules. The General Conditions are used with DBIA's Standard Form of Agreement Between the Owner and Design-Builder (Lump-Sum) (Document 525), and its Standard Form of Agreement Between the Owner and Design-Builder (Cost) (Document 530).

Avoiding Owner-Design-Builder Disputes

Having dispute resolution mechanisms in the agreements is vital in any construction project, whether design-build or not. But in the design-build arena, the parties can do a great deal to minimize the occurrence of disputes by recognizing where problems may arise, and through appropriate contract drafting, risk allocation and contract administration, nip them in the bud.

Partnering. The parties can employ partnering to reduce the occurrence of disputes. The use of partnering is consistent with the overall design-build dispute avoidance and resolution strategy, which is a team approach to all aspects of the project.

Method of Procurement. The design-builder may be selected based on qualifications or on the basis of competitive bidding in response to Requests for Proposals (RFPs). When qualifications form the basis for the selection of the design-builder, the owner is likely to have greater trust in the selected design-builder, so that significant conflict is less likely to develop.

When the method of procurement of the design-builder is on the basis of the bid, more potential problems may arise. In that situation, there is little opportunity to discuss the RFP or the proposal and thus little opportunity to develop trust or have anything other than a formal relationship. Moreover, the expense and time of responding to an RFP can lead a dissatisfied bidder to complain about the procurement process.

To control conflict in this area, the owner must understand what it wants to achieve and define its construction requirements in the RFP. If the procurement system is flexible enough, the owner should consider having the design-builder assist in the development of, or review and comment on, the project requirements. If the owner and design-builder agree on them, there is less basis for disagreement later on. The design-builder then prepares schematic documents and a proposed contract price and schedule based on the owner's criteria.

To minimize bid protests in the selection of the design-builder, the owner should employ a selection process that is not overly complex, and be faithful to selection criteria it selects. Design-builders who wish to bid will evaluate the selection criteria in the RFP in the hope of putting together a successful proposal. The owner should have clear and logical selection criteria. It can be helpful to assign weights to the criteria or list them in order of importance. Providing a specific weight for price can help the design-builder determine what it is willing to offer. The owner should not decide after receiving the proposals to change the weight given to the selection criteria in the RFP.

The owner may find it useful to use an impartial selection committee made up of individuals with the qualifications necessary to objectively review the proposals and determine the reasons behind any major scoring differences among the committee members.

Procurement and Confidentiality. Design-builders who submit proposals on public and private sector projects are often concerned that their unique ideas will be communicated to their competitors or others. This concern often arises when the owner requires revised technical submissions that attempt to normalize the design requirements. These requests ultimately result in a selection process based on the lowest bid on the design. Many design-builders will not furnish the owner with their best concepts during this type of proposal process because there is no competitive advantage in doing so in a process that moves toward price competition.

The owner should be aware of the design-builder's concerns in establishing its procurement process. As a general rule, owners who give adequate assurance that the information provided by a design-builder during the proposal process will be kept confidential have a better chance of receiving the best technical proposals. Regardless of which selection process is used, it is important for both the owner and the design-builder to understand what will happen once a proposal is communicated to the owner and the limits, if any, upon the owner's ability to use this information.

Ambiguity in the Bid Proposal. Procurement of design-build services on a competitive basis creates the potential for ambiguity regarding the scope of the design-builder's contractual obligations. This is particularly true when the RFP contains a mixture of performance and design specifications. To avoid discrepancies between the RFP and the actual proposals, some owners require design-builders to provide a "specific deviation list" with their proposals that clearly identifies how the proposal differs from what is required by the RFP. This puts the owner on notice of what the design-builder intends to provide for the price offered.

Owners also will reduce areas of potential conflict by using performance specifications where possible, rather than prescriptive ones.

In the private sector, the problem of ambiguity is reduced or avoided by having both parties jointly develop, before execution of the contract, a conformed set of specifications that merges the RFP and the terms of the design-build proposal into a single, consistent document.

Contractual Risk Allocation. The pricing of a design-build contract will depend upon what risks and contingencies the design-build team feels can be controlled and measured. If the team is required to assume unreasonable risk, the owner should expect the design-builder to price this risk accordingly in its proposal. The owner should also expect conflict to develop over the interpretation of the risk-shifting clauses. There are many opportunities for conflicts to develop once the design-build contract is executed. Some of these conflicts can be avoided through appropriate contractual allocation of risk.

Meet and Confer. In the design-build process, the owner has the right to review and approve the design as it is developed by the design-builder. The overall project schedule will include the time allotted for the owner to conduct its reviews and give its approvals. There will also be conditions to payment that must be met. This process places the owner and design-builder in a close working relationship. To avoid having such issues as design, schedule and payment lead to contentious disputes, delays and claims, the parties should establish a contractual mechanism that identifies how the parties will deal with each of these issues. The approach endorsed by the DBIA and documents published by the Engineers Joint Contract Documents Committee is having "meet and confer" provisions in the contract. These provisions call for the parties to meet to discuss key issues and procedures. This fosters a team approach, which is more likely to ensure that the parties stay on the same side.

Owner's Role. Most owners have some specific responsibilities that are critical to project success. Examples include providing specifications, surveys and site information, and obtaining permits. An effective way to avoid disputes is to have the contract clearly define what the owner is expected to do on the project. This is particularly helpful when the owner will be using other contractors on the project. On certain types of utility or energy projects, the owner may have additional responsibilities to provide fuel or interconnection services. These responsibilities and the consequences of any delays should be clearly understood by the parties to avoid disputes later on.

Designating Party Representatives. The owner and design-builder each designate a representative to act on its behalf in all project-related activities. The best choices for these representatives, who are often selected at the outset of the project, are individuals who have the personality and skills necessary to deal with and resolve conflict. Senior personnel who see the "big picture" and are not too close to the project are often well-suited to serve as representatives and resolve potential problems.

Changes to the Work. The process of extra work orders has long been a breeding ground for project disputes. These include:

- proposals requested by the owner that are never accepted, leaving the design-builder with unreimbursed proposal costs;
- changes requested by the owner that are performed before the parties agree on their impact on cost and time; and
- disputed scope-of-work items, which the owner directs the design-builder to perform at the latter's own cost.

Each of these situations exposes the design-build team (including subconsultants and subcontractors) to financial loss and reduced cash flow. As a result, it is important for the parties to address each of these situations in the contract and establish a balanced approach to handling them.

The most significant problems with the change-order process occur when the parties disagree on the scope of the design-builder's work. In these situations, the design-builder can be at a major disadvantage, since it is required to perform the work and then proceed through the disputes mechanism of the contract to receive payment. Some contracts require the parties to agree on the commercial terms of a change before implementing it. An approach that does not place the owner at the whim of the design-builder's pricing of the change is to require the owner to pay 50% of the reasonable estimated direct cost to perform the services, without prejudice to either side. This is the approach taken in the DBIA model contracts.

Avoiding Disputes within the Design-Build Team

Much of the discussion about the design-build process focuses on the relationship between the owner and the design-builder. While this relationship establishes the overall structure of the design-build team, the design-builder must look carefully at its relationships with the team and determine how to avoid disputes at that level, since those working for the design-builder will be critical in determining whether the project is successful.

In every project the design-builder should get the major subcontractors involved early. This minimizes the risk that it will be quoting prices based on incomplete designs and inadequate scope definitions. The subcontractors will also be more familiar with the nuances of the design that may affect their actual bids for the work.

The design-builder also must recognize the importance of the design to the overall project and give the architect/engineer a strong say in the overall management of the design phase. It also should determine with the architect/engineer the role the latter is to play during construction to facilitate a conflict-free project.

Finally, the design-builder must develop good relationships with team members, encouraging an atmosphere of trust, cooperation and teamwork.

The unique nature of the design-build delivery system creates some interesting alternatives for the parties in developing dispute avoidance and resolution strategies. Although ADR processes are available, the parties should remember that many owners are driven to design-build for conflict reduction. Creative contracting and administration of both the prime design-build contract and the contracts between the design-builder and its team members can provide ample means of achieving these goals.

V. Waivers of Consequential Damages

Negotiating Consequential Damages Waivers

by Charles M. Sink*

The "waiver of consequential damages" provision became a part of the American Institute of Architects revised standard form construction documents in 1997. Both 1997 editions, of the AIA standard contract between the owner and the contractor (Form A201) and standard contract between the owner and the architect (Form B141), added the waiver provision. These contracts probably are more widely used and copied than any other construction industry agreements. Because these contracts provide for mediation and arbitration, the consequential damages waivers are more likely to be interpreted by the participants in the mediation, or by arbitrators, if the dispute is not settled during mediation.

This article offers practical advice about these waivers and suggests how they can be tailored to the particular transaction.[1]

The addition of the waiver of consequential damages provision was a profound change in the AIA standard form contracts. (Another profound change in these contracts was the addition of mandatory mediation under the Construction Industry Mediation Rules of the American Arbitration Association.) When these revised form contracts were issued, the AIA explained in a news release that "by setting the stakes in a potential dispute more definitively, the contract avoids a rapidly intensifying adversarial atmosphere." Howard Goldberg, counsel to the AIA Document Committee, said of the revised AIA forms, "The mutual

---

* Charles M. Sink is a partner in San Francisco's Farella Braun & Martel, and was recognized a one of the leading construction attorneys in California in *2004 Chambers USA Guide to America's Leading Business Lawyers.* Mr. Sink received his B.A. from Harvard University and his J.D. from Hastings College of Law, University of California. He is the author of *Limitations on Contract and Tort Damages, in* CONSTRUCTION DAMAGES AND REMEDIES, GWYN & SINK (ABA 1998).

[1] A more extensive analysis of this and related damages limitations in arbitration agreements appeared in the CONSTRUCTION LAWYER, Vol. 18, No. 2 (ABA Forum Committee on the Construction Industry). An analysis of all the substantive changes made in the 1997 A201 Document appears in SINK & PETERSON, THE A201 DESKBOOK: UNDERSTANDING THE REVISED GENERAL CONDITIONS (ABA Forum on the Construction Industry 1998).

waiver of consequential damages provision is AIA's first attempt to interject tort reform principles in the construction industry." The waiver can be read very broadly—covering "all consequential damages." [2]

The provision goes on to itemize the types of losses covered by the mutual waiver. Section 4.3.10 (Claims for Consequential Damages) provides:

> The Contractor and Owner waive all claims against each other for all consequential damages arising out of or relating to this Contract. This mutual waiver includes:
>
> 1. damages incurred by the Owner for rental expenses, for losses of use, income, profit, financing, business and reputation, and for loss of management or employee productivity or of the services of such persons; and
> 2. damages incurred by the Contractor for principal office expenses including the compensation of personnel stationed there, for losses of financing, business and reputation, and for loss of profit other than anticipated profits arising directly from the Work.
>
> This mutual waiver is applicable, without limitation, to all consequential damages due to either party's termination in accordance with Article 14 (Termination or Suspension of the Contract). Nothing contained in this Subparagraph 4.3.10 shall be deemed to preclude an award of liquidated direct damages, when applicable, in accordance with the requirements of the Contract Documents.

When drafting construction agreements, the waiver provisions should be evaluated by counsel and client in the context of the particular project. They should consider whether the benefit of having the waiver outweighs the disadvantages. For example, an owner facing substantial financing costs and significant lost income in the event of a delay, may conclude that having the waiver would not be appropriate. (In this case, the owner might opt instead to have an appropriate liquidated damages clause.)

---

[2] *See New AIA Documents Adopt Mediation,* PUNCH LIST, (Fall 1997), at 5.

If counsel and client believe it would be beneficial to include a waiver provision, they may wish to tailor it to suit their transaction. However, construction parties should be aware that the scope of the waiver provision, whether or not they alter it, may be questioned once a dispute arises. This could make the role of the mediator or arbitrator more difficult, at least until better norms are established for the type of damages that may be recovered.

If a construction party wants to retain the waiver and exclude all consequential damages, counsel may wish to add to the arbitration clause a provision that expressly curtails the arbitrator's ability to award consequential losses. For example, this provision might state:

> The arbitrators shall have no authority to award, directly or indirectly, any form of consequential damages, as such damages have been waived by the parties to this contract.

A project owner might wish to specify additional forms of consequential damages that are excluded. A sample clause might provide:

> Such prohibited damages include, but are not limited to: lost profits; home office overhead or any form of overhead not directly incurred at the project site; wage or salary increases; ripple or delay damages; loss of productivity; increased cost of funds for the project; extended capital costs; lost opportunity to work on other projects; inflation costs of labor, material, or equipment; non-availability of labor, material, or equipment due to delays; increased cost of bonding due to delay; or any other indirect loss arising from the conduct of the parties to this contract.

A contractor or design professional might wish to add the following language to the waiver provision:

> Such prohibited damages include, but are not limited to: lost rent or revenue; rental payments for temporary offices; increased costs of administration or supervision; costs or delays suffered by others (unable to commence work or provide services as previously scheduled) for which a party to this contract may be liable; increased costs of borrowing funds devoted to the project; delays in selling all or part of the project upon completion;

termination of agreements to lease or buy all or part of the project (whether or not suffered before completion of services or work); forfeited bonds, deposits, other monetary costs, or penalties due to delay of the project; increased taxes (federal, state, local, or international) due to delay or re-characterization of the project; lost tax credits or deductions due to delay; impairment of security; or any other indirect loss arising from the conduct of the parties to this contract.

Since there is no universal definition of consequential damages, it behooves the drafter of the construction agreement to eliminate, to the extent possible, any potential ambiguity in the scope of waived damages. Thus, the rationale for itemizing consequential damages is to facilitate the arbitrator's understanding of the negotiated limitations, and ensure that they are respected.

Not all parties will wish to waive their right to consequential damages. A party who harbors doubts about the ability of the other contracting party to perform the contract may wish to strike the waiver provision from the agreement and provide in the arbitration clause that "the arbitrators are authorized to award any and all forms of indirect or consequential damages."

To carry out the intent of the waiver provision, the owner, design professional and contractor must stop and consider the potential savings and the possible losses for themselves and the other parties on the project. Setting a limit on the risks being taken is a worthwhile objective, but it will only succeed if those negotiating the agreement realistically consider what could happen if the schedule is not met.

AAA mediators and arbitrators, not judges or juries, will have front-line responsibility for interpreting the terms "liquidated damage" (permitted under the AIA documents) and "consequential damage." The parties should give more rather than less guidance to these neutrals so that they can continue to meet the high expectations of the AIA and the rest of the construction community.

CHAPTER THREE

DISPUTE RESOLUTION BOARDS

I. New AAA Protocol for Dispute Resolution Boards

A New Look at DRBs—AAA Offers New DRB Roster and Protocol

by Robert J. Smith & Robert A. Rubin*

In the toolbox of ADR techniques, there is one dispute avoidance and resolution mechanism that has proved to be effective time and time again in eliminating or resolving construction disputes—the dispute review board. The DRB, which is usually a panel of three neutral, technically qualified individuals, provides the owner and the contractor with recommended solutions to disputes at the construction site "in real time."

Up to now, public sector owners have been the principal users of DRBs. In order to make the process more widely understood and increase its use in both private and public construction, the American Arbitration Association has developed three important resources:

- DRB procedures and guidelines (Guide Specifications);
- A model contract that documents the rights and responsibilities of owners and contractors and the members of the DRB (the Three-Party Agreement); and
- An AAA roster of highly experienced DRB panelists.

The drafters of the Guide Specifications and Three-Party Agreement sought to improve on existing DRB models. Distinguishing features include DRB selection from a roster of experienced construction experts,

---

* The authors are civil engineers, attorneys, experienced DRB members, and members of the AAA's roster of neutrals. They both participated in drafting the original American Society of Civil Engineers' DRB specifications. Mr. Smith co-authored the CONSTRUCTION DISPUTE REVIEW BOARD MANUAL. He is a partner in Wickwire Gavin, P.C. Mr. Rubin is a senior partner in Postner & Rubin.

requiring disclosures by prospective DRB members prior to their selection, and disqualification of any member after the DRB is formed only for "cause." The DRB process in the Guide Specifications also shortens time frames to move the process along, calling for regular board meetings and hearings, as necessary, which serve as a catalyst for negotiation.

A significant feature of the Guide Specifications relies on the AAA's considerable experience as an administrator. While parties may choose self-administration, in most circumstances the perception of neutrality is enhanced by having a neutral organization oversee the selection of members of the board and deal with compensation matters.

Background

Typically the DRB is established shortly after execution of the contract documents, as performance of work on the site begins.

A DRB has two basic responsibilities. The first is to become familiar with the project during construction. This process begins with the board's review of the plans and specifications, followed by periodic visits to the project. These visits are usually made on a quarterly basis.

During these visits, in addition to viewing the construction work in progress, the DRB members meet with the owner's and contractor's staff at the job site to discuss the progress of the work, as well as potential issues on the horizon. These activities on the part of the DRB play a useful role in preventing disputes from arising because the parties are encouraged to clearly and objectively state their positions. They also provide the DRB with valuable background information should it need to hear a dispute.

The DRB's second major responsibility is conducting hearings on any disputes referred to it. At a hearing, which usually is held at the construction site, owner and contractor representatives who have first-hand knowledge of the issues are given the opportunity to present facts, documents, and the rationale in support of their respective positions. Formal recording of the hearing and participation by lawyers are both relatively rare.

Following the hearing the DRB issues a written recommendation or a decision, setting forth its analysis and opinion. If one or both parties elect to reject the recommendation, the issue proceeds to the next stage of dispute resolution under the terms of their agreement.

In practice, however, it is very rare for a party to reject the DRB's recommendation and undergo further ADR proceedings. This is primarily because the parties' needs have been met by having an informed decision from neutral decision makers whose opinions they respect. If nothing else, DRBs are about trust in the judgment of its members.

DRBs were first used about twenty-five years ago. Since then they have been used on over 800 projects, primarily those involving public infrastructure construction. Many public owners in this country (examples are the Washington Metropolitan Area Transit Authority, the Massachusetts Turnpike Authority, and the Departments of Transportation in Florida, California and Washington) have used DRBs extensively. The international equivalent of the DRB is known as the dispute adjudication board and it has been included in the standard conditions of contract of FIDIC (Federation International des Ingeniurs Conseils), the World Bank, and the Asian Development Bank.

DRBs have been credited with a 99% success rate. Given the extraordinary record of DRBs, coupled with the endorsement by major public owners, the NCDRC concluded that the DRB process should be made available to a broader constituency in the construction industry. It sought to promote this process through the creation of state-of-the-art DRB procedures and the formation of a carefully chosen DRB roster as a resource for private and public owners.

DRB Panel and Selection Procedures

Although the AAA Guide Specifications differ from existing DRB models in some respects, they are consistent with them in calling for a three-member DRB. The owner and the contractor each nominate a member to the board. Each must approve the other's nominee. Then the two party-appointed members of the DRB nominate the third member, who must also be approved by both the owner and the contractor.

Unless the parties otherwise agree, the DRB members will be selected from the AAA's DRB roster. The roster currently lists forty-eight individuals with significant hands-on construction experience.

The principal criteria for selecting the members of a DRB are experience and neutrality. Experience includes having the technical and professional background necessary to understand the disciplines involved in the construction contract. It also includes experience with interpreting contract documents and resolving disputes. Normally the contracting parties seek a range of skill sets, e.g., design, construction, and contract management skills.

The Guide Specifications set forth a number of presumptively disqualifying relationships that will preclude a potential DRB candidate from serving on the board. Some of these are having ownership or employment ties with a party to the contract or close business or personal relationships with entities involved with the contract.

The Guide Specifications call for a rapid selection process administered by the AAA. The AAA will provide the owner and the contractor with the names and background information on potential DRB candidates once the process is set in motion. It begins with the filing by the contracting parties of a request with the AAA seeking "DRB assistance." This request, which is to be submitted within two weeks of the effective date of the contract, should describe the type of construction involved, the contract price, the time for performance, and the parties' guidelines regarding DRB compensation and expenses.

The AAA, upon receiving the request, will schedule a conference call with the parties to discuss the desired qualifications for membership on the board. Within two weeks the Association will send the owner and the contractor a list of potential candidates selected from its DRB roster, along with biographical information. Prior to sending the list to the parties, the AAA will obtain disclosures from the prospective candidates to determine whether there is a disqualifying relationship. The owner and the contractor have two weeks after receipt of the list to determine their nominees and notify the AAA. Then they have two weeks to make the decision whether or not to accept each other's nominee.

Reasons for rejecting a nominee are not required to be provided. If a nominee is not accepted, the nominating party must submit another nomination within two weeks.

Next, the AAA will provide the two nominees accepted by the parties with a list of candidates so that they can select the third nominee. They have two weeks to make their decision. Their selection is subject to approval by the owner and contractor.

After all the DRB nominees are confirmed, the parties will execute a Three-Party Agreement and schedule the first on-site meeting.

DRB Operations

Procedures for routine DRB operations, such as scheduling site visits and receiving periodic progress reports, are contained in Schedule A to the Guide Specifications. Procedures relating to board consideration of a specific dispute are contained in the Guide Specifications and Schedule B.

In general, the DRB works with the contracting parties on such pre-hearing matters as scheduling the time and place for a hearing, and establishing a procedure and schedule for pre-hearing submissions, such as reference documents and statements of position.

Each party's contentions and supporting arguments are usually submitted in writing in a pre-hearing statement of position. Thus, at a DRB hearing the claiming party makes a presentation of the facts as it sees them, providing relevant exhibits and documents. This is followed by the presentation of the responding party. This sequence may be repeated several times until the issues have been fully presented to the DRB. The board may ask questions during the presentations or reserve questions until the presentations have been completed.

An authorized representative of each party must be present at the hearing. Lawyers and third-party consultants who lack firsthand factual knowledge of the dispute may participate only with prior notice, subject to the discretion of the DRB.

The DRB's written recommendation is due two weeks after the conclusion of the hearing, unless the parties otherwise agree. The Guide Specifications explicitly provide that the DRB is not bound by judicial forum rules of evidence or by the prevailing burden of proof standards, even though in practice DRBs frequently look to these sources for guidance.

Three-Party Agreement

The Three-Party Agreement is the contractual mechanism establishing the rights and responsibilities of the contracting parties and the members of the DRB. It details the "scope of work" for the board, which may develop its own routine operating and hearing procedures or adopt those in Schedule A and B of the Guide Specifications, subject to approval by the owner and contractor.

The owner and contractor have responsibilities to the DRB, which are also set forth in the Three-Party Agreement. For example, the parties must provide the board with plans and specifications, periodic reports and other information about the project.

The Three-Party Agreement mandates that all board members act impartially and independently. Board members do not advocate for parties.

The neutral role of DRB members is supported by provisions on immunity and indemnification. The contract gives DRB members quasi-judicial immunity for their actions or decisions associated with the hearing and making recommendations with respect to disputes.

Obligations with respect to compensation and expenses are contained in the Three-Party Agreement. The owner and contractor share equally the fees and expenses of the board. Fee collection and disbursements will be facilitated by the AAA, unless the parties opt out of neutral administration.

Disputes arising out of the agreement are governed by the AAA Construction Industry Arbitration Rules.

Tips for Drafters

The AAA Guide Specifications,[1] which detail the purpose, procedure, function and features of the DRB, can be included in the construction contract documents. It bears emphasizing that the Guide Specifications are just that—guides that drafters may choose to follow. At a minimum, drafters may wish to give the following areas some thought when considering appropriate DRB provisions.

Other Dispute Resolution Provisions. It is important to carefully coordinate the procedures for the DRB with other dispute resolution provisions in the contract, particularly those that call for a decision prior to submission to the DRB. An example is a provision requiring a decision by the architect or engineer as a predicate to further review.

---

[1] This effort is the product of the AAA's DRB Advisory Committee, under the aegis of the Association's National Construction Dispute Resolution Committee (NCDRC), whose mission is to provide the construction industry with effective tools to help prevent and resolve disputes. The members of the DRB Advisory Committee, who collectively have had experience on over 100 DRBs, included William Baker, president of the Dispute Review Board Foundation, Susan Tomlinson-Dykens, partnering director and DRB administrator for the Massachusetts Turnpike Authority Central Artery/Tunnel Project, Robert Meade and Mark Appel, both AAA senior vice presidents, Jack Woolf, president-elect of the DRB Foundation, and the authors of this article. The AAA Guide Specifications and Three-Party Agreement can be downloaded from the AAA's Web site at http://www.adr.org.

The Guide Specifications address this issue by providing in paragraph 1.04(B) that if the contract requires a prior decision, the dispute is subject to referral to the DRB when that decision has been issued. If a prior decision is not required by the contract, a dispute is ripe for referral to the DRB when either party believes that bilateral negotiations are unlikely to succeed or have reached an impasse. The Guide Specifications also provide that the DRB is to be an independent entity, formed to assist in and facilitate timely resolution of disputes. It is not intended to let the owner or the contractor avoid good-faith efforts to settle.

Admissibility of Board Recommendation. The Guide Specifications provide drafters with a choice in regard to the admissibility of a DRB recommendation in a subsequent arbitration or legal proceeding. The rationale favoring admissibility is maximizing the DRB's effectiveness by giving the parties incentive to adopt the board's recommendation. The DRB recommendation, although admissible, is not binding on a subsequent forum. Presumably it would be accorded the weight that other evidence, such as an expert report, might be given.

Those who are opposed to admitting DRB recommendations in subsequent proceedings, either because of the lack of full due process rights at DRB hearings or concern that it will tend to make the DRB hearings less informal and more legalistic, can choose the language in paragraph 1.04(L) providing that a DRB recommendation will not be admissible in evidence in a subsequent arbitration or legal proceeding.

Single-Member DRB for Small Projects. The Guide Specifications follow the standard model in calling for a three-person board. That model makes sense in larger projects where the economics justify the additional travel expenses and fees of the board. Recently, considerable thought has been given to extending the value of the DRB to smaller projects. To support that process, the Guide Specifications provide an optional procedure in paragraph 1.02(D) for the appointment of a single-person board.

Self-Administration. The Guide Specifications provide that the AAA will provide administrative assistance to the DRB, schedule DRB meetings and hearings, collect and disburse DRB fees and expenses, and provide meeting minutes and board recommendations to the owner and contractor, as necessary. For many projects, it will make sense to lean on the AAA's considerable administrative experience. Public agencies and others who have already established their own administrative capacity may utilize only the AAA's neutral selection and challenge services.

They may do so by eliminating paragraph 1.07 of the Guide Specifications (AAA Administrative Assistance), as well as references in Schedules A, B and C and the Three-Party Agreement to AAA assistance with scheduling, collection and disbursements of fees, and communication of meeting minutes and board recommendations.

II. Using Dispute Resolution Boards for Real Time Solutions

Dispute Review Boards: Resolving Construction Disputes in Real Time

by Robert J. Smith*

The construction industry is prone to disputes due to such factors as misallocation of risk, ambiguous contract documents, thin profit margins and an ever-changing job site. A single project can generate dozens of disputes. Construction professionals want to avoid protracted, costly methods of dispute resolution. The Dispute Review Board (DRB) is an alternative dispute resolution (ADR) method increasingly utilized for construction disputes. It has compiled an almost 100% resolution rate on many hundreds of contracts aggregating over $23 billion. Issues of interest to lawyers involve whether to provide for a DRB in the construction contracts, and advising parties to contracts with DRB provisions.

A DRB serves two functions. One is timely third-party resolution of claims that have not been resolved by bilateral negotiation. The other is prevention of claims and disputes by (1) promoting early and rational identification of issues, (2) promoting constructive communication, and (3) making available a prompt nonbinding remedy, which promotes bilateral negotiations. The existence of the latter function has been established through post-contract debriefing.[1] A DRB helps address four of the ten leading causes of disputes, i.e. poor communications between project

---

* Robert J. Smith, a civil engineer and an attorney, practices with the firm of Wickwire Gavin, P.C., in Madison, Wisconsin. An active construction dispute mediator and arbitrator, he serves on the AAA's roster of neutrals and on its National Construction Dispute Resolution Committee. He is vice chair of the Construction Industry Dispute Avoidance and Resolution Task Force and serves as contract documents counsel to the Engineers Joint Contract Documents Committee of the American Society of Civil Engineers (ASCE)/American Consulting Engineers Council/National Society of Professional Engineers. Mr. Smith is a fellow in the ASCE and the American College of Construction Lawyers. He is also a co-author of the Construction Dispute Review Board Manual.

[1] It is also consistent with favorable scores for the "process" factors of the Construction Industry Institute's Disputes Potential Index. Diekmann, James E. Girard, Matthew J. & Nader Abdul-Hadi, *DPI—Disputes Potential Index: A Study into the Predictability of Contract Disputes*, REP. TO CONSTRUCTION INDUSTRY INST., 1994.

participants, the failure of participants to deal promptly with changes or unexpected conditions, a lack of team spirit or collegiality, and a litigious mind-set on the part of some or all project participants.[2]

Brief Description of Process

The DRB is a non-adjudicatory third-party dispute resolution process provided more or less in "real time." It is a species of the "standing neutral" family of nonbinding ADR processes. The board is a mutually-selected panel of three neutrals qualified in disciplines relevant to the project. Neutrality is assured by stringent conflict of interest requirements, a detailed disclosure statement, and acceptance of each member by both contracting parties. Even though each party nominates a member, the nominee is not an advocate or representative of its nominator. The output of the process is a written recommendation prepared by DRB members based on information (unsworn oral and documentary testimony) provided by the principal participants in the project.

The DRB is unique among ADR methods in that its members meet with the project participants periodically during the life of the construction project. Typically, at these meetings, which take place about every three months, a standard agenda is followed. This includes status updates, discussion of pending issues, and a tour of the construction project. In between meetings the DRB members normally receive periodic status reports.

The DRB derives from the contractual dispute resolution provisions. Construction contracts typically refer disputes between the owner and the contractor to an architect or engineer for an initial decision. That decision is normally a prerequisite for a referral to the DRB, which, as the name clearly notes, reviews that decision based on information submitted at an informal hearing.

Background

The first known DRB was employed on a tunnel project in Colorado in 1975.[3] Since that time DRBs have been used on several hundred construction projects in the United States, ranging from projects under $7

---

[2] CENTER FOR PUBLIC RESOURCES, PREVENTING AND RESOLVING CONSTRUCTION DISPUTES (1991).

[3] A.A. MATHEWS, ET. AL., CONSTRUCTION DISPUTE REVIEW BOARD MANUAL (1996).

million to several hundred million dollars. (Ten million is generally thought to be the cost-effective threshold.) In this country, over one-half of the DRBs have been on projects with a value of $50 million or less. Most of these have involved public works projects, although a few private owners have employed DRBs. About one-third of the DRBs have been on tunneling and underground construction projects; somewhat more than one-third have involved highway and bridge projects, and the balance have been on building and industrial projects.

DRBs have also been used on construction projects in at least half a dozen foreign countries. The use of DRBs will increase in the future. For example, the World Bank recently made the DRB a requirement of all of its civil works projects with a value of $50 million or more.

DRB Procedures

Bilateral negotiation is an essential prerequisite to referral of a dispute to the DRB for its review and recommendation. If the matter is urgent, a special meeting may be held. Otherwise, the standard practice is for the board to consider the dispute at its next regularly scheduled meeting. Prior to hearing any dispute, a DRB typically will ask the parties to submit short position statements along with the referenced documents, such as correspondence, daily logs, and contract provisions.[4]

The vast majority of DRB issues presented address the subject of merit only. This is because the parties are usually amenable to negotiating the amount at issue in the case of an acceptable affirmative recommendation on merit.

Although termed a hearing, the typical proceeding in which a DRB considers statements and documents from the parties is more like a structured meeting. Recordation of any type normally is not permitted. The job-site managers with firsthand knowledge of the dispute take part. Occasionally, the hearing begins with some "venting" activity, but once this cathartic phase is over, the parties will typically set forth their position. Oral narratives, project documents, graphics and, sometimes, expert reports, may be provided. DRB hearings typically last from a few hours to a couple of days. Each party is given an opportunity to proceed without interruption, with at least one round of responses and questions from the DRB members. Cross-examination usually is not permitted.

---

[4] The documents usually are "Bates-numbered," as in the case of document discovery in litigation.

Typically, the DRB is contractually required to issue its nonbinding written recommendation within a matter of days or weeks following the hearing. DRB members sometimes confer in person at the project site following the hearing, or by fax or conference call after returning to their respective offices. The DRB's recommendation may be as short as one page or several dozen pages long. A typical DRB recommendation summarizes the positions of the parties, states the DRB's recommendation, and explains the rationale. Some DRB provisions provide for reconsideration, or for review of the parties' comments on a draft recommendation.

Anomalies and Concerns

Despite the overall success of DRBs, the operation of an individual DRB can deviate from well-defined norms, such as those in the Construction Dispute Review Board Manual.[5] Perhaps 90% of the problems involving DRBs arise out of 10% or fewer projects. Although some of the practices that have led to problems with DRBs may be well-intentioned, they are counter-productive and should be avoided. These practices are briefly summarized below.

Poor Owner Attitude. There is a mind-set among some owners that virtually no contractor claims have merit and that the decision of an architect or engineer is inviolate. Another problem is that some owners seem unwilling to accept the recommendation of a DRB unless it favors the owner. These owners need to acknowledge that sound risk allocation includes providing for remedy-granting clauses that, in turn, will generate legitimate contractor claims and DRB recommendations favoring the contractor in certain circumstances.

Trying to Fix Something That Isn't Broken. Owners sometimes create problems by tinkering with the DRB process. For example, limiting the DRB's jurisdiction only to technical issues can create jurisdictional disputes. Creating long and burdensome claim/dispute analysis timelines in advance of the DRB process can vitiate the "real time" benefits of the process. "Filtering" communications to the board can create the perception that the owner is controlling the DRB.

Attitude Toward Lawyers. DRBs originated pursuant to contract provisions and procedures developed by engineers. Some engineers have

---

[5] *See supra*, note 3.

a visceral dislike for lawyers, which emanates from a distaste for the adversary process and is driven by the perception (which is often consistent with reality) that attorneys use procedures to unnecessarily complicate the DRB process. Accordingly, some conscious efforts have been made to keep lawyers out of the process, whether as a DRB member or as a participant at the hearing.

Imprudent Economizing. In an apparent effort to reduce the costs of the DRB (typically, 0.3% to 0.5% of the contract value), which are shared equally by the parties, owners will cancel regular meetings, place unreasonably low caps on hourly or daily fees of DRB members, or operate the DRB on an on-call basis. Regular meetings add value by familiarizing DRB members with the project and providing an opportunity for them to inquire into potential issues, thus subtly supporting the preventive function of a DRB.

Fairness and Justice versus Contract Requirements. DRBs sometimes tend to be result-oriented. That is, some DRBs seek to issue recommendations that yield a fair and just result instead of following the contract. To prevent an equity approach, some owners make it a requirement that the DRB members follow and apply the contract provisions.

Length and Content of Written Recommendations. Some DRB members produce copious recitations of what engineers like to call "testimony" and "evidence," followed by lengthy analyses. This "testimony" is, of course, unsworn, and the "evidence" might not pass muster under the applicable rules of evidence. Thus, this material should not be overly sanctified by being included in the DRB's recommendation.

Other Concerns. Occasionally board members will be overly aggressive and exceed their jurisdiction by demanding that the parties appear before them, even though, by definition, the DRB process is consensual. It is not logical to expect that a party unwilling to participate in the process in good faith will be willing to accept the output of the DRB. The willing party should consider pursuing declaratory and injunctive relief in such a situation.

Open Issues

One of the principal issues of concern to counsel for parties to a construction contract is the admissibility of the DRB's recommendation in a subsequent binding ADR forum, such as arbitration.

The DRB's recommendation is essentially the paraphrased summary of both the unsworn testimony heard by the DRB members and the evidence they received, and their professional opinion as to the appropriate resolution of the dispute. Staunch advocates of the DRB process argue that the ability to place the final recommendation of a mutually-selected panel of neutral experts before a subsequent adjudicator will promote settlement. However, counsel for parties are legitimately concerned that this opinion and hearsay not be admitted into any subsequent proceeding. The current guide specification for DRBs takes a narrow view of admissibility; it includes a stipulation that admissibility is limited to: (1) the fact that a DRB considered the dispute, (2) the professional qualifications of the DRB members, and (3) the DRB's specific recommendation, "to the extent permitted by law."

Greater Role for DRBs?

So far as is known, the DRB has not been used outside of the construction industry. However, the potential for its use is there when the right parameters are present. These include:

- a dispute-prone contract;
- a contract performance time of one year or more, involving multiple payments;
- milestones or components of performance;
- unresolved disputes, which can disrupt relationships at the working and management level and lead to protracted and expensive litigation.

These features may be present in a variety of commercial contracts: for example, an aircraft or computer manufacturing contract. Essential to the application of the process is a desire on the part of the contracting parties to eliminate disputes at an early stage and forego the usual mechanisms for resolving disputes long after they have arisen and the business relationship has been harmed.

Characteristics of a DRB

There are over twenty characteristics of a "classic" DRB.[6]

---

[6] Michael C. Vorster, *Dispute Resolution and Prevention: Alternative Dispute Resolution in Construction with Emphasis on Dispute Review Boards*, REP. TO CONSTRUCTION INDUSTRY INST., (1993).

DISPUTE RESOLUTION BOARDS

1. The intention to establish a DRB is noted in the instructions to bidders.
2. The provisions for establishing the DRB are set out in the contract.
3. The provisions for establishing a DRB do not preclude either the owner or the contractor from resorting to other methods for final dispute settlement.
4. Members of the DRB are neutral, and able to serve the owner and the contractor equally with no conflict of interest.
5. DRB members have acknowledged technical expertise in the type of work being undertaken.
6. All parties agree on the selection and appointment of all DRB members.
7. The owner and contractor each nominate one DRB member. These two members select the third member, who acts as chair.
8. DRB members receive regular, written progress reports and remain informed of the status of the work.
9. DRB meetings are held on the job site at regular intervals, not exceeding four months.
10. Presentations to the DRB are made by field project managers completely involved in the construction process.
11. The owner or contractor may appeal any decision, action, order, claim, or controversy to the DRB at any time.
12. Both the owner and contractor are adequately represented at all hearings; rebuttal and requests for clarification are permitted.
13. DRB recommendations are in writing and are made directly to the project participants, who are responsible for accepting, appealing, or rejecting these recommendations.
14. DRB selection and appointment are made within seven weeks of notice to proceed with the contract work.
15. Appeals are made to the DRB as soon as possible and the DRB handles issues current at the time of appeal.

16. Written recommendations of the DRB and the reasoning supporting the recommendations are made available to the project participants within two weeks of an appeal.
17. DRB members do not act as consultants and do not give advice on the conduct of the work.
18. The DRB does not usurp either the owner's or the contractor's authority to direct the work as provided in the contract.
19. The DRB's recommendations are not binding and may be rejected by either the owner or the contractor.
20. The DRB's written recommendations and the reasoning supporting the recommendations are admissible as evidence in any subsequent dispute resolution procedure.
21. The cost of the DRB is borne equally by the owner and the contractor.

III. Experience with Advisory Dispute Review Boards

Expanding the DRB's Role—
The Boston Central Artery Tunnel Project's Experience with Advisory Dispute Review Boards

by Brison S. Shipley*

Much has been learned about dispute avoidance and resolution on the Boston Central Artery/Tunnel (CA/T) project—a $10.8 billion infrastructure project, with multiple prime contractors and numerous contract interfaces. Simply put, the CA/T project, which employs partnering and a dispute review board program, has had remarkably few disputes. It even boasts having had no litigation.

[Editors' note: the author's thesis is no longer as true as it was at the time of original publication. As is now common knowledge, a part of the Boston Central Artery/Tunnel collapsed in July 2006 resulting in a fatality and litigation. See Matthew L. Wald, "Late Design Change Is Cited in Collapse of Tunnel Ceiling," NEW YORK TIMES at A-18 (Nov. 2, 2006.)]

Despite this record of success, there have been concerns about a growing backlog of disputes that could plague the owner and the contractors at the end of the project. This concern has led the CA/T project to experiment with expanding the role of the DRB to provide informal advisory opinions to project participants.

Using DRBs in this manner allows greater use of the expertise and professionalism of the panelists, who are already knowledgeable about the project. The development, expectations and costs of this expanded DRB role are discussed below.

---

* Until very recently, the author was associated with Parsons Brinkerhoff Quade & Douglas, which acts as construction manager for the Massachusetts Highway Department on the CA/T project. During that association, Shipley oversaw the administration of the DRB program. Previously he served as Assistant Attorney General for the Commonwealth of Massachusetts.

Background

Before the completion of the CA/T project, more than 120 separate construction packages will have been awarded and performed over a 14-year period. The day-to-day business of settling claims and disputes on the project occurs within the context of partnering's issue resolution ladder—a hierarchy of authority that identifies the steps and time limits for "advancing" an issue through successive levels of management until one of the following occurs. The issue is either resolved, or an impasse is reached and the matter is referred to a DRB for a formal hearing. Traditionally, this has been the DRB's only role (as opposed to its deterrent effect)[1] in claims resolution for the CA/T project.

A DRB, for the uninitiated, is a panel of three individuals, usually from the construction or engineering profession, who are jointly selected and compensated by the owner and the contractor. The DRB is established at the beginning of the job and it meets regularly at the site for briefings on the work, the construction schedule, and on potential issues that have arisen. When a dispute is submitted to the DRB, it presents fair, informed, timely, nonbinding recommended solutions. The admissibility of a DRB recommendation is generally left to the discretion of the court. However, should the parties not accept that recommendation and decide to litigate, they know, as a practical matter, that a reviewing court is apt to give the DRB recommendation considerable deference or "precedential weight."

Currently there are eleven different DRBs overseeing twenty-six separate construction contracts on the CA/T project. Some of these DRBs oversee just one contract, while others are "consolidated," overseeing anywhere from two to six contracts. The consolidated DRB results from the agreement of the owner and the contractor on a newly awarded contract to extend the jurisdiction of an existing DRB (involving a contract with the same contractor) to the new contract, provided the DRB members agree. The consolidated DRB saves administrative time and operating costs.[2]

---

[1] The parties are naturally reluctant to present a dispute that their peers, the DRB panelists, may perceive as frivolous. This is the "deterrent" effect of the DRB. Its mere presence often motivates parties to make the extra efforts needed to reach settlement.

[2] With DRB members coming from all over the country, and with the typical quarterly meeting lasting no more than five hours, the largest component of DRB expense is airfare and compensation for travel time. In 1997, the owner and the CA/T general contractors jointly developed a "consolidated" DRB program to reduce the number of DRBs. This consolidation has proceeded on a "per contractor" basis.

The Problem

During the past nine years of physical construction, only twenty-two disputes have been formally presented to the project's DRBs. The DRB process involves an intensive effort by both the owner and the contractor. To prepare for the DRB hearing, both the field staff and the contract-administration support staff spend a considerable period of time developing briefing books, charts and graphic displays, schedule analyses, and other exhibits.

The low number of disputes submitted to the DRBs is due to the success of partnering in resolving the bulk of the issues that have arisen. But the concern is that, despite partnering's achievements, there is a growing backlog of unresolved issues.

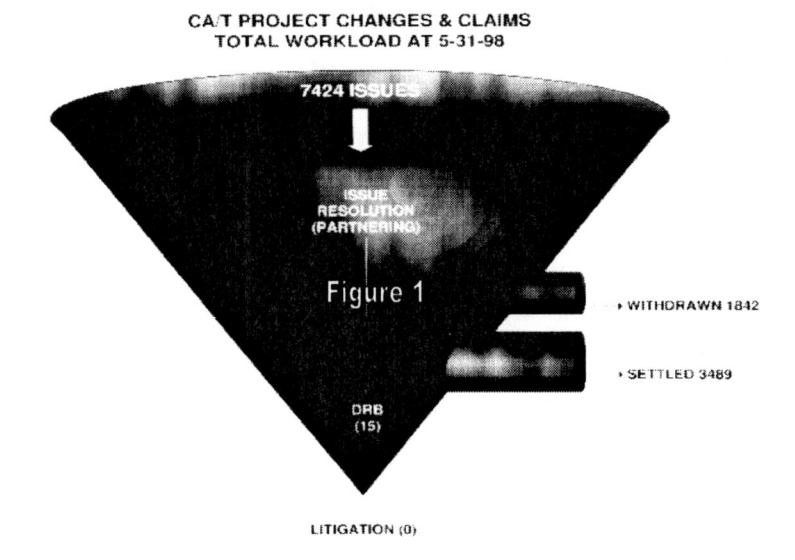

**CA/T PROJECT CHANGES & CLAIMS
TOTAL WORKLOAD AT 5-31-98**

Figure 1

7424 ISSUES
ISSUE RESOLUTION (PARTNERING)
WITHDRAWN 1842
SETTLED 3489
DRB (15)
LITIGATION (0)

Note that approximately 2,500 issues are unaccounted for. This backlog has grown by 500 since 5/31/98. This illustration and the accompanying photos were provided by Dennis Rahilly, CA/T Project.

The backlog grew by 500 claims over a one-year period. [See Figure 1 above.] Extrapolating from this claims experience at the point of 50% construction completion, it is estimated that an additional 7,500 issues could arise before the project is completed, leaving thousands of unresolved claims at the end of the job.

Neither the contractors nor the owner wants to be in this position when construction is completed. There are at least four reasons why this is so: (1) their money will remain tied up in this project; (2) at the end of the job staff resource levels are low; (3) the key participants in the events underlying the original claim have probably moved on; and (4) the momentum for resolving disputed issues is gone.

The Advisory DRB Solution

Borrowing from the recent positive experience of the University of Washington in using DRBs to render early, informal, advisory opinions,[3] the CA/T project began to develop the "Advisory DRB Initiative." The intent was to create a relatively informal process that would provide field personnel with the insight and advice of third-party neutral experts familiar with the job, prior to escalation of the issue to senior management and the subsequent entrenchment of positions.

One impetus for the Advisory DRB Initiative was management's feeling that the benefit of having DRBs was only partially utilized because so few project disputes had been submitted to them for a formal recommendation. The Advisory DRB Initiative offered an opportunity to take greater advantage of the experience and expertise of the DRB panel. The initiative could be done economically, too—by combining the DRBs' expanded role with their regular quarterly meeting agenda. As a result, significant airfare and travel time costs could be saved.

It should be emphasized that the Advisory DRB Initiative was not developed unilaterally by the owner. It was discussed with representatives of the contracting community doing business on the project (which principally includes about eight major heavy civil construction companies —in various joint venture combinations), with which the CA/T project management has maintained an ongoing dialogue. Some of the perceived benefits emphasized during these discussions include increasing contractor cash flow, lessening contract administration burdens on field office staff, and reducing the backlog of unresolved issues.

---

[3] Jim Donaldson was instrumental in providing background materials and his personal experiences with DRBs rendering informal or "rump" advisory opinions at the University of Washington and elsewhere. Donaldson, who serves on the roster of the American Arbitration Association, is president-elect of the Dispute Review Board Foundation, a nonprofit organization dedicated to the furtherance of the DRB concept in the construction industry.

The contractors overwhelmingly supported the concept. But they had several concerns. One worry was that the partnering issue-escalation ladder would be eliminated. The contractors found this feature of partnering to be very useful and did not want to abandon it. Assurances were made that the Advisory DRB Initiative would supplement, not replace, the existing partnering relationships.

The contractors also expressed concern about the precedential weight to be accorded an advisory opinion of the DRB issued pursuant to the new initiative. The dialogue on this issue is still ongoing, and the answer will emerge as the parties gain experience with the new DRB process. Guidelines for the DRB acting in an advisory capacity address this issue in the following manner: "The advice/recommendation of the DRB will be used by those at the level the dispute is at to further discuss and resolve the issue. If the two parties still cannot resolve it, they should elevate the issue to the next level."

What is, perhaps, most important, is that the parties were willing to experiment with the new process even before any agreement on the matter of precedential weight has been reached.

How the Advisory DRB Works

There are several aspects to the new advisory DRB process. The first is who may raise an issue for consideration. Under the guidelines, except as noted below, anyone may do so if (1) good faith negotiations have stalled, and (2) both the owner's resident engineer and the contractor's project manager agree that the issue should be submitted to the DRB for an informal recommendation. If either party opposes the submission, then the issue proceeds through the normal partnering process.

The exception to the above rule concerns issues having project-wide ramifications. For example, a project-wide issue could involve the method of measurement for a particular pay item. When a project-wide issue arises, the owner may obtain senior management review prior to referral to an advisory DRB for an informal recommendation. This approach was taken because senior management is responsible for establishing project-wide policies, and the failure to obtain its input first could lead to confusion and unnecessary tensions between the parties later on.

The requirement of senior management approval does not foreclose the submission of a project-wide issue to the DRB. Senior management might want to hear a DRB's informal recommendation in formulating a project-wide position.

Another aspect of the advisory DRB process involves scheduling meetings. Generally, the owner, the contractor and the DRB panel will identify at the DRB's regular quarterly meeting any issues that will be presented for an advisory opinion at the next quarterly meeting. This allows the parties the needed time to prepare and ensures that DRB members will reserve sufficient time to address the issues.

If a matter arises between quarterly meetings that the parties want to have heard expeditiously, the project DRB administrator will make the necessary arrangements with the DRB members. The guidelines express a preference for giving the DRB panel a minimum of three weeks' notice of new issues before the next quarterly meeting. They also suggest that both parties together submit a one-page joint statement of the issue, with back-up data to be provided as necessary. The logic behind this suggestion is to try to move the parties to agree on the issue to be determined.

The allowance of pre-meeting submittals represents a change from the initial approach, which was to dispense with them entirely in an effort to keep the process simple and informal. The view of submittals changed because several DRB members commented that their time would be better used if they could review relevant documents prior to visiting the site. As a practical matter, the nature and extent of pre-meeting submittals is left to the discretion of each DRB, in light of the objective of avoiding the burdens of preparing for a formal DRB hearing, without prejudicing the right of either party to fairly present its case.

Attendance at the meetings of the DRB is critical to the effective functioning of the advisory DRB process. Party representatives who have the authority to settle the issue must attend the presentation to the panel, regardless of whether the issue is resolved at that time. The guidelines provide that (1) ample time will be allowed for presentation, rebuttal and questions, and (2) the parties will receive feedback the same day.

Following the presentations, rebuttals and questioning, the DRB renders its oral recommendation.[4] The reason for an oral recommendation is to reinforce the informal and contemporaneous nature of the DRB's advice.

---

[4] Donaldson reports that the general consensus among the many DRB members with whom he has discussed this subject is that the board should caucus prior to advising the parties of its opinion and recommendation. This practice not only ensures that the board is speaking with one voice, but also gives it the opportunity to consider carefully how it should phrase its opinion or recommendation to avoid misunderstandings and to exercise diplomacy, where needed.

Depending upon the relationships that have developed, the contentiousness of the parties over a particular issue, and other variables, the board may decide to caucus privately before rendering its advice. This is a matter of group dynamics. Some DRBs recess briefly before giving their oral recommendation. Others formulate and offer their advice as part of one homogenous process of presentation, question and answer, rebuttal, reply, and opinion.

The parties are urged to discuss and question the DRB's reasoning, to assure that all facts and arguments were considered, and that they understand how the DRB reached its conclusions. For example, an issue may not be fully developed when it is presented to the DRB on an informal basis. The guidelines contemplate that the DRB should have the flexibility to address the issue candidly. For example, they should be able to say "Based on what we've seen and heard today, we think party A has a weak position, unless conditions X, Y and Z can be shown."

As previously noted, the DRB's oral recommendation is not binding on either party or on the DRB. The issue may be formally presented to the DRB at a later date pursuant to the "disputes clause" in the construction agreements. Should that occur, the DRB will focus upon the facts and circumstances of the dispute as presented at that time.

Economic Considerations

The current estimate of the total cost of the Advisory DRB Initiative (which is at best only an educated guess) is $1.2 million. This estimate is based on the assumption that (1) every contractor will use the advisory DRB process at every meeting to resolve at least one issue, (2) each meeting will consume six hours of DRB time, and (3) the resolved issues will have a ripple effect so as to resolve other issues.

To put this into perspective, consider the CA/T project's entire construction budget, which is estimated at $7.7 billion. The cost to date of operating the DRB program is 0.05% of completed construction, or $1.9 million (shared 50% by the owner and 50% by the contractors). Extrapolating at the same rate, the total cost of the DRB program, including the advisory DRB process, will be $4.4 million, or 0.06% of the cost of completed construction.[5]

---

[5] This compares favorably with statistics compiled by the DRB Foundation: The "total direct DRB costs generally are considerably less than 0.5% of the final contract price." A.A. MATHEWS, ET. AL., CONSTRUCTION DISPUTE REVIEW BOARD MANUAL 7 (1995).

Performance of the Program

The preliminary results of the Advisory DRB Initiative are quite positive. Since November 1998, twenty-one issues have been informally presented to project DRBs in their advisory capacity. Two-thirds of those issues are now closed. In one case, the DRB's advice allowed the owner to mitigate damages before the contractor incurred costs, by directing the contractor to perform less extensive and less expensive crack repair. In another case, which involved the interpretation of a measurement-for-payment provision, the DRB's recommendation led the resident engineer to work out a method of equitable adjustment via the redesign and re-pricing of a related pay item on work that remained to be performed.

Participants on the CA/T project think of the advisory DRB as insurance, and as an investment in claims avoidance. Only the future will tell, but the benefits experienced in the initial operations are a hopeful harbinger of future returns.

CHAPTER FOUR

PARTNERING

I. The Importance of Trust in the Partnering Process

I Don't Trust You, But Why Don't You Trust Me? Recognizing the Fragility of Trust and Its Importance in the Partnering Process

by Jeffrey S. Busch* & Nicole Hantusch**

Trust has always played an important role in the partnering process as it has in all business relationships. In the following article, Jeff Busch and Nicole Hantusch break through the invisible barriers to trust, and show how partnering can become an easier process when healthy working relationships are able to flourish in a trusting environment.

Vladimir Lenin, leader of the Russian Revolution, said: "Trust is good, but control is better." Today, many people in the business world operate with the same attitude and miss the opportunities for success that are available when they dare to establish trust. Control and lack of trust characterize many personal and working relationships. What is it that makes it so difficult for us to trust other people nowadays?

Often the main perceived barrier to a successful construction project is the contract, which implies that the issue is money. Both parties remain unaware that trust is a more powerful barrier to a successful project than either the contract or the money involved. Experience has shown that if trust has been established, negotiations about the contract and money are fairer.

---

* Jeff Busch is a principal of Pinnell, Busch Inc., and has been instrumental in developing its partnering program which promotes the use of ADR processes. He is an active panel member of the American Arbitration Association.
** Nicole Hantusch is on a business exchange with Pinnell, Busch Inc., where she conducts research in the field of organizational development, focusing on partnering dynamics of construction projects.

But trust is not just needed while negotiating a contract or the price for extra work, it is essential throughout the duration of the project for many reasons. For instance, trust is needed to perceive the intentions of the other party correctly, to exchange important information, or to have confidence in the other party's ability to meet contract obligations. If trust is established between the owner and the contractor at the beginning of a project, respect, commitment, and accountability become part of their relationship.

However, building trust is not an easy task, especially in the construction industry, where the relationship between parties is often characterized by shifting risk, contract language, and adversarial perspectives.

What Is Trust?

Trust plays an increasingly important role in the partnering process, and in all business relationships. There are many different definitions of trust, which do not contradict each other, but rather are focused on different aspects of trust. Doney, Cannon and Mullen[1] make the effort to develop a single definition of trust. They define it as:

> A willingness to rely on another party and to take action in circumstances where such action makes one vulnerable to the other party.

In their opinion this definition incorporates the notion of risk as a precondition of trust, and it includes both the belief and behavioral components of trust.

Other authors also suggest that a perceived risk is required for trust to influence one's decisions and actions:

> A fundamental condition of trust is that it must be possible for the partner to abuse the trust.[2]

> Trust is an attitude based on the past and extending into the future; it reduces the complexity of the world for us, but leaves us with some risk.[3]

---

[1] Patricia M. Doney, et. al., *Understanding the Influence of National Culture on the Development of Trust*, 23 ACAD. MGMT. REV. No. 3, 601, 620 (1998).
[2] NICKLAS LUHMANN, TRUST AND POWER (1982).
[3] TRUDY GOVIER, DILEMMAS OF TRUST (1999).

The Dilemma of Trust

Why is it often difficult for us to trust someone we don't know or someone we know who has disappointed us once? Why is it so difficult to make the first step to a trustful relationship? The answer to these questions is "the paradox of trust."[4] Simply stated, before you are trusted, you first must trust others.

Trust is an essential value of all human relationships, but it is also a fragile good, which is hard to earn and easy to destroy. It creates a situation of potential disappointment, and consequently, many people distrust others. It is not easy to take the first step towards a trustful relationship, but the only way to be trustworthy is to trust the other party. The other party has the same concerns and fears as you and probably will not venture the first step.

The so-called dilemma of trust is present in the construction industry since the relationship between owner and contractor is often characterized by a long-term adversarial relationship. It is therefore important to put additional emphasis on the necessity of trust at the start of the partnering process, to give both parties the opportunity to overcome their prejudices, and to start the project in a new atmosphere of mutual understanding.

The Benefits of Trust

Trust has been called "social capital," a social good that facilitates economic growth and development.[5]

Research by Caudron[6] shows that a high level of trust equals aspects such as:

- Better customer satisfaction.
- Lower costs.
- Quicker response times.

---

[4] J. Sullivan, *Walking the Talk*, PM Network, p. 16 (Nov. 1999).
[5] Govier, *supra* note 3.
[6] Shari Caudron, *Rebuilding Employee Trust*, 50 TRAINING & DEV. No. 8, 18 (Aug. 1996).

Research also finds that in a trustful environment people spontaneously help others to solve their problems as they arise. It is difficult to measure the worth of these actions, but they enhance every organization's or project's ability to overcome unexpected difficulties,[7] which otherwise could lead to total failure.

For example: Parks, Henager & Scamahorn[8] found that low trusters reacted to a competitive message (demanding) by decreasing cooperation, but were unaffected by a cooperative (friendly) message. In contrast, high trusters reacted to the cooperative message by increasing cooperation but were unaffected by the competitive message.

Kramer also points out that many empirical studies show the importance of trust in people's willingness to engage in positive behaviors like:

Contributing their time and attention towards the common goals, sharing useful information with other members, and exercising responsible restraint when using valuable but limited resources.[9]

These positive behaviors contribute to many positive actions, like handling change orders or the altered conditions of a construction project quickly and in favor of the project. They can prevent the project from getting stuck because both parties are working in the same direction and want to make the process as easy as possible.

Another benefit is the high satisfaction and motivation of people who work in a trusting atmosphere. Without having to be afraid of unpredictable reactions or behaviors of the other party, everybody can focus their attention and energy on the success of the project.

Trust in the Partnering Process

Partnering is the creation of a working relationship, primarily between a building owner and a contractor, which should promote mutual and beneficial goals. Partnering further involves subcontractors, design professionals, and other agencies. The central objective is to encourage

---

[7] R.M. Kramer, *Trust and Distrust in Organizations: Emerging Perspectives, Enduring Questions*, ANN. REV. PSYCHOL. 569(1) (1999).

[8] Craig D. Parks, et. al., *Trust and Reactions to Messages Intent in Social Dilemmas*, 40 J.CONFLICT RESOL. No. 1, 134-51 (1996).

[9] Kramer, *supra* note 7.

contracting parties to establish their project-specific business plans, leading to an attitude that fosters risk-sharing and win-win resolutions.

Partnering allows parties to review their ways of doing business. It provides an opportunity for both parties to gain insights into the business practices of other companies. To learn valuable information related to a common project, each party has to be trusted. Inevitably, partnering means that both parties must take risks and expose their vulnerabilities. This risk-taking leads to strength and knowledge. Without trust, the success of the project is in great danger because the effects of distrust waste too much energy, labor, and money, which would be better spent on the project.

The other key elements in the partnering process are: commitment, communication, conflict resolution, consensus on goals and objectives, equity and win-win thinking, issue resolution, and empowered people. A total partnering culture cannot fully exist in an environment of distrust because trust is its foundation.

In their 1997 study, E. Larson and J.A. Drexler, Jr., found that professionals in the field view trust as crucial.[10] Analyzing 187 responses to the question: "What are the major barriers to successful partnering in construction projects?" they identified five major impediments to the success of Partnering processes. The most mentioned barrier was trust, making up 29% of the responses. An additional 9% mentioned that mistrust resulted from past adversarial relationships and training, and another 2% mentioned fear of past adversaries. Other constraints mentioned were attitudes and interpersonal barriers, project structure barriers, partnering process barriers, knowledge and skill barriers, and commitment. Larson and Drexler concluded that the perceptions of the respondents: "reflect a general level of mistrust between owners and contractors engendered by years of viewing and treating each other as potential adversaries."

Fairness and Good Faith

Every construction contract has an implied basis of fairness and good faith. If the parties don't trust each other, they tend to break this contract rule and calculate how far they can go with being unfair in order to win. At some point this behavior will affect the project and consequently turn the situation into a lose-lose situation for both parties. To turn the project

---

[10] E. Larson and J.A. Drexler, *Barriers to Project Partnering: Report from the Firing Line*, 28 PROJECT MGMT. J. No. 1 46-52 (1997).

around again, both parties must learn to treat each other fairly. If they continue to push the limits with each other, they will kill the project.

Based on Pinnell, Busch's experience in conducting over 150 partnering sessions, it was found that when trust is broken effective communication stops. The parties then try to find out who caused the problem, rather than solving it. Instead of talking with each other, they start writing formal letters, referring to the contract and pointing out the other party's responsibility. Kept busy with the contract language, neither party is able to address and solve the on-site problems. Many times the result is a severe dispute, claim, or lawsuit.

Deciding Whether to Trust or Distrust

Distrusting people is a black hole. Every day people make assumptions about others' intentions, behaviors, attitudes, and abilities. But what is the basis for these assumptions, which lead to the decision of whether to trust or distrust a person or party?

The most important precondition to building trust is the interaction with other individuals or organizations. To determine if a party is trustworthy, people must interact on a personal level—and frequently. Interaction is needed to experience the other party's predictability until trust can be established between them. If this happens, the parties can start working together without as much personal interaction, because they don't have to observe and test each other anymore. However, to maintain this relationship, both parties have to continually reinforce trust. Because of its fragility, trust can turn into distrust more quickly than it is established.

Kramer describes six elements of trust that can be found within organizations. These factors influence our cognitive trust-building processes. They influence our assumptions about the trustworthiness of other people and our own willingness to engage in a trusting behavior.[11]

1. Dispositional Trust

Research suggests that people differ in their general predisposition to trust or distrust other people. Rotter proposes that people take from their early trust-related experiences to build up general beliefs about other people.[12]

---

[11] Kramer, *supra* note 7.
[12] Julian B. Rotter, *Interpersonal Trust, Trustworthiness, and Gullibility*, 35 AM. PSYCH. No. 1, 1-7 (1980) *in* Kramer, *supra* note 7.

2. History-Based Trust

Some authors[13] call this "knowledge-based trust." It is when people predict the future behavior of others based on past actions. The consistency of a party's past actions and the extent to which the actions are congruent with the party's words indicate the degree to which the party can be trusted. According to Lewicki and Bunker,[14] the greater the knowledge about the past actions of the other party, the higher the chance their behavior is predictable. In particular, the mutual or cooperative interchange of favors, privileges, or rights can enhance trust, while the absence or violation of reciprocity erodes it.[15] And, the expertise and competence of one party assures the other party that their partner has the capability to meet their expectations.

3. Third Parties as Conduits of Trust

Trust can also be built through the transference of information about a party by a source that is known as trustworthy.[16] Uzzi observed that "third parties acted as important go-betweens in new relationships, enabling individuals to roll-over their expectations."[17]

The construction industry resembles a huge network, which connects owner, contractor, and design firms with visible and invisible links. Recommendations and the exchange of information often lead to new working relationships. If an owner is satisfied with the work of a specific contractor or designer, he will likely talk about it and let other owners know about the good work.

4. Category-Based Trust

Category-based trust is predicated on membership in a social group or organization. Studies show that in dilemma situations people trust members of their own group more than others. For example, contractors

---

[13] Debra L. Shapiro, et. al., *Business on a Handshake*, 8 NEGOTIATION J. No. 4, 365-377 (1992) *in* Doney, *supra* note 1.
[14] ROY J. LEWICKI AND B.B. BUNKER, TRUST IN RELATIONSHIPS: A MODEL OF DEVELOPMENT AND DECLINE. (1995).
[15] Kramer, *supra* note 7.
[16] Doney, *supra* note 1.
[17] Brian Uzzi, *Social structure and competition in interfirm networks: The Paradox of Embeddedness*, 42 ADMIN. SCI. Q. 35 (1996) *in* Kramer *supra* note 7.

usually trust other contractors more than they trust owners because they share the same interests, problems and perspectives with members of their own group.

The construction contract tends to reinforce this categorization, making the trust-building process more difficult. The goal of partnering is to break down this invisible wall between parties to create a new category called "project" that unites the parties.

5. Role-Based Trust

This focuses on the specific role a person occupies in an organization, e.g., regional manager or project manager. It is not based on knowledge about the person's capabilities, dispositions, motives, or intentions. Trust develops from a common knowledge regarding the barriers to entry into organizational roles. People rely on their assumption that people will behave as expected because of their role within an organization. This reduces the necessity for personal interactions to test trustworthiness. When role-based trust and category-based trust are well-established, they can help to reduce the costs for other trust-building processes.

On the other hand, role-based trust can fuel distrust. If, for instance, top management is not committed to the partnering process, the other party may distrust not only top-management but also the project managers. Proceeding from the importance of role-based trust, the trust-building process in partnering can be seen as a top-down process. Consequently, top managers should pay attention to creating trust and commitment among themselves and the project managers at the beginning of the project.

6. Rule-Based Trust

"Rule-based trust is predicated on shared understandings regarding the system of rules and appropriate behavior."[18] Hewlett-Packard can be used as an example of trust creation. HP encouraged their engineers to take equipment home for personal use. This act demonstrated management's trust in the cooperativeness of the employees, and as a

---

[18] Gary J. Miller, *Managerial Dilemmas: the Political Economy of Hieuanuchies* 254 (1992), *cited in* Kramer, *supra* note 7.

result the employees tended to trust HP in return.[19] Kramer emphasizes that "by institutionalizing trust through practices at the macro-organizational (collective) level, trust becomes internalized at the micro-organizational (individual) level."[20]

In the construction industry, top management might demonstrate trust in their project managers by giving them more authority without countermanding it at a later time. Being trusted with responsibility motivates the project managers to give their best and to trust in return. It also encourages them to trust their field team and to relinquish more authority. This process of developing new authorities does not just demonstrate that people trust each other—it can also help simplify decision lines and processes to keep the project going.

Barriers to the Process of Building Trust

Trust is difficult to obtain and maintain. There are two main reasons for the fragility of the trust-building process:

- Trust-destroying events are more visible and noticeable than trust-building events. Positive events are taken for granted in contrast to negative events.
- Trust-destroying events carry more weight in judgment than trust-building events.[21]

Unfortunately, most of the elements that build trust can become powerful barriers to trust. The following are barriers to the trust-building process that can be found in organizations and construction projects:

1. Interaction History

History is one important barrier to the trust-building process in the construction industry. Often an owner and contractor have had bad experiences with past projects and are not able to start a new project without holding prejudices and resentments against each other. Combined with barriers like social categorization and generalization, it is understandable that both parties think they can never fully trust each other.

---

[19] *Id.*
[20] Kramer, *supra* note 7.
[21] *Id.*

2. Social Categorization

People tend to categorize other people if they do not have much information about them. A category might be gender, nationality, profession, or employment status. People use these categories to simplify their decision-making processes.[22]

Participants of a partnering project may place other members in categories of contractor-people and owner-people or engineer-people and agency-people. If they do, they are likely to trust members of their own category more than members of another. Brewer shows that people evaluate out-group members as less honest, reliable, open, and trustworthy than members of their own group.[23]

3. Generalizations and Role Models

People tend to generalize from the actions of one person to the intention of the whole group to which this person belongs. For example, if one contractor does not meet the expectations of an owner, that owner tends to think that all contractors are likely to disappoint, and he or she may distrust contractors in general. Also the behavior of role models, like top managers, is observed attentively by the other party. If the top managers of a company are perceived as not to be trusted, their employees will not be trusted either.

Barriers Specific to the Construction Industry

4. Contract Obligations and the Issue of Hierarchy

The conditions of construction contracts lead automatically to perceived hierarchies between parties on a project. Money and who-gets-how-much mainly determines this hierarchy. A recent study conducted by Pinnell, Busch showed that contractors often feel they stand in a low-status position in relation to the owner, while owners indicated that they have a higher status because they have the money.

---

[22] *Id.*
[23] Kramer, *supra* note 7 (citing M.B. BREWER, ETHNOCENTRISM AND ITS ROLE IN INTERPERSONAL TRUST, 345-59(1981)).

5. Time Constraints

Every party needs time to collect information about the other party in order to measure the predictability of the other side's behavior. Several interactions with the other party must occur before trust is developed.

Construction projects usually don't have, or make, this time available. Projects start with a specific time frame, and move at top speed to a series of deadlines. There is little time prior to the project start or during the project to establish trust. In addition to the element of time constraint is the fact that construction parties do not usually work with each other continuously over a period of years. As a result, the trust-building process has to start at the beginning over and over again.

How to Build and Restore Trust

Govier says that "we often fail to distinguish between lies and disagreements about the facts or between unreliability and cultural differences."[24] Simple misunderstandings or misinterpretations can lead to deep distrust, and the other party will never know when and why this distrust emerged. Lack of communication may even lead to the belief that the other party lied.

Despite the challenges and constraints of building trust, somebody must venture the first step.

The First Step

The challenging first step to establish trust is trusting others. This means that you allow yourself to become vulnerable to disappointment and that you are prepared to take a risk. It also means that you developed and demonstrated courage.

Self-trust is the most important factor in having the courage to take the unpredictable step of risking trust.[25] Self-trust means that we trust our professional capabilities and that we have positive beliefs and expectations about what we can do. If a contractor submitted solid estimates of costs on past projects, he will be confident in his estimating abilities for the next project. Armed with this self-confidence, it is easier to trust the other party because our vulnerability isn't so much at risk.

---

[24] Govier, *supra* note 3.
[25] *Id.*

Horsburgh labels the idea of trusting somebody as the best way to engender trust as "therapeutic trust." Therapeutic trust is:

> ...based on the assumption that people who are explicitly entrusted with certain tasks or goods will feel an obligation to live up to the expectations of others, and guilt if they do not do so. It is based on the human desire to reciprocate goodness and to live up to what others expect.[26]

It does not mean that you should automatically trust everybody all the time. It is a single act that gives a start to a trustful relationship with the goal of inspiring trustworthy behavior from the other party. "By regarding the other as a worthy and potentially trustworthy being, by approaching him in this light and responding to mistakes with a forgiving attitude, we can encourage him to develop in positive directions."[27] The assumption of therapeutic trust gives us the chance to overcome fears and to inspire cooperative behavior in the other party.

How do you encourage the other party to trust you? According to Govier: "We cannot control the other party's actions and attitudes, but we can control our own."[28] To build trust we must turn our focus from the perceived insufficiencies of the other party to our own insufficiencies and work on our own behavior and actions.

Partnering should encourage parties to be more agreeable, forgiving, open, and less greedy. To venture the first step would mean that the owner—especially at the start of the project—demonstrates trust in the calculations of the contractor by accepting more easily than usual a change order. In return, the contractor would know that on the next change order he will not have to exaggerate his calculations to obtain reasonable compensation. On the other side, the contractor can start building trust by providing more details than usual in the change order to make it easier for the owner to accept it. Both parties should not ask for everything the first time, rather they should show that they are interested in a fair solution and willing to compromise.

Unfortunately, acting and behaving in a trustful manner does not necessarily mean that the other party will respond in the same way. People

---

[26] H.J.N. Horsburgh, *The Ethics of Trust*, 10 PHIL. Q. No. 41, 343-54, *cited in* Govier, *supra* note 3.
[27] *Id.*
[28] Govier, *supra* note 3.

who expect close reciprocity in relationships are almost certain to be disappointed. In the construction industry, it may be hard to "scratch your back if you scratch mine" when the contract does not allow for it or when the other party's perception of the value of the favor differs from yours.

Action Plans

The following actions and behaviors will help reinforce and maintain trust in a relationship.

1. Consistent and Predictable Behavior

You have to behave as you communicate in order to be predictable to the other party. If your behavior is predictable, the other party has nothing to fear and can start trusting you. To be inconsistent in behavior is the quickest way to lose trust.

It is easier to build trust through behavior than through just talking. Behavior is the translation from communicated commitments into action. If you set rules, you are the first person who has to follow those rules. For instance, you have to return phone calls when promised or be on time for meetings if you expect other people to be on time. If you fail to fulfill your promises, you not only fail to build trust, you lose the trust other people might have had in you before.[29]

2. Honesty

It is an absolute requisite to have honest intentions when you strive to build trust. Without honesty people will never trust you completely. Be honest in everything you do and say. Like Peters cautions: "Nothing destroys trust quicker than the failure to tell the unvarnished truth."[30] To admit to a mistake can also be a powerful method for building trust. Caudron calls it "the magic of an apology."[31] To apologize symbolizes openness and respect for the other party. If the other party sees that you can admit mistakes, you open the door for them to do it too without being afraid to be vulnerable.

---

[29] Sullivan, *supra* note 4.
[30] Caudron, *supra* note 6.
[31] *Id.*

You must also be open to criticism and do not try to rationalize a mistake or to justify behavior. Keeping promises and commitments is important and if doing so is not possible, admit that you are not able to keep them.

3. Clear Communication

Behavior can only be perceived as consistent if communication of the intended behavior is clear.

Often people do not ask for clarification when they don't understand something, either because they are afraid to appear incompetent or they fear causing conflict. To prevent misunderstandings or different interpretations, clarification must be sought and communicated effectively.

Effective communication is candid, clear, at the right level of detail, timely, relevant to the interests and needs of the participants, involves the right people, and ensures mutual understanding of content and conclusion.[32]

Following are some recommendations on how you can make your communication more effective:

- Resist over-talking.
- Empathize with the other person's situation.
- Control your anger.
- Avoid the statement "you have got a problem here."
- Avoid hasty judgments and assumptions.
- Ask a lot of questions.
- Use good eye contact.
- Compliment whenever you can, but only sincerely.
- Keep judgments to yourself.

4. Active Listening

Listen attentively to the other party and make this clear by maintaining eye contact and affirming the other. To listen actively shows respect and can create mutual understanding. You should not interrupt or formalize a response until the other party is done speaking. By paraphrasing what you understood you can make sure that your

---

[32] G. Pitagorsky, *Building a Communication Infrastructure*, PM NETWORK, 41-46 (1998).

interpretation is correct and it shows the other party that you paid attention to what he or she said. If you don't understand something ask the person to explain it again instead of making your own assumption about what the person might have meant.

5. Share Information

Sharing important information shows the other party that you trust them not to take advantage of you and encourages them to share important information with you. Avoid surprises and inform the other party early about decisions, changes, and other information they may need to know. If you are not sure what information they need, ask them. It would be negligent on your part to assume which information is important to the other party. You might be wrong.

Action Plans for Top Management

Horton and Reid[33] especially encourage the top management to establish a new, more trustful relationship with their middle management by:

- shifting emphasis from deal-making and short-term results to long-term planning;
- practicing the corporate values they preach (don't talk about empowering employees and then overrule their decisions);
- interacting and avoiding isolation (communicate with as many people as possible, ask what they think, especially if it's negative. Listen to their ideas, problems, and solutions. Communicate goals and visions—everybody must operate from the same perspective);
- making an ongoing commitment that gives life to slogans; and
- restoring and respecting ethical values.

Enhanced Strategies of Partnering

The dynamics of the construction industry and its ever-changing projects require dynamic and full-contact partnering. Over the last decade, focused strategies for implementing partnering on construction projects have evolved. These strategies place emphasis on building the

---

[33] THOMAS R. HORTON & PETER C. REID, BEYOND THE TRUST GAP (1990).

process by working more with small groups rather than with the whole team. The partnering sessions are project-specific: actual project issues are solved at the session.

Direct Application Method (DA)

The goal of the direct application method is to establish at the beginning of a project a project manager-level team, which consists of three-to-six key project manager-level individuals. This team would have leadership and responsibility for designing and implementing the partnering processes on the particular project.

To be successful, the team needs to understand the concept of "project first thinking." That means focusing on what they want and not getting caught up in what they don't want. A prerequisite to making this happen is that the PMs commit to supporting the project's focus.

Exchanging perspectives and working together on action plans to solve issues will create mutual understanding and is the foundation of a trustful relationship between the PMs. In this relaxed and "safe" environment of the partnering session, PMs get the opportunity to try and test what happens when they trust the other party while discussing real issues.

Once a PM-level team is formed, it leads the partnering effort by scheduling and leading the meetings, the issue resolution and feedback processes, and other key partnering protocols. Every problem the team they successfully solves together enhances the level of trust among the team. It is the team's responsibility to expand the team by inviting the participation of new members and spreading the idea of "project first thinking."

When trust is established, all participants identify themselves with the project and the project develops its own identity and culture.

Executive/Sponsor Involvement

Leading the partnering process and serving as a role model is a new position for most PMs, and requires training. They cannot make the necessary changes and meet project partnering expectations unless their top management supports them with the needed commitment, resources, and organizational structures.

One of the commitments the top management needs to make is to relinquish a part of their authority to their PMs, in order to expedite processes and as a sign of trust. Neglecting to do this can become a main constraint in the trust-building process, since it is an indication that top management fears losing power.

Intervention Partnering

Intervention partnering or project realignment is an alternative dispute resolution technique designed to realign a project that is off course. At this point in a project, trust may be completely broken down and both parties are unable to talk reasonably about the issues. People are focused on protecting interests, defending positions, and cutting losses or impacts to their organization instead of trying to rescue the project.

For a project to get back on track, trust must either be reestablished or, in some cases, established for the first time. Project realignment can put processes in place that promote trust by building cross-organizational teams for project planning and for issue resolution. The project may need to employ a full-time independent expert for a short while to facilitate the teams through tough issues. It may even bring in a team of experts to provide guidance and immediate solutions.

The goal of the realignment process is to create an environment of fairness in which people can establish trust, honesty, and a degree of professionalism that will allow them to work through tough issues regarding risk and dollars.

The realignment process is built on:

- refocusing the project manager-level team to collectively do what is best for the project;
- working to reestablish an environment of good faith and fair dealing;
- addressing and resolving all outstanding contractual or people issues on the project in the immediate time frame; and
- resolving "project killer" issues and disputes.

Conclusion

Distrust has become part of "business-as-usual" and is an accepted form of behavior in the construction industry. As more risk and higher dollar amounts become involved in a project, the less trust is evident between parties. Distrust can be an invisible but powerful barrier to the success of a project or a company. Since the impact of trust or distrust cannot always be measured in precise numbers or dollars, many people overlook distrust as a main barrier to success.

The partnering process has prevented a lot of construction projects from realizing major losses in the past. But at the beginning of every project, partnering usually has to deal with a lack of trust between parties. To make partnering more effective and successful, it needs focused strategies. After attending a partnering session, each participant should know what he or she must do next to make the project a success. One of the first actions must be to start building trust.

II. AAA Task Force Guide to Partnering

Building Success for the 21st Century:
A Guide to Partnering in the Construction Industry

Report of the Dispute Avoidance and Resolution Task Force of the American Arbitration Association

The American Arbitration Association's Dispute Avoidance and Resolution Task Force (DART) of the construction industry convened a commission of prominent industry professionals to clearly define the process and provide guidelines for those who would implement a partnering strategy. Drawn from both the public and private sectors, the group has used partnering and is committed to belief in the value and utility of the process when creating and sustaining successful construction projects.

The commission's ultimate aim was to gain wider understanding, acceptance, and use of partnering, thereby improving the cost effectiveness of the industry's design and construction processes. This document is meant to help the industry effectively implement the partnering strategy and to challenge us all to take it to the next level.

The Partnering and Value Equation

Gone are the days when design and construction inefficiencies could be ignored and buried in project costs. Buyers of construction services, whether private or public, demand ever-increasing value from the limited dollars that are available. The industry must respond to this challenge and continue to develop innovative ways to work together that create added value through increased productivity.

With margins and costs heavily influenced by market forces, improved cost effectiveness and productivity are where a business or agency has the most potential for positive impact on its return on assets or program budgets. What's more, business arrangements based on mutual gain, like partnering, yield improved relationships and lead to increased trust. Studies by the Construction Industry Institute (CII) indicate that increased trust results in reduced project costs and schedules, ergo, effective partnering yields improved productivity resulting in increased value. Additional evidence follows almost daily from surveys of project teams that use partnering as a key improvement strategy:

- Ninety percent of the participants surveyed said partnering improved the quality of the project.[1]
- Five partnered projects with total installed costs of $492 million averaged 7% savings.[2]
- Of thirty partnered projects with a total cost of $684 million,[3] 83% completed early or on time.

What Is Partnering?

Partnering is a voluntary, organized process by which two or more organizations having shared interests perform as a team to achieve mutually beneficial goals. Typically, the partners are organizations that in the past worked at arm's length or may have had competitive or adversarial relationships with one another. Generally, the more partners that are involved, the better the overall results.

Partnering is also a collaborative process that focuses on cooperative solving of problems participants have in common. Properly applied, it yields reconciliation (win-win) as opposed to either compromise (lose-lose) or concession (win-lose). It is not a social process that simply promotes courtesy and politeness among participants, but rather good faith joint resolution of problems.

Partnering is a nonbinding process. It neither alters the contract documents nor the relationships between the parties. Instead, it is a commitment between the parties to use the agreed-upon partnering process and to deal with one another as true partners by:

- Participating in organized, facilitated team-building sessions and joint indoctrination to acquire the skills and attitudes needed to work together as a team.
- Removing organizational impediments to open communication at all levels, from owner through specialty trade contractors.
- Providing open and complete access to information (except

---

[1] Western Council of Construction Consumers (WCCC) (1992).
[2] Construction Industry Institute (CII) (1994).
[3] Harnett Partnering Consultants (September 1993).

information specifically excluded by law, regulations or ethical considerations).
- Training (empowering) front-line staff members to resolve quickly as many issues as possible.
- Reaching decisions through consensus whenever possible and achieving dispute resolution in a timely manner by following an agreed-upon process.
- Taking joint responsibility for maintaining, improving and nurturing the partnering relationship.

Partnering is a process that must be initiated in a disciplined manner at the beginning of a project if its maximum potential is to be realized. While it usually requires increased staff and management time up front, overall benefits accrue from a more open and innovative environment, thus assuring more successful project results and less staff and management time during project execution.

The value of early engagement can be seen in the cost influence curve. An active partnering process during the preparation of project basics can result in significant cost improvements. Similar relationships for key project parameters such as quality, schedule, and safety can also be drawn.

If the partnering process is to be successful, senior management must establish the proper environment and expectations for individual interaction. Specifically, the partnering participants must:

- Be personally committed to achieving the team mission.
- Lead by example through living the philosophy and principles of partnering.
- Contribute tangibly through time, resources, expertise, legal authority, or potential influence.
- Demonstrate an up-front commitment to be part of the team instead of waiting until decisions are made before deciding whether to support them.
- Accept, and keep, all commitments.
- Support the team and the interests it represents.

The Partnering Process

The partnering process encourages all stakeholders to resolve problems at the lowest level of authority possible. The process works to eliminate barriers between stakeholders and to build relationships among individuals involved in a project.

Partnering has several factors that are critical to its success. The process can be adapted to meet many different circumstances, but to ensure optimal application, several basics must be in place. These critical success factors are:

1. All needs must be clearly defined and documented prior to initiating work.
2. All leaders must be directly involved in all aspects from the outset through project completion.
3. Knowledgeable committed facilitator(s) must be engaged from the outset through project completion.
4. A comprehensive charter must be prepared, published, and signed by all stakeholders.
5. All work processes, systems and structures must be clearly defined and documented.
6. Ground rules must be specified, agreed to by all parties, published, and used to guide the relations between the parties.
7. Communicate, communicate, communicate.
8. Celebrate, celebrate, celebrate!

A barrier to successful partnering is the attitude that building relationships among the individuals involved from the various stakeholder organizations is a luxury—something to be done when there is plenty of time and nothing else really important to do. Actually, it is the investment in these relationships that assures maintenance of the partnering attitude by avoiding problems and the extra, nonproductive work that results from miscommunication, claims and other disputes.

For partnering to be successful, it is necessary to involve all affected participants and convince each of them that they have common goals and needs. Sincerity and commitment to the partnering process is essential.

The essential elements to successful implementation of the partnering process are listed below and illustrated on the next page. It is common practice to use facilitators or third-party consultants to implement the process. Omission of any of the activities will result in an ineffective implementation and a waste of time and resources.

PARTNERING

Phase One—Define the Overall Long-term Strategy. Partnering must be based upon sound strategy established by senior management using goals and objectives that are measurable. Key activities during this stage are:

- Attend leadership, strategic planning and partnering sessions;
- Define a long-term vision with supporting strategies and measurable goals and objectives; and
- Implement training across all involved organizations.

Phase Two—Enlist Project Participants. Key activities include:

- Educate the organization on the partnering process;
- Make a financial commitment and define objectives clearly for each participant;
- Assess leadership and technical issues; and
- Define the specific process to be implemented.

Phase Three—Team Formation. Participants convene and begin the process of teaming and relationship building. Key activities required:

- Orient new stakeholders and define roles;
- Establish project charter (see key components);
- Create evaluation mechanism and continuous review procedure;
- Establish issue-resolution process (see key components);
- Develop problem-solving process and action plans; and
- Practice interaction and communication skills.

Phase Four—On-site Implementation. Time committed to partnering peaks during this step. Key activities during this phase are:

- Hold regular Partnering Leaders meetings;
- Secure weekly or monthly assessments evaluation and feedback (see key components);
- Engage in daily proactive problem-solving;
- Encourage creative thinking throughout the team;
- Resolve difficult technical/financial issues;
- Modify the issue resolution process so that its effectiveness is maximized;

- Call partnering review meetings to improve the process;
- Support skill-building/monitor behavior;
- Call formal team meetings;
- Implement action plans for transition to operation phase; and
- Celebrate successes and recognize individual accomplishments;

Phase Five—Project Close-out. When done correctly, partnering yields hundreds of innovative practices. These lessons should be incorporated in the conceptual stage of future design and construction efforts. Key activities at this time include:

- Review team goals, both successes and failures;
- Develop best practice improvement plans;
- Recognize individual contributions;
- Continue the process on future projects; and
- Celebrate success.

Regularly scheduled project-level meetings are a vital element to successful partnering. At these meetings, it is important that stakeholders discuss ways to improve their partnering efforts. They also should use the meetings to identify and resolve present as well as potential problems.

For partnering to work, the parties must bring up current and potential problems to be worked on by the team. There also must be an open exchange of information about all aspects of the project during the meetings. This will ensure that everyone is fully informed and eliminate the surprises that contribute to lack of trust among stakeholders.

By identifying potential problems in advance, teams can use project meetings to activate problem-solving procedures.

Once in place, it is essential that the team stay focused on keeping the partnering process viable, otherwise stakeholders will slip back into their old ways and habits. The most effective way to enhance the partnering spirit is to have project leaders set the right example.

Each party must be objective and fair with each new issue. When a team member feels that his or her counterpart has not been reasonable it is important for that person to bring the issue to the attention of the other party. This frank discussion is essential in developing better understanding of each other's views, and ultimately improves future communication.

When trying to find a win-win solution to an issue, all team members who may be able to contribute to a problem's resolution should be involved.

Partners need to avoid "letter wars." An effective technique is to review a draft of letters with the receiving parties in advance and to incorporate their ideas on how to express an issue. That way the final letter becomes a joint product and greatly reduces the need for a formal reply.

Letters should be limited to the essential aspects, avoid argument, and be viewed as opportunities to build understanding and trust.

Key Partnering Components

When implementing partnering, team members must develop and use the following key components. They are required if the team is to stay focused and accountable.

Project Charter. The "Charter" is comprised of a Mission Statement and list of specific goals. Together they define the team's commitment to their project and their resolve to work together. At the conclusion of the workshop, all participants must sign the charter, which is then posted in prominent locations at all job sites. The charter must express and be compatible with the legitimate needs of all the stakeholders.

Team Assessment. The assessment is a tool to measure the performance of the team and to encourage mutual accountability. Team members should fill out an evaluation survey each month. It should measure the success of the team in meeting partnering goals and identify opportunities for improvement.

Issue Resolution Process. Stakeholders must commit to openly identify all actual or potential problems or major issues.

Often the best approach is a detailed problem-resolution matrix or chart. This involves designating project participants by name from each stakeholder organization with a commitment for involvement in the resolution process. Another key element is the commitment to a maximum length of time for an issue to be deliberated before it is escalated to the next level.

The issue resolution chart, with its escalation requirements, should be a flexible procedure that can be changed by consensus throughout the life of the project.

Selecting Facilitators

The use and selection of the facilitator is a business decision which should be made jointly by all stakeholders. Before choosing a facilitator, the stakeholders need to understand not only the potential benefits, but also the training and support they will need prior to starting the partnering effort. It is crucial that the facilitator remain involved throughout the life of the project.

The following checklist can help in selecting the right facilitator.

A good facilitator should possess:

- A basic understanding of construction;
- Strong communication and listening skills;
- Solid organizational and people skills;
- Demonstrated team-building skills; and
- Well-developed problem-solving/conflict management skills.

A good facilitator does:

- Assist the group in focusing on common problems and goals;
- Create an environment of openness and trust;
- Build consensus and commitment on all topics;
- Establish credibility and trust;
- Match the "personality and style" of the project stakeholders;
- Maintain flexibility;
- Control the process; and
- Generate participation.

A good facilitator will:

- Briefly state qualifications, work experience, and training;
- Explain roles, responsibilities, and objectives;
- Help stakeholders set ground rules;
- Remain objective, positive, and neutral;
- Serve as a positive role model;
- Organize all workshops;
- Know and understand the background of the stakeholders and the project;
- Keep all meetings focused on issues at hand;
- Encourage participation in an open dialogue;
- Have a recorder appointed to take notes;
- Keep the discussions moving and pertinent;
- Listen to participants;
- Help the group reach consensus;
- Recognize and constructively channel conflict; and
- Avoid personalizing discussions or taking positions on issues.

Again, the facilitator's role should not end with the conclusion of the first partnering meeting. Successful partnering projects have ongoing educational evaluation. The facilitator should help the parties stay focused, smooth out stumbling blocks, bring newcomers up to speed on the partnering process and improve the process so future projects will be able to realize even greater advantages.

Final Thoughts

Seldom are we given an improvement tool that offers the flexibility, breadth of application and value-added potential as does partnering. It is equally effective on projects that are large or small, domestic or foreign, fixed price or cost-plus, R&D or commercial, or fast-track. It can be tailored easily to meet any user's specific needs and is a proven value generator for all committed participants. With careful and consistent use of partnering, we in the construction industry can, and must, forge a leadership position in continuously delivering more value from each project dollar. Through partnering's unique capacity to enable groups to develop actionable consensus, leading to that type of commitment which ensures successful outcomes, we can today create the functional reality of Henry Ford's philosophy from almost three quarters of a century ago:

Coming together is a beginning;
Keeping together is progress;
Working together is success;
Partnering together, we can "Build Success for the 21st Century."

III. The Benefits of Partnering

The Benefits of Partnering

by James H. Keil*

The construction industry has been undergoing many changes due to developments in technology, environmental concerns, and changes in laws and regulations. In order to address the problems created by these changes, the author recommends using "partnering," as illustrated by his experiences as lead facilitator on the Tren Urbano project underway in Puerto Rico.

The construction industry has been dramatically and negatively affected by numerous changes to the laws and regulations controlling it over the past three decades. Environmental considerations alone have impacted individual projects, as well as entire construction-related industries, such as logging, transportation, and marine-use projects, to name a few.

Construction is a very dynamic industry. Developments in computer technology are coming fast and furious, and every advance creates new frontiers in joint design possibilities on projects. These joint ventures on design and construction include creative combinations and uses of CAD (Computer-Aided Design), CATO (Computer-Aided Take Off), and electronic transmission of files. This increased use of computer technology in one sense drastically reduces the potential for miscalculations, yet creates even greater potential for bigger disasters, since one errant keystroke can take away volumes of material instantly.

Virtual reality is now frequently used to measure and calculate use of spaces before they are actually created. Being able to measure the confines of a space in "real time" before attempting to assemble it in the field is a tremendous advantage. The surface has only been scratched on the use of this "fourth dimension" in construction.

---

* The author is an experienced mediator and arbitrator. He is a former policy-making official of Maine state government, having directed a 260-person bureau, and has been instrumental in leading the state of Maine into development of a total quality management (TQM) program. He is on the AAA's commercial mediation and arbitration panels and is a member of the AAA's Construction Advisory Council.

From a design and review perspective, linking many computer terminals together has given us tremendous progress in quality and volume output of work. But, from a legal perspective, the linking of terminals will make the question of ultimate responsibility for failures that occur more challenging.

ADR neutrals will likely need to be educated and experienced as much on the overall construction process as on the judicial process. Panels of mediators, arbitrators, and facilitators must be strengthened worldwide, and contracting authorities must become more willing to invest in supporting the improvement of these processes, which means more up-front legal counsel on contract provisions. Further, attorneys for the owners must be willing to support the need for "soft" conflict resolution processes in addition to litigation and other third-party resolution methods.

ADR is rarely a "stand-alone" method of dispute management and resolution, and most often works in concert with litigation. Considering the number of civil and criminal cases that settle before being heard in court, ADR seeks simply to make these settlements occur earlier in the process.

One ADR process that is already in use and continues to be refined and improved is called "partnering," and a derivation of that is called construction alliances. Both operate on similar principles. Both are forms of risk management, in which participants are encouraged to develop an interdisciplinary vision of the project, then to use that vision to more clearly identify, discuss, and thus, manage the risks.

As an example of the way partnering can become part of an overall system of dispute resolution management, we might consider the following case study.

Tren Urbano Project, San Juan, Puerto Rico

Tren Urbano is a regional rail transit system now under development in San Juan, Puerto Rico. The initial 11-mile line will run along one of the most densely populated corridors in the U.S., serving an estimated 115,000 travelers per day. The Puerto Rican Department of Transportation and Public Works (PRDTPW) received approval of the environmental impact statement and the record of decision for the project in 1996.

Recognizing the difficulties associated with bringing the necessary expertise together to build such a large and complex project, the PRDTPW determined to invest significantly in building a dispute resolution system into the project from the earliest stages. Not only did they have to face the usual communication problems of the construction industry, but this project attracted international joint ventures, which then introduced a significant management concern over cultural differences among the players.

Contract documents included provisions for the establishment of dispute review boards as a means to have swift justice readily at hand when issues cannot be resolved by the parties.

Dispute review boards are standing boards of industry professionals with specific process knowledge related to each contract. The boards meet quarterly to keep pace with its assigned contract. Should an issue warrant a third-party decision, the board stands ready to hear evidence and render a decision while work progresses.

The American Arbitration Association is a dispute resolution administrator large enough to maintain an international panel of construction experts to serve on such boards. The AAA was also specified in the contract documents as the provider of partnering facilitation services for all of the contracts in phase one of the project.

Partnering sessions were held on five major contract segments totaling more than $1.3 billion during 1996. A systems and test track turnkey (ST3) contract was awarded to one of five major consortia submitting proposals for the innovative design-build-operate contract. This was the first such contract ever conceived to implement a major transportation infrastructure project in the U.S. Other design-build contracts were awarded as rights of way were acquired and cleared. The ST3 contractor is coordinating and monitoring the work of the design-build contractors, and the entire operation is being overseen by the project's general management and architectural and engineering consultant (GMAEC) and Tren Urbano Office.

All of the partnering sessions designed and implemented were geared to accomplish the following minimum objectives:

- Identify project risks from all perspectives;
- Improve inter-disciplinary communication and vision;
- Promote teamwork among participants;
- Minimize cultural differences and the negative impacts they can have on projects;
- Develop a common vision of the "big picture";
- Provide dynamic feed-back loops to monitor project progress;
- Guide participants in making their own process adjustments where needed;

- Provide increased management of project risks by all participants;
- Establish uniform project goals for each contract segment; and
- Anticipate and avoid costly disputes by discussing alternatives early, and agreeing to attempt informal mediation before proceeding with any other legal process of resolution.

Although it is still too early to completely assess the value of partnering to the Tren Urbano project, comments received from participants are extremely positive. Follow-up sessions are currently underway, and a number of issues have been successfully dealt with through informal mediation.

A review of some of the action plans developed in the facilitated sessions on this project are indicators of the kinds of risks identified by teams that are being managed successfully.

Teams on one project recognized a need for an improved submittal process, and determined, among themselves, that the best adjustment would be for an advance submittal copy to be submitted. Even though the contract was silent on that issue, there was nothing limiting this agreement among the parties.

Another team was concerned over external factors, such as neighborhood coalitions, advocacy groups, etc., that could have a negative impact on the project, and established a smaller work team to identify and quantify these issues and bring them back to senior management through "feed-back loops" they established for the purpose.

Still another team, consisting of owners, designers, and contractors developed a method for assurance of design quality during construction. This team continually strives to find the best "engineering solution" to problems, rather than to blindly follow the contract terms alone.

Partnering Workshops

A typical partnering scenario begins with an initial strategic management session with the principals involved in the three elements that are common to all projects: specifically, design, constructor, and owner (through a contracting authority).

The principals themselves are encouraged to take an active role in the development of partnering agendas, project management goals, and the preparation of the invitation lists. This meeting usually takes place toward the end of a workday several weeks ahead of the initial partnering session. All partnering sessions, including the strategic management session, are retreats, held away from offices, telephones, and daily business interruptions. Cell phones and radios are put aside for the duration of the sessions, and adequate breaks are provided for management of messages. This undivided concentration on the project is crucial to partnering success, as is the positive attitude of senior managers toward the process. In fact, neither partnering nor construction alliances can be successful without it.

Management strategy sessions involve significant discussion on who should be invited as "stakeholders" to the process. Inclusiveness is usually preferable to exclusiveness, although no one should be invited to participate without accountability. It is no longer enough just to have an opinion. Participants must be willing to hear other arguments and work together with adversaries to find the best "engineering solution" to problems identified.

Groups that would otherwise work diligently to stop or delay projects often put their own experts to work on project details when invited into the negotiations. When invited to participate in strategic sessions, many groups organize themselves and send a spokesperson representing all. The spokesperson plays a role selling the strategic plan to group members.

Once agendas and invitation lists are determined, the principals establish a partnering oversight body (of its own design) that is representational of the three project elements. This informal oversight body provides the best opportunity for the establishment of loop-back performance links that will stay with the project for the duration.

These loop-back performance links keep the partnering oversight body informed, and provide them with opportunities to take action, rather than observing and reacting. Actions taken may include, but are not limited to, additional partnering sessions, mediation sessions on specific issues, arbitration on specific issues, bringing in an umpire, dispute review boards, or anything else the body determines to be productive.

All partnering sessions have some similarities in that they are, first and foremost, informal, outside the legal confines of the contracts involved (in some parts of the world, construction alliances are being used as the basis for contracts), and are intended to offer opportunities for questions and answers in a group setting. Expectations for internal processes are formulated by the group itself.

Even though contract terms and conditions often limit the ability or willingness of participants to alter situations, it generally increases the understanding participants have of why things are the way they are. In the real world, people underestimate or do not fully understand the risks they take every day. This leads to misunderstandings and eventual problems.

Under any typical contract delivery system, opportunities for questions across disciplines have been limited, rather than increased, over the past three decades or so. Pre-construction meetings rarely consist of more than the "owner" making a statement to the contractor and his subs, often quoting verbatim sections of the contract, most likely having to do with liquidated damages.

Opportunities for questions are limited, and, more importantly, such meetings are not conducive to open communication. Contractors, and, especially subs, are often very intimidated. Partnering, on the other hand, for the first time in years, provides an opportunity to shift that momentum favorably.

Conclusion

Through partnering and construction alliances, risks are better identified, understood more clearly by more people, and can thus be managed, rather than reacted to. Through a series of strategic sessions and follow-up work sessions throughout the pre-design, design, final design, and construction phases of a project, quality, safety, and on-time delivery can be improved.

It is the opinion of many involved with huge, complex projects such as the Central Artery Tunnel Project or Tren Urbano, that the work could perhaps not be accomplished at all without partnering, and its resultant increased communication. Constructors lose sight of the fact (if they ever understood it) that every shovelful of earth is someone's driveway, church parking lot, or backyard.

While nothing is perfect, a managed process is possible through partnering and construction alliances, and the common vision of the project can be improved by all the participants. This common vision of the project is particularly important on complex, inner city projects, where the real story of the project is not told at neat presentations with computer-generated audiovisual graphics, but, rather, is told in the post office, drug store or supermarket, where project participants interact with neighbors.

If they have not worked to develop a common vision for the project, including expectations of dates for certain major accomplishments, it quickly becomes evident to outsiders, and the seeds have been sown for community distrust. Lack of community trust can lead to unforeseen work interruptions, unsafe conditions, or other kinds of problems.

Strategic Risk Plan (S.R.P.) Check List

Development of a strategic risk plan for any construction project is a necessary step that should be undertaken at the earliest possible point of development.

Partnering During Concept Phase

- Use a trained, experienced project neutral to facilitate discussions among team members and legal advisers.
- Create "corporate oversight structure," or "advisory council" for project duration.
- Determine who should be involved in concept development.
- Establish a joint vision for the project among all disciplines.
- Establish loop-back performance links that keep the "corporate oversight structure" apprised of successes/failures. (Loop-back performance links are small work groups with specific assignments, or they could include the establishment of a project Intranet Web Page, as two examples.)
- Discuss the dispute management techniques best suited for this project and their incorporation into design contract language.
- Identify, quantify and discuss the risks as seen by various project disciplines with the guidance of a trained, neutral facilitator.
- Cross-check development of project timelines.

Partnering During Design Phase

- Use a trained, experienced project neutral to facilitate discussions among team members.
- Create a new "corporate oversight structure" to carry through the design and construction phases.
- Determine who should be involved in design development (including outside stakeholders).
- Refine joint vision for the project as the design develops.
- Manage input into project design through the "corporate oversight structure."

- Monitor and add/delete loop-back performance links as required.
- Discuss and develop ADR (dispute management techniques) for incorporation into construction contracts.
- Continue identification, quantification, and discussion of risks as seen by various project disciplines with the guidance of a trained, neutral facilitator.
- Continue cross-checking development of project timelines.

Partnering During Construction Phase

- Use a trained, experienced project neutral to facilitate discussions among team members.
- "Corporate oversight structure" continues.
- Determine who should be involved in design development (including outside stakeholders).
- Allow designers to help in refining joint vision for the project as construction begins.
- Monitor and add/delete loop back performance links as required.
- Continue identification, quantification, and discussion of risks as seen by various project disciplines with the guidance of a trained, neutral facilitator.
- Continue cross-checking performance against project timelines.
- Maintain partnering gains through facilitated project follow-up meetings as directed by "corporate oversight structure."

Follow-up Sessions

- "Corporate structure" determines schedule for follow-up sessions, "as needed."
- Facilitator available for a few hours pre-meeting to talk with any partnering participants.
- Facilitator then develops follow-up agenda and project principals.
- Project principals (only) participate in follow-up meetings to save time and costs unless otherwise directed by "corporate structure."

IV. Using Partnering to Manage Construction Disputes

Partnering and the Management of Construction Disputes

*by Steve Pinnell**

Too many construction disputes end up in the courts, argues Steve Pinnell. He recommends integrating partnering with a comprehensive dispute management program that will resolve disputes "far more effectively than an adversarial approach." This article is a step-by-step guide to what is needed to make a dispute management program achieve the ultimate goal of avoiding litigation and maintaining a healthy business relationship.

Too often conflicts between owners and contractors escalate into litigation, or contractors absorb cost overruns to avoid protracted disputes and damaged business relations while owners pay too much for extra work. Construction disputes should never escalate into litigation. The need for a rational, non-adversarial, and cost-effective approach to resolving construction disputes is evident.

To help avoid disputes, partnering is rapidly being adopted in the U.S. construction industry. Partnering is a formal process for building teamwork among the owner, contractor, designer, subcontractors, and others. In many ways, partnering is a return to how business relationships used to be.

Partnering improves attitudes, reduces conflict, and facilitates settlement. It starts with securing a commitment from all parties and brings everyone together in a pre-construction workshop. The project team defines a mission statement with common goals, implements improved communication, establishes conflict resolution procedures, and then works together to complete a successful project.

Partnering helps avoid disputes but isn't always well-implemented; contractors sometimes feel reluctant to press for legitimate change orders which could threaten long-term business relationships, while owners sometimes overpay for changes in order to maintain the partnering

---

* Steve Pinnell is a construction and project management consultant in Portland, Oregon with Pinnell Busch, Inc. The following article is adapted from his book, HOW TO GET PAID FOR CONSTRUCTION CHANGES: PREPARATION AND TECHNIQUES (1998), which was published recently by McGraw-Hill.

process. In addition, contractors' records are frequently inadequate for determining the facts and quantifying costs, and the owners' records lack sufficient detail to verify contractor claims. If claims are pursued, contractors, owners, and their attorneys are often forced to rely on claim consultants, who frequently have difficulty substantiating their professional opinions. The result is excessive financial and emotional costs, ill will, and discord.

Dispute Management Program

What's needed is a combination of partnering and a comprehensive approach to construction disputes. This comprehensive approach, which we call a dispute management program, is the subject of this article. It is equally applicable to contractors, owners, and designers of capital projects. It can also be adapted by any industry (manufacturing, software, consulting, etc.) that delivers a product or service under contract. A dispute management program will prevent most contract problems, limit conflict when it occurs, and resolve those disputes that do develop—far more effectively than an adversarial approach.

A dispute management program provides a framework and specific techniques that support a partnering approach. Everyone benefits. Contractors get paid and project owners pay no more than a fair price for extra work and legitimate construction impacts. Project designers, construction managers or contract administrators, and owner representatives are able to focus on building the project while avoiding haggling and potential liability for alleged errors. The project delivery process becomes less contentious, more efficient, and personally satisfying.

How to Achieve Improved Project Results

How do you achieve this comprehensive approach to avoiding and resolving disputes?

Establish Partnering as the Basis of Your Working Relationships

The first step is to realize that a partnering approach to business relationships will be more successful than an adversarial or win/lose approach. This is true even if the other party does not initially subscribe to partnering, as long as you preserve your contract rights. Both parties must continue to perform their contract obligations when partnering.

Most parties who do not initially buy into a partnering approach will quickly see its advantages. A dispute management program will protect you from those who don't.

Many contractors are reluctant to pursue legitimate construction claims for fear of damaging working relationships and their reputation in the industry. By using a partnering approach to changes, they can collect these costs while maintaining their reputation. Owners can use partnering to avoid inflated claims and to minimize costs or delays. Everyone benefits.

Implement a Dispute Management Program

The second step is to implement a dispute management program which integrates partnering with a comprehensive set of techniques for avoiding and resolving disputes. These techniques transition from pro-active to re-active, as described in Figure 1.

Dispute management programs for a contractor and project owner will have a common philosophy and techniques, but each will have slightly different goals. For example, a contractor's dispute management program:

- Identifies and limits contractual risks from onerous contracts;
- Ensures that estimating and cost-accounting systems track extra work and impacts costs;
- Provides procedures and systems for better communication, record-keeping, and dispute resolution;
- Trains personnel to identify extra work, give timely notice, and track extra costs;
- Develops in-house expertise in preparing change-order requests and claims; and
- Is compatible with partnering, while ensuring fair and prompt payment for extra work.

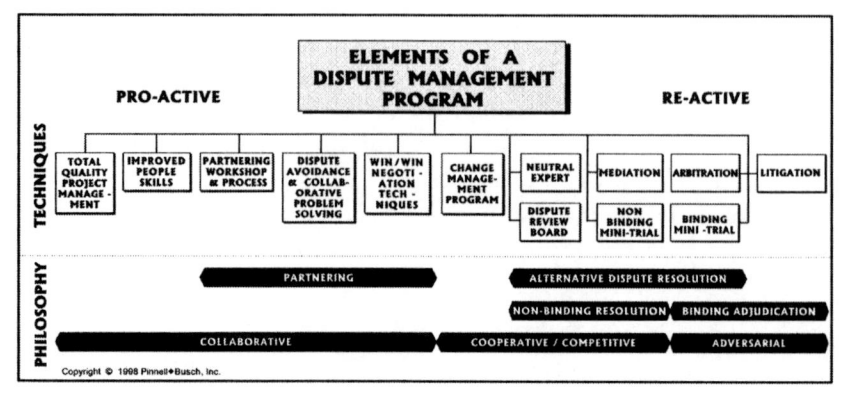

Figure 1

The Techniques of a Dispute Management Program

The techniques of a dispute management program are applied sequentially as needed, with the final step being binding arbitration instead of litigation. They include:

1. Total Quality Project Management policies, procedures, skills, and teamwork ensure projects are better managed, with fewer errors, changes, or other sources of conflict. Many, if not the majority, of construction problems (and the resulting disputes) occur because of poor project management practices.

Project owners sometimes don't plan ahead and end up rushing projects—with poorly defined scope, too-short schedules, and inadequate budgets. Designers face similar problems with poor project management leading to design errors, poor drawing coordination, or running out of time and money before the work is done. Contractors also have problems with poor project management. Bid errors, inadequate scheduling, and poor cost controls all lead to delay, cost overruns, and then claims.

Better project management is an important step towards avoiding claims. It includes setting a clearly defined scope of work, developing budgets and schedules based on that scope and the resources available, following the plan, tracking progress, and taking corrective action when actual results differ from the plan.

At Pinnell/Busch, we have found that short training sessions in scheduling, contract administration, or project management are invaluable for improving the quality of project management. In addition, they can double as informal needs assessments that identify an organization's strengths and needs. This requires an interactive learning process that teaches immediately applicable skills while explaining basic concepts and obtaining feedback on current problems. Even though many personnel are familiar with the basic tools, e.g., critical path scheduling, few are expert and all need to fully understand the tools and speak the same language. Well-designed training leads to further beneficial changes—including documentation and improvement of project management procedures and ultimately more successful projects.

2. Improved People Skills by all project team members lead to improved communication, more productive interpersonal dynamics, less tension, and fewer conflicts. Some construction disputes are caused solely by personal conflict and poor communication; many disputes are exacerbated by poor people skills. Training project personnel in better people skills will go far in minimizing these problems and in helping partnering succeed.

3. Partnering is both the overall philosophy for dispute management and one of the tools for avoiding disputes. Partnering promotes a more successful project environment where all parties work together and claims are avoided or readily resolved. Lack of partnering often leads to adversarial relationships when conflicts occur. Partnering should be implemented on all projects and should include subcontractors and key vendors in addition to the project owner and designer. Regulatory agencies and neighborhood associations may also need to be included.

Partnering is essential for both dispute avoidance and collaborative problem-solving. The environment of trust generated by the partnering process is also needed for win/win negotiation, a more successful change-order management program, and for the most effective use of a neutral expert or dispute review board. It can also help in mediation, if that becomes necessary.

Partnering is not always successful, but succeeds more often when the facilitator has:

- Enough experience in construction to relate to and understand the problems of contractors and owners' field personnel;

- Time for regular follow-up, in order to identify problems before they get out of hand; and
- Construction expertise and the ability to craft solutions to the problems that do occur and claims experience to aid in describing the consequences of not resolving disputes.

As an example of the benefits of partnering for contractors and owners, 30% of our firm's work used to be helping contractors resolve disputes with the Portland District of the U.S. Army Corps of Engineers. Since partnering was implemented by the district, that workload has fallen to zero. Other organizations have achieved similar results. They still have change orders, but the change requests don't escalate into disputes, resolution is directly between the parties without the need for outside help, and the settlements are more reasonable.

Dispute Avoidance and Collaborative Problem Solving techniques help the parties avoid disputes and jointly solve problems—even problems that impact only one party. Working together to solve problems builds a sense of teamwork. It also leads to faster, more economical, and better quality projects as the project team finds improvements to existing plans and procedures. Collaborative problem solving often results in creative value engineering proposals that reduce costs while maintaining or enhancing the function being performed.

4. Win/Win Negotiation includes looking for mutual benefits and seeking increased value in order that both parties can better their position. The parties look at basic interests instead of positions on an issue and try to craft a solution that meets each party's interests.

5. Change-Order Management Programs help contractors and project owners identify, track, document, and negotiate settlement of extra work and impacts without adversely affecting partnering. This includes being prepared with a plan in place and having personnel trained. It also includes a recognition that some change-order requests will be rejected and claims may be necessary. They need not lead to adversarial relationships.

Claims are similar to change-order requests, with the primary differences being the greater level of detail and the focus on proving entitlement for a claim. A claim is just a continuation of a change-order request that hasn't yet been accepted. Both should be fact-based, non-adversarial but firm requests for an equitable adjustment. They must be of professional quality but need not be prepared by a consultant. With proper training and support, a contractor's employees can prepare more successful change-order requests and claims that do not damage the partnering process. These change-order requests and claims will be easier for the owner's employees to evaluate and negotiate an equitable adjustment.

Unfortunately, there has been a history of poorly supported and inflated claims. In today's partnering environment, all change-order requests and claims need to be handled professionally. Thorough documentation, timely notice of change, careful preparation and prompt submittal of change-order requests (and claims) contribute to successful partnering and a successful project.

Rational, fact-based analysis techniques are essential to a successful change-order request or claim, especially when working in a partnering environment. Contractors need to understand and use these techniques to avoid inflated or unsupported claims. The techniques can be as simple (and powerful) as:

- Identifying and prioritizing the issues in dispute as part of a preliminary analysis;
- Organizing documents chronologically with the oldest on top so that the reviewer understands the project as it progressed;
- Tabbing important documents by issue (or copying for an issue file) and highlighting the relevant content for easier retrieval and review;
- Recording pertinent facts as summary notes with the date of the event or document, a reference to the source document for later retrieval, and a code for the issue covered; and
- Sorting the summary notes chronologically and selectively printing by issue for review. A chronological review of the summary notes (or issue file) for only a single issue is infinitely easier than trying to understand the issue when reviewing the entire project file.

The techniques can also be as sophisticated (but easy to use) as the detailed as-built schedule. The detailed as-built schedule is used to create an as-built schedule when the contractor's schedule wasn't updated during construction, or when more detailed information is needed to determine the cause of delays. It is an integrated, multisource document reconstructing the project on a day-by-day basis. It synthesizes numerous sources, each by itself insufficient for determining the events that happened, into a coherent, single document that describes what happened and why. It can be prepared by a contractor to develop a scheduling claim or by an owner to defend against one.

Detailed as-built schedules are usually built from the contractor's daily reports, the inspector's daily logs, personal diaries, minutes of meetings, and correspondence by all parties. They also use the contractor's weekly labor reports or timesheets, test reports, delivery tickets, weather records, etc. In addition to the as-planned schedule and reconstructed as-built activities, they can include rainfall histograms, tabular daily crew sizes for each trade, comments on major events, and any other data to aid in analysis.

The detailed as-built schedule is an accurate, complete, and detailed record of what happens on a project and why. Its advantages over other techniques are:

- It is easier to understand. A claim preparer, reviewer, or fact finder can (with careful review) understand the flow of activities, their relationships, and how they were affected by events.
- It eliminates unsupported opinion, sloppy analysis, or unjustified assertions. Each daily event constituting an as-built activity is described and referenced to a source document for verification.
- It can prove or refute alleged concurrent delay and identifies or explains apparent contractor errors.
- It identifies additional issues that had been overlooked but become apparent when all of the pertinent facts are organized and presented graphically.
- It establishes credibility when negotiating or testifying, provides a foundation for your conclusions, and intimidates opposing parties who wish to contest the facts with bluster or unsupported opinions.
- It provides all pertinent as-built information on a single drawing, allowing quick responses to unanticipated questions during negotiations or cross-examination that can be substantiated with the referenced source documents.
- It isn't that difficult to prepare, with the proper training and software templates and macros.

6. Standing Neutrals, either a neutral expert or a dispute review board (DRB), are experienced construction experts who monitor progress in order to understand and help resolve problems as they develop.

A dispute review board is retained jointly by both the contractor and owner (with subcontractors and the designer sometimes participating). The board normally starts at the beginning of a project, but can start midway through. It meets regularly, reviews progress, hears disputes, and recommends settlements. Dispute review boards on smaller projects may consist of a single individual if the parties have a high degree of confidence in the individual.

The parties need not accept the findings and recommendations, but almost always do so. Dispute review board recommendations are admissible in litigation. That seldom occurs as the courts and arbitration panels are reluctant to disagree with the findings of mutually selected industry experts who were involved in the project and familiar with the dispute.

A neutral expert functions similarly to a dispute review board, but takes a more pro-active role and uses his or her technical expertise to aid the parties in determining the facts and crafting solutions. Neutral experts can also assist a dispute review board with research on technical issues or assist mediators when the parties can't reach resolution due to uncertainty about the facts. The advantages of using a neutral expert, which can be an individual or team, over each side having their own expert include:

- A higher level of confidence in the results;
- Fewer exaggerated claims and unfounded counter-claims;
- Reduced resolution costs (only one expert needs to be paid);
- More accurate data due to the expert having access to all parties' records;
- Compatibility with partnering.

Neutral experts are normally involved from the beginning of a project, but can be brought on later. On one recent project, we were retained as the neutral expert by a partnering facilitator midway through a long-overdue project. The partnering facilitator first won the confidence of the parties and then helped them build trust among themselves. The resulting spirit of cooperation and our access to all parties' records enabled us to develop detailed recommendations for the allocation of $1.6 million in current and projected cost overruns. The dispute was settled 45 days after the parties agreed to the process. In addition, the pace of construction increased, and potentially serious construction deficiencies were resolved by the parties working with the masonry and concrete sub-consultants on our neutral expert team.

The recommendations of neutral experts can be non-admissible in arbitration or litigation (if the parties agree), although few disputes brought before them fail to settle. Their recommendations are usually admissible before a dispute review board.

7. Mediation involves a neutral third party who facilitates resolution of disputes while allowing the parties freedom of decision-making. Mediation can also benefit from the rational, fact-based analysis techniques described above. One of the major reasons for unsuccessful mediation is lack of sufficient, reliable information available to one or both of the parties.

One example of successful mediation is a recent case between an engineering company and their client on a $200 million food-processing facility in the Midwest. Relations had deteriorated to the point that another firm was brought in to finish the drawings and coordinate construction. The owner refused to pay our client's bill and counter-claimed $1 million-plus when our client filed for arbitration. After an investigation of the facts, we assisted legal counsel in mediation that resulted in payment of most of the contested bill, some reimbursement from our client's insurance company, and a new contract to redesign portions of the plant. Not only did they receive most of their money, they were able to resurrect an important business relationship.

8. Arbitration instead of litigation, is recommended if the parties find that they are unable to resolve an issue.

Conclusion

Contractors and owners and their attorneys need to re-evaluate their approach to dispute resolution and adopt a partnering philosophy and a comprehensive approach to managing disputes. Disputes will occur in construction. It is inherent in the process and a natural part of human interaction. The goal is to deal with conflict and disputes in a professional and non-adversarial manner through a dispute management program that leads to fair and prompt settlements.

V. Effective Partnering

Practical Tips for Effective Partnering

by Bruce Johnsen*

Partnering is a process that does not end after the workshop is over and the mission statement, goals and dispute resolution ladder have been developed. It is only after the workshop, when the project is underway, that the stresses and challenges of the project must be faced by the stakeholders.

Inadequate plans and specifications, schedule delays, payment delays, cost overruns, a variety of unforeseen conditions, weather problems, defaults by suppliers or subcontractors, changed government requirements—these are only a few of the potentially troubling problems that can arise on a project. Not surprisingly, a few partnering projects have had to be re-partnered because of inadequate follow-up. Seeing that the necessary follow-up occurs, so that the various participants communicate effectively with each other to work out disputes before they escalate is critical to the success of partnering.

Here are some practical tips from my experience as a partnering facilitator that will help all stakeholders maintain the follow-up effort throughout the project and ensure that it yields the maximum return.

Just After the Workshop

Spread the word about how the partnering effort should be carried out on the job. Spend time with your staff from the outset to coach them in the clear communication and the positive attitude they will need throughout the project. Since many of the key field people, subcontractors and suppliers may not have attended the partnering workshop, they will think that it's "business as usual." To dispel that impression, inform them about what occurred at the workshop and advise them about the skills they will need to work with other team members

---

* Bruce Johnsen is a Monterey, California-based partnering facilitator. He is a founding member of the AAA's partnering panel and a member of the Dispute Avoidance and Resolution Task Force (DART) national commission.

and achieve the partnering goals. As other subcontractors and suppliers begin on-site work, take them aside to bring them up to date on partnering for this project and what that will entail.

Create evidence demonstrating to the team that you're serious about partnering. There should be enough evidence that if partnering were a crime, you would be convicted. Get the field people involved in disseminating this evidence. It would be a good idea to ask your field representative to get together with your partners on the project and devise ways to let everybody know that this job is going to be different because it is being partnered. A partnering billboard on the jobsite, copies of the mission statement in all the job trailers, tee-shirts, hard-hat decals, and media releases are some of the ways to document to those involved in the project that partnering is a serious endeavor that has the complete support of management.

For the Life of the Project

Be on your best behavior at the jobsite and encourage your team to do the same. Be positive and constructive at all times in your comments and behavior toward other team members. If you are, they will follow your example. When mistakes are made by your partners, don't explode into anger. If you do, your team will wonder what you mean by partnering and cause them to question how they are supposed to act.

Build awareness of partnering and what it can do. If you and your managers talk about partnering at each visit to the jobsite, the team will stay interested in it. The model for this technique is in the area of safety. Safety improves on a jobsite when leaders continually talk about it with their people. The same is true of partnering. On jobsite visits, have your managers ask what they can do to help the partnering effort. This communicates the idea that management is serious about partnering and that the team should push it every day, not just at weekly meetings.

Measure results regularly during the project using the "Partnering Process Evaluation" forms from the workshop. Although the project superintendent or owner's representative may think there are more important things to do than sending out these forms, explain the importance of gathering data on the success of partnering. Measuring results helps you discover how the partnering process is working.

Monitor the volume of correspondence. If your staff is generating a lot of correspondence "for the record," find out why. Are there problems with suppliers, with the specifications or with subcontractor delays? If so, get your staff back to a more constructive discussion of how to solve these problems and away from less productive documentation. Excess correspondence can choke a project's progress, much like water in a fuel tank.

Encourage your partners. Compliment them on milestones completed and their other accomplishments and offer your assistance when they need it. For example, if one of your subcontractors had a lost-time accident, your staff should ask the subcontractor if there is anything you can do to help. Your partners should know that you are in the project together. Don't take them for granted. They will appreciate your recognition and the partnering spirit that you convey to them. This will encourage them to continue to meet your partnering goals, which will enhance the likelihood that the project will be completed successfully.

Have fun together. Spend social time with the team, either at organized sports or other company events. This can help to smooth the rough spots that arise and strengthen the partnering relationship.

When Problems Arise

Turn off your ego when someone on the jobsite does something that strikes a raw nerve or something undesirable occurs on the job. This is the time to get serious about joint problem-solving and try to reason a solution to the problem, rather than blaming. How many problems are solved by blaming?

Focus on the positive when bad things happen. For example, if a planned bridge move was only half completed, instead of groaning to the team about how far behind schedule the project is and how much it is going to cost to start again tomorrow, reinforce the idea that progress was made and that even greater cooperation will be needed tomorrow. Whether the problems are due to unexpected weather conditions, political pressure, personnel changes or other difficult events, it is important to take stock of the good that exists and build on it. That will get better results in the long run.

When the Project Ends

Have a warm-up session to find out what was learned during the project. Identify what went well and should be done again and what went wrong and should not be repeated. This information is worth its weight in gold. Take the time to pan for it.

The partnering workshop is an upfront investment that can yield a quality outcome. These tips can help get the best possible return on that investment.

VI. "Beware of Partnering"

Team Players-Not "Partners"!
"Partnering" Does Not Create "Partners"

*by Robert S. Peckar**

When the term "partnering" was created to describe the process now used so often by members of a construction project team to create a path to positive relationships and dispute avoidance, it was not surprising that many participants in that process would begin to describe themselves as "partners." Some enthusiastic partnering participants even referred to their relationship with other participants as a "partnership." However predictable this development, it is an unfortunate one because it can lead to serious misunderstandings and adverse consequences in a project that has employed partnering.

Project team members, who participate in the partnering workshop, subscribe to the partnering charter and believe in the value of its appropriate application to their performance on the job, are not partners or members of a partnership. What they are, and should be referred to, are "team players" or cooperators. But "partners"? No!

The dictionary definition of the term "partner" may have abetted the lay perception of a partnering participant as a partner in the ordinary sense of a colleague or an associate. In the MERRIAM WEBSTER COLLEGIATE DICTIONARY (10th ed. 1993), this term has several meanings, one of which is "one associated with another, esp. in an action: associate, colleague" and "one of two or more persons who play together in a game against an opposing side...."

Despite this popular usage, in the world of construction contractual relationships the nouns "partner" and "partnership" have very different meanings from the verb "to partner" (as in the partnering process). When those meanings are misunderstood or, worse, misapplied, serious problems can arise.

---

* Robert S. Peckar, Esq., is the senior partner in the construction law firm of Peckar & Abramson in River Edge, N.J. Mr. Peckar serves on the Steering Committee of the Construction Industry Dispute Avoidance and Resolution Task Force (DART).

The term "partner" describes a specific legal relationship and implies a state of affairs that does not usually exist in the typical construction project. Partners usually share in the investment and in the gains and losses of their partnership. In addition, partners usually place their own self-serving needs aside in favor of fairness to their partners. In a partnership, even if the partners' rights are allocated by percentage, it is "one for all and all for one."

This is completely different from the partnering relationship. Even though project participants may walk out of the partnering workshop enlightened and excited about the possibility of having an enjoyable, cooperative project experience, they have not been converted into legally recognized partners by reason of this experience. The partnering process typically occurs after the contracts establishing the parties' legal relationship have been drawn and signed. The purpose of that contract is to allocate responsibilities and risks. Even when the partnering participants agree to carry out that contract in a cooperative and constructive manner, the terms of the contract are not changed. They are exactly who they were when they walked into the workshop. Their legal relationship to each other did not change.

Thus, provisions with respect to notice, waiver and rights to compensation, along with provisions allocating risk and legal liability, operate regardless of equity or fairness and are fully effective notwithstanding the partnering charter.

How does the use of the term "partners" by participants in partnering create danger? These examples may provide insight into this problem:

- Perceiving the project owner as a "partner" dedicated to fairness, equity and friendship, one project manager elected to rely upon oral discussions with the owner at job meetings with respect to his company's needs for additional time and compensation. Much later in the project, it became obvious to the project manager that the owner had taken advantage of him and concealed the real intent to resist the project manager's requests. At that point, the project manager realized for the first time that he may have waived contractual rights and otherwise prejudiced his company with a weak written record. His response? "How could a partner treat me this way?"

- In another case, a contractor who considered the owner to be his "partner" proposed a contract adjustment near the end of the job.

He said, "Look, as you know, because we "partnered" this job and we committed to act like "partners," my company worked through some pretty tough situations without banging you over the head for extras, time extensions and the like. You knew our situation and we knew yours [*i.e.*, concern about a weak market for the sale of the condominium units] and your vulnerability with your lender. But now that the market for your units is really good and it is obvious you are going to make a huge profit, I would appreciate your living up to your part of the partnering promise and treat[ing] me as a partner in the same way I treated you. I want a contract adjustment of $2 million."

What did the owner say to this? "Are you nuts? You think you were my partner in this deal? Where were you when I had to make a cash call to my real partners when the deal was going sour? Hey, if you have claims, you should have put them in writing and submitted them to me when they arose. But I have to tell you, if you plan to submit any claims now, like the $2 million claim you are hinting at, you are barking up the wrong tree. And, by the way, don't count my money!"

Partnering is a wonderful process. However, the flaw is that participants in the process may be misled into believing that they are "partners" and act in ways that are not in their own interest. The fervent wish of contractors, owners and designers for dispute-free projects seems to push some of them into this fantasy. Whatever the most appropriate term to describe partnering participants, it is clear that the term "partner" should not be used.

VII. The Limitations of Partnering

The Truth About Partnering—Limitations and Solutions

by Allen L. Overcash[*]

Some years ago when partnering burst upon the construction scene, it was heralded as a miracle cure for dispute-plagued construction projects. Among other benefits, it was claimed that partnering would avoid litigation, control costs, facilitate on-time completion, improve functional and aesthetic quality and create a cooperative and safe working environment.

Not surprisingly, partnering has become very popular in certain branches of the construction industry, particularly on larger and more complex projects. The process has succeeded in opening lines of communication and enriching the quantity and quality of communication between parties to the construction process. In this respect, it has certainly helped avoid disputes.

Critic's Views

But even if partnering's achievements have been substantial, the process has not been a uniform success. It is not uncommon to hear criticism of partnering in interviews with veterans of the process. "The other side did not seriously participate in the spirit of the sessions." "There was no meaningful follow up." "The people who should have been there weren't." "The partnering sessions were simply job-site meetings which did not change the attitude of the parties." "There was no real commitment to the concept." These and similar statements reflect frustration over the fact that partnering did not succeed in preventing disputes on the project.

Concerns about the process also have been raised in the legal community. Is the informal cooperative atmosphere of partnering inconsistent with the parties taking adversarial legal positions? Are friendly discussions inconsistent with formal notice letters? Were statements made in partnering sessions admissions that could be used against

---

[*] The author is a partner at Woods & Aitken in Lincoln, Nebraska. He serves on the American Arbitration Association's roster of neutrals.

the partnering party in a later court proceeding? What about differences between conclusions developed in the partnering session and the terms of the contract between the parties?

Many of the criticisms of partnering can be addressed by adhering to the principles and structures recommended for the process. The Dispute Avoidance and Resolution Task Force of the Construction Industry (DART), for example, in its publication *Building Success for the 21st Century, A Guide to Partnering in the Construction Industry*, set forth a number of practical guidelines which partnering participants should follow. Following these suggestions undoubtedly improves the prospects for success of the process.

But many disputes between the parties cannot be resolved by partnering. This is apparent from the major disputes involving partnered projects that still find their way into court or arbitration. Instituting partnering on a project does not ensure the project against disputes. Further, disputes arising on a partnered project can be just as divisive and irreconcilable as pre-partnering battles, and carry the additional frustration of the failure of partnering "to work."

If partnering is not the single solution to construction disputes, what needs to be done to prevent ruinous disputes from disrupting projects and bankrupting the contractors, owners, architects and engineers involved in them? I offer these suggestions.

Improve the Process

We should not blame the concept of partnering for failing to produce dispute-free projects. Partnering clearly has been oversold as a cure for construction disputes. The process generally was thought to create a new relationship between the parties to a construction project, one in which cooperation was to replace adversarial posturing, to the benefit of the project and the parties building it. As a result of this expectation, some attorneys were concerned that the days of lucrative construction disputes were at an end.

Partnering is really a process of communication. It is intended to break down the traditional adversarial barriers that have prevented construction people from talking to each other in a meaningful fashion. It has been widely successful in breaking these barriers and, because of this, it is now commonly used on both public and private projects to facilitate on-site communication.

But partnering alone does not create a different relationship. Even on partnered projects, the parties remain loyal to their interests and positions. While they generally adhere to the slogan of completion of the project on time and within budget, each continues to have its own independent concerns. The owner may be concerned with both the time frame and the budget, as well as the need to change the project to match developing conditions not fully anticipated at the start of the project. The contractor may be concerned about absorbing the cost of conditions it (rightly or wrongly) did not anticipate while still profiting from the project. The architect and engineer commonly have their own budget, yet they too must respond to changes proposed by all parties.

While partnering may encourage these parties to discuss their concerns, it does not ensure the discussion will be productive or even cordial. Even so, we should not abandon an effective means of communication because of irreconcilable differences. To abandon partnering is to shoot the messenger rather than cure the ill.

Partnering on some projects has also been under-performed. It is easy to find flaws in the way the process was conducted on particular construction projects. The real decision makers may not have attended the sessions. There may have been little follow-up to the initial session. The process may have started after a dispute had arisen and after the parties had taken adversarial positions. The sessions themselves may have deteriorated into ordinary project meetings without neutral leadership and without any partnered goals in mind. Such deficiencies need to be corrected if the full potential of partnering is to be realized.

Combine with Other ADR Tools

While partnering can benefit the atmosphere of a project, there are certain attributes it lacks. For example, partnering generally does not offer the services of an active intermediary or a final decision maker. When parties who fail to use their partnering skills to resolve all their disputes adopt hard-line positions, meaningful communication between them tends to disappear. On-site personnel who meet daily on project matters may be loath to discuss their major differences. They may even lack the authority to resolve disputes.

Moreover, once the parties become convinced of the veracity of their respective positions, it is often hard to relieve them of their strength. Although the parties may talk, they usually will not accept criticism from each other, which they perceive as self-interested and advancing the criticizer's own cause.

Parties can be swayed away from hardened positions by an objective, knowledgeable, active intermediary through such mechanisms as a standing neutral or mediation. In some cases the dispute will require a knowledgeable, skilled decision maker to reach a resolution.

Yet many contracting parties apparently view the partnering process as the only ADR effort to be made on the project. Thus, disputes that are not resolved during the partnering process go the same way as disputes which existed in the pre-partnering age. They are left to the courts or to arbitration to resolve.

This dichotomy is unfair to the concept of partnering. While partnering can help to create both a communicative relationship and a more cooperative atmosphere between the participants, the seeds of a dispute may need more than communication and cooperation to prevent their growth. The goodwill of those attending a partnering session is often not enough to settle problems that may have resulted from decisions or other factors beyond their immediate control. Simply leaving these matters to litigation or even arbitration is impractical.

Partnering should be considered only one of a number of ADR tools that should be used on the project. Because it may reasonably be expected that partnering alone will not dispose of all potential disputes, parties to construction projects should write other ADR measures into the contract. Depending on the particular needs of the project, consideration should be given to including such measures as step negotiations, standing neutrals, dispute review boards, mediation, and arbitration. Often the existence of another procedure is an impetus to parties to make a more serious attempt at solving the dispute.

Inconsistencies with Legal Instruments

The partnering process calls for different behavior than the contract provisions the parties signed and may well be inconsistent with those provisions. For example, partnering's encouragement of direct verbal communication when there are problems on the project seems to many people to differ from the precepts of contract provisions requiring written notice of claims in order to prevent a waiver. Direct communication between parties who have no privity of contract also may be inconsistent with the contractual pattern. Understandings reached through partnering that are not promptly memorialized in contract amendments also pose problems. Not surprisingly, attorneys for the parties to a partnered project even frown upon party representatives admitting fault or partial fault for construction problems.

Some perceived inconsistencies between the construction contract and partnering conduct can be reconciled. For example, confirming verbal advice in writing, as the contract requires, need not be considered contrary to the partnering process. Other aspects of partnering, however, raise more serious conflicts with the contracts. This is because an informal team-oriented approach to construction differs fundamentally from the adversarial contract scheme parties have traditionally used. This accounts for some attorneys' aversion to the expression "partnering," which connotes a different legal relationship than the term "independent contracting party." The suggestion has been made to use, instead, such terms as "team building," which have less serious implications.

Ultimately, we must ask whether the differences between partnering philosophy and contractual agreements indicate a problem with partnering or with the contracts themselves. For years we have followed the concept that the position of the parties on construction projects should be solidified into detailed instruments that describe how the projects will be built. In so doing we have failed to recognize the difference between static agreements (such as the sale of a horse) and relational contracts (such as a construction contract).

The division between the dynamic construction process and static legal agreements has become more pronounced under current market conditions. Rather than the traditional "plans and spec" projects, "fast track" construction is now the rule. In this market, owners cannot wait for, nor afford, the luxury of completed design preceding construction. To the contrary, building must move ahead on the basis of "conceptual plans" that will be finalized as the project is constructed. The eventual design will result not only from the input of the owner, the architect and the engineer, but also from input by consultants, equipment manufacturers, suppliers and other parties. Even the contractors and their subcontractors and suppliers are expected to play a roll in design.

Addressing the Inconsistencies

More certain than death and taxes, particularly in this fast-track construction market, are changes in construction. The changes in the circumstance of the project may be small or large. Often, the nature, size and frequency of these changes are such as to allow parties to absorb the cost and time involved without changes in compensation or time. In many cases, however, the changes are subtle and their impact on the project is not immediately grasped by the parties. In any event, whatever their color or nature, it is a sure thing that changes which can form the seeds of a disagreement will arise.

Since virtually no project will be performed exactly as written, shouldn't the contract concentrate more on the dynamics of the process than its fixed elements? If anything, construction contracts should be regarded more as charters setting the broad parameters of a long-term relationship and providing for adjustments in that relationship as new conditions develop. Thus, the "contract/charter" governing the project and the relationship of the parties should focus more on how the project will absorb and allocate the responsibility of changes and changing circumstances, and how it will handle disputes. The framing of this document should start from the premise that construction is a dynamic changing process, rather than a fixed static arrangement.

To the extent partnering conduct conflicts with common legal agreements and principles, it may well be that it is the agreements and principles which should be changed.

Conclusion

Construction's move toward fast-track "evolving" projects has users of construction services looking for the best systems to match their needs. Partnering has proved its worth in opening communications and facilitating the step toward a less conventional relationship between parties to the project. Partnering used in the context of a non-static construction contract that reflects the relational aspects of construction projects, together with on-site and other ADR systems, can fulfill these needs.

CHAPTER FIVE

ARBITRATION

I. **Drafting Arbitration Clauses**

Dangers in Drafting the Arbitration Clause

*by Stanley P. Sklar**

Two cases in the last five years, one from New York, the other from California, point out problems associated with poor drafting of the arbitration clause. If the decision to use the clause is an afterthought, or a "boiler plate" ADR clause from another transaction is used without considering the ramifications, the end result could be litigation, instead of a speedy, efficient, cost-effective dispute resolution process.

The problematic ADR clause in *Maggio v. Windward Capital Management*,[1] provided that any controversy or claim "shall be settled in accordance with the Code of Arbitration of the American Arbitration Association." Windward, the party that drafted the clause, argued that "in accordance" meant only that AAA rules had to be applied, and did not mean that the hearing had to be held "before" the AAA. Reversing the trial court, the California Court of Appeal made a sound analysis that showed that by referring to the AAA rules the parties agreed to have the Association administer the proceedings. Thus, arbitration conducted "in accordance with" the AAA Construction Industry Dispute Resolution Procedures, or the AAA Commercial Dispute Resolution Procedures, must take place before the AAA.

What drafting lessons may be gleaned from this case? First, make sure you know the name of the rules under which you wish to operate. There is no "AAA Code of Commercial Arbitration." There is a Code of Ethics for Arbitrators in Commercial Disputes promulgated by the AAA,

---

* The author is a partner in Bell Boyd & Lloyd in Chicago. He serves on the American Arbitration Association's roster of neutrals for construction disputes.

[1] 96 Cal.Rptr.2d 168 (Cal. Ct. App. 2000).

the American Bar Association and the Society of Professionals in Dispute Resolution (SPIDR), but it contains ethical guidance, not procedural rules. The AAA promulgates Construction Industry Dispute Resolution Procedures (including mediation and arbitration rules), and rules for other types of disputes. Know which one applies.

The mistaken reference to the "code of commercial arbitration" was not fatal to the proceedings in *Maggio*. But the reference to a set of rules or to an organization that does not exist at the time the claim is filed could lead a court to nullify the ADR clause. A simple Internet trip to the AAA's Web site at http://www.adr.org will provide the needed information, and there the relevant rules can be downloaded with the stroke of a key.

A second lesson is to use caution in the use of language. For example, the clause in *Maggio* stated that any controversy shall be "settled...." Could one party have argued that this required mediation rather than arbitration? Had the parties called for any controversy to be "resolved" or "decided" under the AAA's rules, that clearly would have indicated that the process they intended to select was arbitration.

The problematic ADR clause in *Diagnostic Radiology Ass'n v. Brown*,[2] called for ad hoc (i.e., non-administered) arbitration by a particular sitting district court judge. In the event that he was unable to serve, the clause authorized him to designate a substitute. The parties never advised the judge of his appointment in their agreement, but had they done so he no doubt would have declined because Canon 5E of the Code of Ethics for U.S. Judges does not permit a federal judge to act as an arbitrator or mediator or otherwise function in a private capacity. Had the judge accepted the assignment, he could have been disciplined under 28 U.S.C. §§ 332(d)(1) and 372(c). Thus, a bit of legal research or a simple telephone call would have saved the parties from this clause.

The court seemed to want to help the parties out of their dilemma by engaging in a bit of legal legerdemain. The only way their ADR clause could become operative would be to have a judge before whom the case was pending appoint a successor. The designated judge could not appoint the successor, despite the authority in the ADR clause, because the case was not before him. To remedy this situation, the court decided *sua sponte* to transfer the original action to federal court where the designated judge was sitting, thus setting the stage to permit him to name a successor.

---

[2] 193 F.R.D. 193, 2000 WL 573127 (S.D.N.Y. May 10, 2000).

Cases such as these can teach valuable lessons. The main lesson is that dispute resolution clauses must be given as much attention by drafters as the substantive portions of the agreement. If there is a significant economic risk involved, it may be advisable to consult with an ADR expert or litigator. There is plenty of literature on drafting ADR clauses that the drafter could consult. The AAA's excellent booklet entitled *Drafting Dispute Resolution Clauses—A Practical Guide* can be downloaded from its Web site. A few hours of careful research and drafting will cost the parties significantly less in the long run by avoiding challenges to the operation of the clause.

II. Effective Construction Arbitration Advocacy

Tips on Advocacy in Arbitration Before an Industry Arbitrator

*by Jorge R. Cibran**

"How can I improve my skills in presenting a case to an arbitrator who is a construction industry professional?" I am often asked this question, probably because I am an architect who frequently serves as an arbitrator. For the most part, I believe counsel in construction disputes strive to present a thorough and effective case. Nevertheless, I can't deny that there's always room for improvement and toward that end, here are some tips to keep in mind.

Know the facts and issues in your case and how to arbitrate. Successful advocates in arbitration understand that arbitration differs from litigation, and that this is even more true when the arbitrator is a construction industry professional. In such a case, the arbitrator is already knowledgeable about construction principles and may even have expertise in the particular type of dispute. Thus, it is essential for counsel to "get up to speed" to present a convincing case. The arbitrator with construction experience and expertise knows when the attorneys are unprepared or lack an understanding of the facts and issues.

It also is critical to know the arbitral rules that apply. Judicial rules of procedure and evidence are relaxed, unless the parties' arbitration agreement otherwise provides. Arbitrators who are construction professionals have a lower regard for attorneys who try to turn arbitration into a courtroom proceeding; they prefer to rely on arbitration's key benefit—a quick resolution at a lower cost.

Argue the facts. Most decisions by construction arbitrators are fact-driven. Too often attorneys focus their presentations on legal issues, failing to pay adequate attention to the key construction facts in the case. For example, in a delay-damages case involving phased completions, focusing almost completely on the contract language to support a claim for liquidated damages may cause the lawyer to overlook facts that make the

---

* Architect Jorge Cibran is vice president of The Architectural Partnership in Miami. He serves on the American Arbitration Association's roster of arbitrators.

liquidated damages clause inapplicable. It is counsel's responsibility to ask the client the right questions and learn the nuances of the facts of the case.

Respect the industry arbitrator's expertise. An elementary review of the ABCs of construction is usually necessary when explaining a case to a judge or jury. But this is not necessary when the arbitrator is a construction professional. The attorneys should tailor their presentations to the level of the arbitrator's (or panel's) construction expertise. Counsel also should prepare witnesses to testify at the same level of expertise. Testimony intended to educate the arbitrator is best directed toward areas that are outside of the arbitrator's general construction knowledge and experience.

Retain a qualified expert witness. Sometimes attorneys miss the mark in selecting an expert witness. They should seek an expert who will present a logical, well-organized, even-handed evaluation of the dispute. Since an industry arbitrator will recognize legitimate issues raised by each side, the expert should acknowledge and address these issues while analyzing the dispute from both parties' perspective, not just from the client's point of view.

The expert's ability to present a concise evaluation will win points with the industry arbitrator. For example, in one case I recall a contractor's expert led the arbitrators through a one-day presentation, using graphics, charts, matrixes, and person-hour calculations to demonstrate the percentage of work that had been completed and the amounts due under the contract. By contrast, the owner's expert made a two-hour presentation comparing payment requisitions to aerial and non-aerial photographs depicting the work in place. The owner's presentation was not only more efficient, it was also more effective.

Attorneys sometimes fail to consider the industry expertise and experience of the arbitrator when they select an expert. If the person selected has less construction experience than the industry arbitrator, the expert's presentation is likely to have little or no impact.

Attorneys should always put themselves in the arbitrator's chair and imagine what he or she would expect of the expert witness' presentation.

Less is more. The well-known architect Mies Van der Rohe once suggested that "less is more" in connection with the modernist style of architecture. This statement could also be applied to complex arbitration in which parties seem to think that their chance of prevailing grows with the amount of discovery they conduct. This approach can be counterproductive, overwhelming the arbitrator with voluminous amounts of repetitive evidence which distracts from more important issues and facts.

To be sure, it is important for attorneys to make a thorough presentation and tell the whole story. But this story should be appropriately edited, focusing on the most important evidence and testimony.

Attorneys should feel completely comfortable with industry arbitrators as long as they remember that they are arbitrating, not litigating. Those who adapt to arbitration rather than trying to change it into litigation will better serve their client's interests and pocketbooks.

III. Selecting an Arbitrator

Unilateral Selection of the Arbitrator

by Robert J. MacPherson* & Sarah B. Biser**

Can a public entity, or any other contracting entity for that matter, contractually appoint its own representative as the sole arbitrator of disputes arising under a contract? In a recent decision raising this issue, the New Jersey Appellate Division concluded the answer is "probably not."

The court held in *Gothic Construction Group Inc. v. Port Authority Trans Hudson Corp.*,[1] that a clause in the Port Authority's standard form contract, designating its chief engineer as the sole arbitrator, was subject to attack on the basis of potential arbitrator bias. The court reversed the dismissal of a suit brought by Gothic against the Port Authority for breach of contract. The lower court had dismissed the action on the basis that the dispute must be submitted to the chief engineer.

The clause at issue, which the court held was the equivalent of an arbitration clause, provided in relevant part:

> To resolve all disputes and to prevent litigation the parties to this contract authorize the chief engineer to decide all questions of any nature whatsoever arising out of, under, or in connection with, or in any way related to, or on account of, this contract... and his decision shall be conclusive, final and binding on the parties....[2]

The Appellate Division found the contract had the hallmarks of a contract of adhesion, that Gothic had no real say in its provisions and that utilizing one's own representative as arbitrator "presents a conflict of interest, especially since the chief engineer has "unbridled decision making power under the dispute resolution clause."

---

* Mr. MacPherson is a member of Postner & Rubin, New York and Holmdel, New Jersey.
** Ms. Biser is a partner at Seyfarth Shaw, LLP in New York.
[1] 711 A.2d 312 (N.J. Super A.D. 1998).
[2] *Id.* at 314.

The court's ruling was not surprising given earlier New Jersey cases on the issue of arbitrator partiality and the appointment of one's own arbitrator to arbitrate disputes.

For example, in *Chimes v. Oritani Motor Hotel, Inc.*,[3] the court held an arbitration clause in a musician's union contract between a singer and a hotel, providing for binding arbitration of disputes before the executive board of the American Federation of Musicians, was void against public policy. The court said:

> In the circumstances, we conclude that the so-called arbitration provision, giving the board power to decide disputes between its members and defendant, is contrary to public policy. The relationship between the board and its members is obviously too close to assure the dispassionate and impartial resolution of disputes between AFM members and nonmembers.[4]

The *Chimes* court also noted that "complete contractual autonomy in the choice of an arbitrator must give way to the common law requirement of fair procedure."[5]

What is surprising about the *Gothic* decision is that the court did not flatly declare that the Port Authority's chief engineer could not be the sole arbitrator of disputes. Instead, it sent the case back to the trial court for a determination on the potential "bias issue." It is unclear whether the hearing on that issue will be limited to the potential generic bias of anyone in the position of chief engineer or whether it will focus on the potential bias of a specific chief engineer. In any event, the authors understand the Port Authority has asked the New Jersey Supreme Court to hear the matter.

Contracting agencies across the Hudson and Delaware Rivers are given more leeway in selecting a sole arbitrator. In *Westinghouse Electric Corp. v. New York City Transit Authority*,[6] New York's highest court held that a contractual dispute provision authorizing an employee of one party to make a final, binding decision did not violate public policy as long as some judicial review, even though limited in scope, is available. And in *Gauntt Construction Co./Lott Electric Co. v. Delaware*

---

[3] 480 A.2d 218 (NJ App. Div. 1984).
[4] *Id.* at 222.
[5] *Id.*
[6] 82 N.Y. 2d. 47 (1993).

River & Bay Authority,[7] a New Jersey court held that Delaware law does not prohibit such a provision.

To achieve a workable ADR solution to disputes involving public contracts, we believe public employers should strive to incorporate procedural fairness into the dispute resolution process and avoid imposing a partial sole arbitrator on the parties with which they contract.

---

[7] 241 N.J. Super 422 (N.J. Law Div. 1989), *reversed on other grounds,* 241 N.J. Super 310 (App. Div. 1990).

IV. Avoiding Litigation over Arbitrability

Removing Roadblocks to Arbitration

by Paul M. Lurie*

Parties to construction contracts often agree to include pre-dispute arbitration clauses because they have decided they want their disputes resolved quickly and economically by individuals experienced in construction matters. The irony is that arbitration clauses, which are supposed to expedite the resolution of differences, can sometimes be the cause of litigation between the parties over the arbitrability of the dispute. Fortunately, a properly drafted arbitration clause can help avoid this problem.

This article highlights some areas in which pre-arbitration litigation has occurred and offers suggestions for drafting arbitration clauses in construction contracts so as to avoid roadblocks to arbitration.

Why Pre-Arbitration Litigation Exists

It is not foolish to ask why there is arbitrability litigation when the parties have agreed to a pre-dispute arbitration clause. Have they changed their minds? Why are they now arguing over whether the dispute is arbitrable?

Scope of Arbitration Clause. Arbitrability litigation has sometimes resulted when parties limited their arbitration clauses to certain issues, leaving other items to be litigated. This occurs because at the time a dispute arises, the parties are no longer in agreement as to the meaning of the scope of the arbitration agreement they signed. For example, an arbitration clause allowing for arbitration only of disputes "during the course of construction" led to arbitrability litigation to decide whether the clause applied to disputes prior to the commencement of construction. In *U.S. Insulation v. Hilro*,[1] the court held that disputes arising before construction commenced were arbitrable.

---

* The author is the senior member of the construction law group at Chicago's Schiff Hardin & Waite. He serves on the AAA's National Construction Dispute Resolution Committee.

[1] 705 P.2d 490 (Ariz. Ct. App. 1985).

Another type of jurisdictional limit in arbitration clauses that has produced arbitrability disputes is monetary limits. Both *Frucon Construction Co. v. Southwestern Redevelopment Corp.*,[2] and *ACF Property Management, Inc. v. Chaussee*,[3] involved clauses limiting arbitrable disputes to disputes under $200,000. In *Frucon*, the court refused to aggregate claims under $200,000, thus finding the jurisdictional limitation on arbitration was not exceeded. In *AFC Property Management*, the trial court ordered the case to arbitration, where the arbitrator found that the damages were greater than $200,000. The arbitrator awarded $200,000 and referred the matter back to the trial court to consider the damages in excess of the award. But an appeals court voided the entire award because the jurisdictional limit on arbitration had been exceeded.

Applicability of Conditions Precedent. Arbitrability litigation has also arisen over whether the arbitrator, or a court, has the power to determine whether noncompliance with conditions precedent, which are frequently found in construction contracts (such as notice requirements, statutes of limitations, and requirements that submittals be made to design professionals for initial decisions), bars the arbitration from going forward.

An example of such litigation is *Village of Carpentersville v. Mayfair Construction Co.*[4] The Illinois court held that under the Illinois version of the Uniform Arbitration Act, the issue of the timeliness of the claim was procedural and initially for the arbitrators to decide.[5] However, in *Donaldson Acoustics, Inc. v. N.Y. Institute of Technology*, 671 N.Y.S.2d 114 (N.Y. App. Div. 1998), the court reached a contrary result, holding that the court should determine whether a claim was time-barred. Who decides the timeliness of a claim has been widely litigated, and courts in different jurisdictions have reached widely divergent outcomes.

Other Issues. Arbitrability litigation has also arisen out of the inclusion of choice-of-law clauses in arbitration agreements. This occurs because the scope of the incorporated law is not clear from the agreement. Well-known examples are *Volt Information Sciences, Inc. v. Board of Trustees of Stanford University*,[6] and *Mastrobuono v. Shearson*

---

[2] 908 S.W.2d 741 (Mo. Ct. App. 1995).
[3] 850 P.2d 1387 (Wash. Ct. App. 1993).
[4] 426 N.E.2d 558 (Ill. Ct. App. 1981).
[5] *Accord.*, Nielsen v. Barnett, 485 N.W.2d 666 (Mich. 1992).
[6] 489 U.S. 468 (1989).

Lehman.[7] In *Mastrobuono* (which involved post-arbitration litigation), the U.S. Supreme Court, applying the Federal Arbitration Act, held that a New York choice-of-law provision in an arbitration agreement did not constitute an election of New York case law barring punitive awards in arbitration. Thus, arbitrators could issue punitive awards in arbitrations governed by the FAA, unless the parties' agreement unequivocally said otherwise.

Incorporating an arbitration clause by reference to another agreement may create ambiguity which could also lead to arbitrability litigation.

Tips on Avoiding Pre-Arbitration Litigation

So how does a practitioner avoid having an arbitration clause become the source of litigation? A properly drafted clause that strives for broad applicability and addresses threshold issues will help parties avoid unnecessary litigation, delay and expense. Here are some tips.

- Use a broad form arbitration clause that has been court-tested for soundness. The pre-dispute arbitration clause recommended by the American Arbitration Association, which calls for arbitration under the AAA's Construction Industry Arbitration Rules, is a good example.
- Avoid using an arbitration clause that carves out arbitrability exceptions.
- Avoid the ambiguity that can be created by incorporating an arbitration clause by reference to another document.
- When appropriate, specifically provide that the Federal Arbitration Act will govern the agreement. There is no doubt that the case law that has developed under the FAA heavily favors arbitrability.[8] Therefore, an arbitration agreement interpreted under the FAA will be less susceptible to arbitrability litigation than one interpreted under a state arbitration statute. Since most construction materials and services are procured across state lines, most construction contracts "involve interstate commerce," which invokes the applicability of the FAA.[9] Drafters of

---

[7] 514 U.S. 52 (1995).
[8] *See* Moses H. Cone Memorial Hospital v. Mercury Construction Corp., 460 U.S. 1 (1983).
[9] *See* Allied-Bruce Terminix Cos., Inc. v. Dobson, 513 U.S. 265 (1995).

construction contracts that meet the "interstate commerce" test may find the following clause to be helpful:

The parties acknowledge that the performance of services necessary to complete the Project involves "interstate commerce" and therefore the arbitration shall be governed by the Federal Arbitration Act, 9 U.S.C. §§ 1-16, which shall supersede contrary state law. Any ambiguities concerning the arbitrability of any dispute shall be resolved in favor of the dispute being arbitrable.

- Provide in the arbitration agreement that the arbitrators have broad powers to determine the arbitrability of all issues. Rule 8 in the revised American Arbitration Association Commercial Arbitration Rules addresses the arbitrator's authority to rule on arbitrability. It provides that the arbitrator "shall have the power to rule on his or her own jurisdiction, including any objections with respect to the existence, scope or validity of the arbitration agreement." A clause addressing arbitrability issues in the context of a construction agreement issue might read:

The arbitrator(s) shall have the authority to decide all issues concerning the fulfillment of any conditions precedent to arbitrability of the claim or defense; the amount of damages to be awarded, if any; and the arbitrability of the issues presented.

- Consider the effect of any incorporated choice-of-law clause carefully. State laws that limit the validity of arbitration agreements will not be given effect under the FAA.[10]

- To minimize the likelihood of post-arbitration litigation, the parties should be counseled to accept the fact that the award will be final and non-appealable. The parties will be more accepting of the finality of arbitration if they are actively involved in the selection of experienced and trained arbitrators.

---

[10] Doctors Associates Inc. v. Casarotto, 116 S. Ct. 1652 (1996).

V. Guidelines to Writing Explanatory Awards

The ABCs of Writing a "Reasoned Award"

by James R. Holbrook*

There are three common forms of award in arbitration.[1] The first is a standard award (a simple statement of who won any relief granted) or, if the award is issued under the Construction Industry Arbitration Rules of the American Arbitration Association, a concise written breakdown of the award.[2] The second is a reasoned award or, as described in the AAA construction rules, "a written explanation of the award." (These rules provide that the parties may request, in writing, a written explanation of the award prior to the appointment of the arbitrator.[3]) The third is an award based on findings of fact and conclusions of law.

In the past, arbitrators were advised to issue a naked standard award because of concern that a detailed written opinion "might expose the award to challenge in the courts, jeopardizing both the speed and finality of arbitration."[4] More recently, however, arbitrators have been encouraged to issue the type of award the parties want. For example, the AAA recommends: "In instances where both parties request an opinion, an arbitrator should comply."[5] Thus, arbitrators should give the parties the type of award specified in their arbitration agreement. If none is specified but the parties referenced the AAA construction rules, arbitrators should write the kind of award the rules require. However, under AAA rules, arbitrators have the discretion to write an explanation of the award if they believe it is appropriate to do so, even if the parties

---

* An experienced arbitrator, the author serves on the AAA's roster of neutrals and teaches ADR at the S.J. Quinney College of Law at the University of Utah.

[1] AAA *Report of Preliminary Hearing and Scheduling Order.* ¶9(a) (referring to three forms of award).

[2] American Arbitration Association (AAA), Construction Industry Arbitration Rule R-45(b).

[3] *Id.*

[4] GABRIEL M. WILNER, DOMKE ON COMMERCIAL ARBITRATION 436 (rev. ed. Clark Boardman Callaghan, 2000).

[5] AAA, AWARD BRIEFING SHEET FOR ARBITRATORS, 2.

have not requested it.[6] Because parties usually do not specify the type of award when they enter into project documents, arbitrators should raise this issue during the prehearing conference.

In my experience as an arbitrator, most parties (80%) have requested a reasoned award at the preliminary conference. Half of the remaining 20% desired a standard award and half asked for findings and conclusions. Most lawyers prefer a written explanation of the award so their clients can see why I ruled as I did. Moreover, they realize that preparing detailed findings and conclusions takes time and therefore is costly. Accordingly, the balance of this article discusses my views on writing an explanation of the award, commonly called a reasoned award.

Definition

Exactly what a reasoned award means apparently has not been determined by any American court. One meaning given under English law is that "the loser should be told not only that he has lost but also why he has lost."[7] Also, according to a 1981 English case, in a reasoned award "the arbitrators should set out what, on their view of the evidence, did or did not happen and should explain succinctly why, in light of what happened, they have reached their decision and what that decision is."[8]

The only case to address the definition of a reasoned award in the context of an arbitration under AAA rules is *The Bay Hotel and Resort Ltd. v. Cavalier Construction Co.*[9] The award at issue in this case stated, "On the basis of the testimony and evidence of the parties, the Arbitrators find that Respondent breached the Agreement...by unreasonably interfering with and delaying [Claimant's] performance... by requiring [Claimant] to perform work beyond the scope of the Contract without compensation, and by failing to make payments as required." The award also stated how much money was required to be paid on the claims. A supplemental award addressed costs and legal fees.

---

[6] *See* American Arbitration Association, *supra* note 2.

[7] The Bay Hotel & Resort Ltd. v. Cavalier Construction Co. Ltd., (Lords of the Judicial Committee of the Privy Council, July 16, 2001) at ¶42, *available at* www.privycouncil.org.uk/output/Page50.asp.

[8] *Id.* at ¶25, *quoting* Bremer Handelsgellschaft v. Westzucker (No.2), 2 Lloyd's Rep. 130, 132-33.

[9] *See* Bay Hotel & Resort Ltd., *available at* www.privycouncil.org.uk/output/Page50.asp.

The English court determined that this was a reasoned award for purposes of the AAA rules, because a reasoned award and a written explanation of the award are expressions with the same meaning. In reaching its decision that this award contained sufficient reasons, the court relied heavily on the expert testimony of Prof. Carl Sapers, who "provided evidence that there was no necessity to tell the loser why he lost, and that that was not the purpose of a reasoned award."[10]

Parts of the Award

Turning to the practical aspects of writing a reasoned award, it may be helpful to examine its five parts.[11]

1. *The caption.* This states the parties' names, the case number, the name of the tribunal (e.g., the AAA Construction Arbitration Tribunal), and the name of the award (e.g., Award of Arbitrator).

2. *The preamble.* This usually references the parties' arbitration or submission agreement; the arbitration rules that apply; the appointment of the arbitrator; the names of the parties' attorneys; the names and dates of relevant court orders (e.g., an order compelling arbitration or determining arbitrability); the names and dates of the parties' pleadings; and the date, place and length of the scheduled arbitration hearing.

3. *The body of the award.* This addresses the merits of the dispute.

4. *The closing.* This is essentially a declaration that the award is in full settlement of all claims and defenses submitted to arbitration.

5. *The signature and notary statement.* The last part of the award includes the arbitrator's signature line (three lines for a three-person panel; a majority of the arbitrators must sign the award), a notarized statement or affirmation by the arbitrator (if one is required by applicable law), and a certificate of service on the parties (only if served by the arbitrator).

---

[10] *Id.* at ¶26, *quoting* the Court of Appeal of the Turks and Caicos Islands, from which the appeal was taken.
[11] *See* AAA, AWARD PREPARATION FACT SHEET, 1.

Preparation and Drafting

People have different approaches to writing tasks. However, there are some formulaic aspects to writing an award. Each award has the five parts referred to above, although the facts and parties differ. Arbitrators can prepare the caption, preamble, closing and notary sections before the hearing.

Because writing anything other than a standard award involves significant arbitrator time, the process should be as efficient as possible. The arbitrator should have easy access to the key facts and relevant documents. I use a loose leaf notebook to keep materials relevant to the hearing. These materials include copies of the parties' arbitration agreement, the prehearing order, the applicable arbitration rules, relevant court orders, the arbitral pleadings and any stipulation of material facts not in dispute. The notebook also holds a list I prepared of the elements of the parties' claims and defenses. (A list of claim elements helps when considering the evidence to determine who the prevailing party is.) In addition, it holds my notes of the hearing. I tend to take extensive notes, including a description of all exhibits, affidavits and depositions received into evidence, the names of witnesses, the date and time of their testimony and whether it was in person or by telephone. I also take detailed notes of testimony on direct and cross examination and of the parties' closing arguments. (I highlight the portions of the testimony and documents tending to prove or disprove the elements of the claims and defenses with a highlighting marker.) Having these materials handy makes it much easier to find the relevant evidence when I am drafting the body of the award.

Three principles should guide the drafting of the award:

1. The award must be clear and definite, leaving no doubt as to what the parties must do to comply.
2. It must decide every claim and defense submitted to arbitration.
3. It should not rule on anything beyond the scope of the arbitrator's authority.[12]

---

[12] AAA, AWARD BRIEFING SHEET FOR ARBITRATORS, 1-2.

The process of drafting the body of the award should begin as soon as possible after the hearing, while the evidence is still fresh in the arbitrator's mind. In my view this process should begin before the parties submit any post-hearing briefs and the transcript (if any) of the hearing becomes available. (If these documents later become available, the arbitrator can supplement or revise the award, as appropriate.)

The body of the award generally begins with a statement of the case. This is usually a brief statement of the parties' claims and defenses found in the parties' pleadings.

The case statement is followed by a concise statement of the facts. This statement answers the questions about "who, what, when and how" the dispute happened.

It is followed by the decision of the arbitrator. This is where the arbitrator focuses on the parties' claims and defenses, states who is the prevailing party, provides both an explanation of the award and a written breakdown of the relief awarded, and allocates arbitration expenses and arbitrator compensation.

Since the statement of facts and the decision of the arbitrator are more challenging to draft, they are discussed below.

Selecting the Relevant Facts. The first step in drafting the statement of facts is to identify the facts that are essential to support the decision. John W. Cooley, whose Arbitrator's Handbook includes the subject of award writing, says, "The master opinion writer earns his or her reputation by knowing which factual details to select, how to state them as facts, and where to arrange them in the opinion."[13]

To identify the essential facts, I review the pleadings, the important documents and my notes about witness testimony and closing arguments. I select only relevant and credible facts that support the arbitrator's rulings and the relief granted. Relevant facts are those necessary to prove or disprove the elements of the parties' claims and defenses. Credible facts are those established in the record by stipulation or the weight of the evidence.

The facts chosen may be presented in different ways (e.g., chronologically all together, as in a short story, or marshaled separately, claim by claim), but the presentation should be as succinct as possible. It is important to remember that a statement of facts is not the same thing as findings of fact.

---

[13] JOHN W. COOLEY, THE ARBITRATOR'S HANDBOOK 184 (Nat'l Institute of Trial Advocacy, 1998).

Drafting the Decision. The decision is the most important part of the award, for it is here that the arbitrator states his or her conclusions about the merits of the dispute and provides the reasons for the decision. The Bay Hotel award referred to above exemplifies a very brief explanation of the award. In that case the arbitrators stated their conclusion that one party breached the contract and then identified the conduct that constituted the breach. The brevity of this award landed the award in court. Providing more explanation may avoid subsequent litigation. It is up to the arbitrator to decide how extensive that explanation will be.

I generally approach drafting the decision claim by claim (e.g., breach of contract, negligence, etc.). I briefly restate each party's position on the claim, then present my conclusion as to liability, followed by the reasons for that decision. In giving reasons I may refer to testimony, language from the contract, or the specifications. I may also refer to the burden and standard of proof, and any controlling statutory or case authority, even though these are more typically found in findings of fact and conclusions of law.

Providing a written explanation of an award tests the validity of the arbitrator's conclusions. It focuses the arbitrator on assessing the weight and credibility of the evidence. In hard cases, the arbitrator may change his or her opinion on a claim or defense during the drafting process.

After concluding the reasons for the decision, the arbitrator should break down the relief granted in a separate paragraph or paragraphs. This is required under the AAA construction rules. Although arbitrators have wide discretion under these rules with respect to relief,[14] any relief granted must be within the scope of the arbitrator's authority and consistent with the parties' arbitration agreement. Moreover, the parties' performance of the relief in the award must be possible. The award cannot require performance by a non-party.

If a monetary award is issued, the amount should be clearly stated along with any time limits for payment. In addition to any damages awarded, the award should state how administrative expenses and arbitrator compensation are to be allocated. The arbitrator also should respond in the award to any request for prejudgment and/or post-judgment interest, attorneys' fees and costs. These may be authorized by the parties' arbitration agreement or by applicable law.

---

[14] AAA Construction Industry Arbitration Rule R-46.

The end of the award should always state: "This award is in full settlement of all claims and defenses submitted to arbitration."[15]

Stylistic Tips and Editing the Award

The goal is to have an award that is clear, concise and definite, decides all the claims and defenses submitted to arbitration, provides a principled explanation of the arbitrator's rulings, and leaves no doubt as to what the parties must do to comply with the award.

A clearly written award is best achieved if the writer uses short, declarative sentences, writes in the active voice, and avoids jargon and clichés. It also helps if the arbitrator uses the same word throughout the award to refer to the same person or thing.

When writing an award, humor should be avoided. Arbitration is serious and the parties expect to be taken seriously. It also is important not to denigrate parties, witnesses, or lawyers who have participated sincerely and in good faith.

Clarity can be facilitated by using appropriate subheads and discussing different subjects in separate paragraphs. Each paragraph should build on the one before. I like to number the paragraphs of my awards because it helps me organize them, especially during the editing process.

An award is not finished just because the arbitrator has a first draft down on paper. First drafts are "[o]ften imprecise and almost always wordy" and "require revision to make them say exactly (and only) what we mean."[16] Editing gives the arbitrator the opportunity to revise, reorganize and clarify. During the process the arbitrator should simplify long, complex sentences, replace esoteric words with more familiar ones, eliminate unnecessary words and details, check citations and any quoted material, and correct inconsistencies and spelling errors. It is not prudent to rely on a computer's spell-check function to catch misspellings.

While editing the award, the arbitrator should verify that there is a principled basis for every ruling and that each fact presented is supported by the record. When the editing is complete, the arbitrator should read the award out loud several times. Hearing it can help the arbitrator decide if the award uses language that is easy to understand and makes the intended points.

---

[15] AAA, "Award of Arbitrator" for Construction Industry Arbitration Tribunal.
[16] Gertrude Block et al., *Writing Style*, in JUDICIAL OPINION WRITING MANUAL 38. (American Bar Ass'n, 1988).

Conclusion

The award is the most important part of arbitration, so great care should be taken in its preparation. Before submitting the award, the arbitrator should be comfortable that the award demonstrates to the parties, their attorneys and any reviewing court that all of the important issues were fairly considered and fully decided.

VI. Jurisdictional Labor Disputes and Subcontracting

Between the Devil and the Deep Blue Sea — Subcontracting and Jurisdictional Labor Disputes

*by Gregory R. Begg**

This is a cautionary tale about a general contractor who subcontracted work in breach of a labor agreement. The conclusion of this true story was a federal court ruling that required the contractor to abide by two conflicting awards: one by the National Labor Relations Board (NLRB) assigning the work to one union (the figurative devil), and the other by an arbitrator awarding damages to the "unemployed" union (the figurative deep blue sea). As a result the contractor had to pay twice for the same work!

Our cautionary tale comes from a federal court in Wisconsin. The general contractor subcontracted work to a subcontractor who had a collective bargaining agreement (CBA) with another union. The general contractor's union contended that the subcontract was made in violation of its CBA and threatened a job action, triggering the NLRB's jurisdiction to assign the work to one of the competing unions under § 10(k) of the National Labor Relations Act (NLRA). Later that union commenced arbitration against the general contractor, seeking lost wages and benefits. The NLRB awarded the work to the subcontractor's union. But unfortunately, in the arbitration, the arbitrator awarded the general contractor's union back pay and damages.

Realizing the gravity of its situation, the general contractor petitioned the federal court to vacate the arbitration award on the ground that it conflicted with the NLRB's determination. The court declined to vacate the award, finding that the subcontracting grievance was a distinct, nonjurisdictional claim, separable from the jurisdictional issue decided by the NLRB. Since the contract grievance arose immediately upon subcontracting to a nonsignatory, the court found that it was irrelevant which union eventually did the work.

---

* Gregory Begg is a partner in the River Edge, N.J., office of Peckar & Abramson, PC.

The court noted that the contractor's obligation to pay two unions for the identical job, while admittedly harsh, was solely attributable to the contractor's decision to enter into agreements with conflicting obligations.

"Jurisdictional" labor disputes and "subcontracting" disputes arise from the tangle of potentially conflicting contractual obligations in CBAs. Subcontracting disputes arise from a provision in the CBA precluding the subcontracting of work to a nonsignatory contractor. Jurisdictional disputes involve the contractor and competing unions with respect to a work assignment. Such a dispute may arise if the contractor has labor contracts with more than one trade that arguably cover the same type of work and it assigns work to one trade to the exclusion of the other trade. A jurisdictional dispute may also arise if the general contractor, in violation of the "no subcontracting" clause, assigns work to a nonsignatory contractor that has its own labor contract, resulting in a claim by both unions to the work. Jurisdictional disputes may be resolved by an arbitrator, a federal court or the NLRB, often with painfully conflicting results.

NLRB jurisdiction to decide a dispute between competing unions claiming a right to the work is triggered only if the union ousted from the work threatens to picket or strike. The NLRB has no jurisdiction over subcontracting disputes, or disputes between competing trades in which no job action is threatened.

Suppose a union loses a jurisdictional dispute before the NLRB. Can it obtain damages and lost benefits from the contractor in arbitration?

Our cautionary tale indicates that this is where the contractor may meet the devil and the deep blue sea, having to pay twice for the same work. If the losing union alleges a violation of a "subcontracting" clause, the court will view this grievance as a nonjurisdictional claim separable from the work assignment issue addressed by the NLRB. Thus, there would be no conflict between an NLRB award requiring the subcontractor to use one union and an arbitral award ordering the contractor to pay damages to the unemployed union. Thus, the damages award would be enforceable.

But if no violation of a subcontracting clause is alleged, the unemployed union may not be able to obtain damages and lost benefits. In many jurisdictions (including New Jersey), the federal courts have held that ordering payment of lost wages and benefits is equivalent to ordering a reassignment of work to the unemployed union. For that reason, they will not enforce such an arbitration award.

What if the NLRB does not step into a jurisdictional dispute because there has been no job action? In that case, the unions competing for the same work may each commence arbitrations against the contractor, under their respective CBAs, seeking an award of the work and other relief. In this situation, the federal courts will generally rescue the contractor by ordering the competing unions and the contractor to arbitrate before a single arbitrator. The court will certainly take this course if the parties' CBAs clearly provides for arbitration of jurisdictional disputes before the same arbitration panel, and the parties have agreed to be bound by the panel's ruling.

Even without such provisions, many courts will order one arbitration so long as the arbitration clause does not expressly exclude jurisdictional disputes. They reason that since the parties have agreed to arbitrate, they might as well submit the jurisdictional dispute to a common arbitrator. In such a case, the court will fashion a procedure through which an arbitrator agreeable to all parties can be selected.

A single arbitration eliminates the possibility of conflicting awards by different tribunals. And while it is theoretically possible for the arbitrator to assign work to one union and grant back pay to the other, that result is unlikely.

Contractors can avoid labor disputes by understanding the terms of their CBAs. They should address problematic "work assignment" and "subcontracting" clauses with their union when the CBAs comes up for renewal. Contractors also need to pay attention to their subcontractor's labor agreements in order to avoid taking actions that may create conflicting contractual obligations under these agreements. When conflicts cannot be avoided, they should try to negotiate a resolution before work begins or before a dispute causes a delay.

CHAPTER SIX

MEDIATION

I. Successful Mediation

Recipe for Success in Construction Mediation

by John P. Madden*

One reason parties choose mediation over litigation and other forms of ADR is its high success rate. More than 85% of those who mediate their disputes settle successfully. This level of success creates pressure on the part of the mediator who must live up to the high expectations of disputants. The following article is based on the author's presentation at the International Arbitration Super Conference in Salzburg, Austria.

My first mediation training in 1990 left me with the feeling that the mediation process seemed vague and remote. I wondered if there was any practical application to be seen, at least on a wide-scale basis, in the construction industry, my area of legal practice.

Three years later, I was invited for the first time to serve as a mediator and to meet with two parties for a $25 million dispute. The representative of the arbitral institution that invited me described the two parties and their legal advisors as ready for a pitched battle whenever everyone was in the same room, and advised that I would probably only last about fifteen minutes before I or someone else left the room refusing to proceed. I set about meeting with the parties to explore whether they knew enough about their dispute to be ready for mediation. After four hours, it was apparent that an audit needed to be conducted before either party could feel a sense of certainty with regard to the costs expended on the construction project. I recommended that they conduct such an audit,

---

* John P. Madden, Esq., BSCE, MSCE, FCIArb, a 30-year veteran of the construction industry, first as a structural engineer and later as a construction attorney, conducts a national mediation practice specializing in resolving substantial, technically complex, multi-party design and construction disputes.

and if they so chose to, to contact me again in the future. I truly never expected to hear from them again.

Six months to a year later, I received a telephone call from the chambers of a judge of the U.S. federal court in New Orleans.[1] The legal advisors with whom I met previously as well as two other parties involved in the same project were now inquiring as to my availability for "global mediation." Apparently, the federal judge who was to preside over what was to be a two-month trial was disinclined to tie up his courtroom for such a lengthy, complicated case, and requested that the parties resolve their dispute another way.

Within weeks of the call, the matter was resolved through mediation with the consent of all parties. In fact, the parties reached a final settlement after an hour of discussion on the fourth day of the process.

Achieving a full and complete resolution of this dispute in essentially three consecutive days sparked the amazement of the lawyers, experts, the parties' representatives themselves and, without question, this mediator. I saw how acrimonious and antagonistic groups of individuals could unite into a single team with a common goal to resolve the matter then and there. In fact, when the matter was not resolved at the end of the allotted three days and I announced that it was time to close the mediation, the unified group urged me not to stop. They had come such a long distance toward resolution (though still far apart financially) and the only conduct on my behalf that was acceptable to them was to see the process through to its conclusion. This, of course, I did. The dispute was resolved in one hour on the fourth day by conference calls.

This was the first time that I had witnessed the "magic" of mediation. Over the years I have come to know that, with the right recipe and the right ingredients in the melting pot, there is an overwhelming likelihood of success in mediation. Experienced mediators commonly report success rates of about 85%, sometimes higher.

It is not quite magic, but it sure appears that way when such contentious disputes are resolved in such short periods of time. Successful mediation comes about by recognizing the process for what it is, preparing for it adequately, choosing a competent and experienced mediator, and having the right ingredients in the cooking pot.

The purpose of this article is to provide practical and useful information on mediation, including a discussion of the decision to

---

[1] A full report of this mediation has been published by the American Arbitration Association in 18 PUNCH LIST No. 2 (Spring 1995).

mediate, the selection of a mediator, and the identification of the essential elements for a successful mediation.

What Is Mediation?

Mediation is a structured and facilitated settlement process involving a neutral, professional facilitator. In the commercial world, mediation is an extension of business negotiations. It is a commercial process, not a judicial process. Most commonly, it is a process largely progressed, with the guidance of the mediator, by the senior commercial representatives of the disputing parties, and not by the attorneys for these parties. There are some, particularly judges, who have difficulty discerning the difference between a judicial settlement conference and mediation. It should be clear that mediation is not merely a conference, but in fact, a creative, dynamic process.

First, mediation is generally a voluntary process. Parties are free to withdraw from the mediation at any time without either penalty or adverse effect. However, in recent years, more and more commercial arrangements contain a requirement that the parties engage in mediation prior to litigation or arbitration. The process is still voluntary, though the participation may not be. In other words, there is no requirement to make any agreement on terms that are not satisfactory to the participants. Because the mediator is not a judge or an arbitrator, only the parties can decide the acceptable resolution to the dispute.

The mediation process is only binding on a party that agrees to accept the terms reached during the course of the mediation. If there is an agreement on settlement terms, the mediation is binding. If there is no agreement on settlement terms, the mediation is nonbinding. Thus, a party never attends a binding mediation unless that party is satisfied that the terms are suitable and acceptable.

Second, there is an ongoing philosophical debate in the mediation community over whether the process should be purely facilitative or whether the mediator should provide some form of evaluation of the dispute. Depending on the mediator's expertise in the field in question, adding a level of evaluation to his duties may be more or less appropriate. This is not to say, however, that the evaluating mediator should impose his judgment on the parties. Rather, a mediator with significant knowledge of the industry in question can provide a "reality check" of the strengths and weaknesses of the parties' arguments.

Frequently, mediation offers the first opportunity for the senior decision-maker of a party to confer with an informed and unbiased individual regarding the strengths and weaknesses of the case. Usually, participants in such discussions have been, on one side, the staff of the executive biased in favor of the arguments being advocated and, on the opposing side, the staff of the adversarial parties biased against the arguments being advocated. At some point, all become deaf to each other. With the appropriate background, the mediator not only facilitates discussion between the factions, but also keeps the allegations and remedies to realistic levels.

The Decision to Mediate

The potential value of mediation to a disputant is best drawn from comparison. Typically, the disputant has the choice between mediation and either litigation or arbitration. Sometimes, however, the option is more muddled because of a necessary future relationship between the parties. For example, the disputant may be embroiled in a controversy with a joint-venture partner in the early stage of a long-term construction project. Litigation or arbitration would likely drive the parties apart and make future dealings either miserable or impossible, rather than bring the parties together to allow the continuation of a working relationship.

Therefore, from a practical standpoint, there are several features to consider when choosing whether to mediate. On the positive side, mediation offers a low-risk possibility to involve the parties in creating their own solution to the dispute, as well as the opportunity to save time and money, bring information to light, and generate a final, binding agreement. There are, in addition, possible drawbacks to mediation: the additional expense required for participation in the process and any risk associated with information disclosure to the opposing party.

Beginning with the positive aspects, there is little or no risk to participating in mediation. The parties retain control of the outcome and work towards their own resolution of the dispute. Thus, there is no turning the matter over to a third party and "rolling the dice" on the outcome. Furthermore, the nature of the process is such that it is non-adversarial. Though it may start out as adversarial, in the hands of an effective mediator, the dynamic transforms the group into a "team" working toward a solution. The outcome is by agreement of all concerned. Mediation also offers the opportunity for creative solutions that would in no way be available in arbitration or litigation. The process brings together informed party representatives who are ready to explore, without interruption and with great focus, all of the strengths and weaknesses of the parties including their own. This allows the ability to move toward an understanding of the needs and values of all concerned and, more importantly, to recognize and foster resolution.

Second, mediation provides the opportunity to curtail attorney, expert and consultant expenses, as well as the hidden expense of the involvement of the corporate staff in litigation or arbitration. It has been my experience that the time from the day the parties select a mediator until the matter is resolved is usually a period of about 60 days. In addition, while clearly there are costs to waging the wars of litigation in terms of attorneys and consultants, it is less obvious costs that mediation reduces so successfully. This is the emotional toll, and the disruption of corporate operations. The inability to work on profitable activities because executives, managers, and other workers are tied up in preparation for court or arbitration proceedings is the expense that is so unpredictable and so damaging to smooth-running corporate operations. In fact, it is frequently this feature that, at the end of even a "successful" arbitration, causes the senior executive to pause and wonder whether his company was really "successful" from a commercial standpoint. Further, mediation also reaches an end, thereby diminishing any interest expense that might be payable as a result of an arbitration award.

Third, mediation provides the opportunity to obtain information that could be useful in litigation or arbitration. This can be viewed as both a positive and negative aspect. There are those that criticize the process by saying this amounts to "free discovery" of the other party's documents and positions. And that may be true. Yet the possible benefit to be obtained is a very high likelihood of success in the mediation process. Given its 85% success rate, the risk is relatively modest. Furthermore, should the mediation talks fail, the parties would often still be required to provide this same information to the other party in a traditional dispute resolution process.

Another positive element of mediation is its finality. There are no appeals. There are no awards to convert to judgments. There is no chasing payments. In addition, in many instances, the parties can resume working together productively and profitably. Years spent battling through an arbitration or litigation often build up enormous rancor and acrimony, and create indelible markings of mistrust that are rarely ever repairable. Yet the speed, low cost, and finality of non-adversarial mediation reduce the chances of this kind of rift, and allow companies to return to their profit-making endeavors. Last, this finality is achieved with confidentiality, a fact that allows all parties to move past the dispute more quickly and easily. This confidentiality can be maintained in mediation in a way that is often not possible in arbitration and not ever possible in litigation in a public forum. For parties wanting to keep the details of their dispute private, mediation is an excellent choice.

Looking to the negative side, there is an expense to participating in mediation. The cost to mediate disputes of $200,000 to $50 million could range from $3,000 to more than $20,000 per party.[2] The use of corporate staff time comes into play as well, but it limited in terms of both time and expense, because the mediation process is completed, successful or otherwise, in a very short time frame. A second possible negative feature is the information disclosure issue discussed above, though the benefits generally outweigh the risks.

Selecting the Mediator

To a considerable extent, the success of the mediation will depend upon the skill of the mediator. The qualities of a good mediator are not easily identified or measured. Persistence, patience, and continued optimism come to mind as mediator virtues. The mediator can command the respect of the parties and their representatives through a display of leadership qualities. The mediator needs to possess a strong personality while displaying humility, empathy, and understanding for the burdens that the disputing parties have had to endure. Tenacity, particularly when the likelihood of success is bleak, is also essential. In my experience, the breakthrough to success has frequently followed the darkest period in the mediation. Perhaps it is because when parties feel that all is lost, there is some compelling factor that causes them to soberly re-evaluate their positions and continue the process.

Prior to my experience as a mediator, I never realized the benefit of the "cheerleader's" approach that I have learned to maintain during mediations. This struck me only after completing several mediations in which parties or their attorneys advised me that it was my frequent

---

[2] For a summary of diverse cases mediated through CEDR, along with specifics on costs and time involved, *see* EILEEN CARROLL & KARL MACKIE, INTERNATIONAL MEDIATION—THE ART OF BUSINESS DIPLOMACY, Appendix V (2000).

encouraging remarks that inspired them to continue to believe that resolution was possible if they persisted.

Given the mercurial nature of the above characteristics, it is important to turn to more objective criteria. A clear priority should be finding a mediator with a successful record of mediating disputes of a nature similar to your own. This can be achieved by making use of references provided to the interested parties in order to evaluate the style and experience of the mediator. In addition, a mediator with knowledge of the parties' industry is an extremely valuable asset. In my view, it is frequently better to have a grasp of the technical expertise that forms the underpinning of a party's presentation than it is to have a grasp of the law at issue in the dispute.

Other important considerations in selecting a mediator are assessing his of her availability, fee, and any potential conflict between the mediator's interests and the interests of the parties in the dispute. Normally the latter is done by revealing the identities of the parties, subsidiaries, etc., to the mediator, who can then make any appropriate disclosures. One important note on this subject: a mediator is not a judge. There have been instances where a former senior executive of one party has served as a mediator because both parties respected the mediator's judgment. As long as there is disclosure, the opportunity for neutrality can be assessed properly.

Recipe for Success

The mediation process includes three steps: the preparation for mediation, the mediation itself, and the acceptance of a final agreement. Once a mediator is selected, he or she typically takes over the direction of the process until its conclusion. The first step is to foster the parties' readiness for mediation. There are four essential elements of a successful mediation. These are:

1. Commitment to the process by the parties;
2. Authority of all parties to act;
3. Knowledge of the facts of the dispute; and
4. Expertise.

If all four of these ingredients are present at the mediation, the likelihood of success is somewhere between 85% and 100%. The second step is mixing these elements of the recipe for success in the mediation melting pot. The last step is closure, which is obtaining a written agreement signed by the parties' representatives before leaving the mediation.

Preparation for Mediation

The decision to engage in mediation can come at any time, even as a full-fledged lawsuit is on the courthouse steps ready for trial. Sometimes it may come even later than that. Back when mediation was held in less regard by litigators than it is today, mediation was elected by the parties as a last-minute, "last-ditch" effort to resolve the dispute before turning it over to a third party for ultimate resolution. I have found, thanks to a better appreciation of the benefits of mediation in the legal and business communities, that more and more parties are opting for mediation in the early stages of a dispute.

Where there is a considerable amount of commercial interest involved, I think it illusory to believe that the parties' decision-makers will be willing to make agreements in such matters without ample knowledge of the facts and supporting law of their position as well as the positions of the other parties to the dispute.

Moreover, in the construction industry, as well as other industries, there is usually a need for expert reports, either formally or informally, to assist the decision-maker in evaluating his or her position. Hence, the preparation phase should be used to ensure that the four required elements—commitment, authority, knowledge of the facts, and expertise—will be in place for the duration of the mediation.

From a practical standpoint, one or sometimes two pre-mediation conferences are necessary to assess the readiness of all parties. Before the conference, typically the mediator will receive preliminary information explaining the nature and amount in dispute, as well as the remedies sought.

The meeting is usually conducted four to six weeks before the mediation session and provides the opportunity for the mediator to get the elements of the recipe into the kitchen, that is, at the mediation. Commitment, authority to act, knowledge of the facts, and expertise all must go into the melting pot. This meeting is sometimes the only opportunity for the mediator to assess whether he or she will have what is needed at the mediation. The more obvious purpose for the meeting, however, is to present the who, where, why, how, and what of the mediation procedure itself.

At the conference, the mediator has the first face-to-face opportunity to work with the parties to assess their commitment to the mediation. Frequently, this is also an opportunity to build the level of commitment to the process in each of the parties. Thus, at such a conference, I would recommend the attendance of the chief executive officer, the experts, and the legal counsel.

If, in the mediator's judgment, all parties are not ready to mediate because they lack any one of the essential elements, the mediator should indicate no intent to proceed, as in my earlier example of the case requiring an audit.

Focusing on the aspects of virtually no risk, limited financial expenditure compared to the alternatives and a short timetable is generally very encouraging to the parties, and may help to solidify their commitments. Some reference by the mediator to his prior successes in similar matters also builds and encourages the parties' commitment to the mediation process.

One important note: false optimism about the power of mediation, and proceeding without all four required elements, have two detrimental effects. They will not only result in a failed mediation, but also result in poisoning the view of the parties and their representatives towards the use of mediation in the future.

Elements of the Recipe

Commitment. The higher the level of commitment to the mediation process, the higher the likelihood of success. The level of commitment should be clear, and can be manifested in various ways. Alone, the agreement to mediate stands as a commitment, as does the selection of a mediator. In addition, the use of the pre-mediation conference to agree on information exchange by certain deadlines heightens the level of commitment from the parties. As silly as it sounds, even the payment of the mediator's fee in advance creates a psychological commitment because there is an investment in the success of the process on both sides of the dispute.

In a nutshell, I ask two things of the parties: the commitment to (1) participate in the process and (2) follow my lead with regard to procedure and my requests for information exchange. I ask for the parties to give me leeway to use my imagination into developing hypotheticals, worst- and best-case scenarios, timelines, chronologies, and other tools to assess the strengths and weaknesses of each side's arguments. I ask them for a commitment to answer questions, in private caucus if necessary, to the best of their ability. I do not ask for any more. With this level of commitment, I have one of the first elements that I need to proceed successfully.

Authority to Act. Mediation is a nonbinding process unless both parties agree to the terms of the settlement. There will be and can be no such agreement unless each party has a representative with the full authority to act present at the mediation. Most typically, this involves financial authorization, the level of which is often very difficult to predict. Thus, it is essential to obtain this element with absolute assurance at the pre-mediation conference.

In small companies, this can be simple. The president of the company is frequently authorized to act alone on behalf of the company. However, the managing director of a larger corporation may need to report to a board of directors for financial clearance. In that case, ensuring that the necessary level of authority will be present becomes a little more difficult. Here, the skill and experience of the mediator are crucial in assessing whether the particular individual designated as the senior representative of a party has an adequate level of authority. A candid conversation with that representative in a private side caucus during the pre-mediation meeting can be most useful, and is sometimes essential, to uncovering whether he or she has adequate authority. There is no shortcut here. Without this element, the likelihood of success at mediation is undeniably crippled.

In my experience, the most challenging parties with which to deal as to the aspect of authority are government agencies. The mediator must be creative in dealing with this problem. For instance, in one matter wherein I served as a mediator, I discovered that the governing board was composed of five people, none of whom was planning to attend the mediation. Thus at the pre-mediation conference, I made arrangements with the chief executive officer of the government body to have available by telephone at least three of the five board members throughout the mediation so that an immediate vote could be taken on any settlement reached. They could authorize the chief executive to sign the settlement agreement on the spot. I am pleased to say that, at the end of the second day of mediation for this $5 million dispute, we reached a point where the calls were made and the settlement agreement was signed.

Knowledge of the Facts. Frequently I find that the attorneys for the parties do not have an extensive grasp of the facts of the case. Yet, it is the attorneys that engage in the settlement discussions. Even when the parties' staffs themselves get together for meetings, often there is an "institutional truth" that has come to exist about key facts in the case. By this I refer to allegations of the culpable conduct of the "other party" that are repeated so often for so many years. At some point, everyone in that particular institution or the company becomes convinced without question that the conduct is fact, not allegation, and no one searches out the truth. The concept is almost as though if you say it often enough, it just becomes the truth.

This will unquestionably mar any assessment of the facts of the dispute upon which senior representatives of the parties must rely for decisions about settlement terms. It is squarely the job of the mediator to begin to purge the false information and misunderstandings that ordinarily exist in the dispute scenario.

This starts with directing each party to develop clear and concise information by retrieving documents or creating summaries that portray accurately the history of the relationship between the parties. Examples include the contract documents, project documents (daily logs, etc.), the parties' contentions, witnesses' identities and statements, anecdotal evidence, and any cost assessment or other financial documents. Typically, operational representatives such as field managers or foremen are great warehouses of first-hand knowledge of the project.

A mediator is in a position to help bridge the abyss that exists frequently between the operations people and the chief executive officer by virtue of the buffer of middle management. Watching the face of a chief executive officer listening to a blue collar worker discuss the day-to-day problems and what was done about them can be an enlightening experience for the mediator. This is precisely the type of discussion that should be conducted in a caucus. The bottom line is that a complete knowledge of the background of the dispute is an essential element of the recipe.

Expertise. In my experience in engineering and construction cases, the strength of the positions in a technical dispute rise or fall on the validity of the expert's opinion as to the cause and effect of the problems and the damages incurred by the disputants. However, this is not to say that an outside expert is necessary. Frequently the parties themselves have adequate expertise to explain the technology at issue as well as the bases for their conclusions. Moreover, this expertise can provide an evaluation of the opposing expert's assessment. The most important expert report besides those analyzing technical and engineering issues is the accounting and damage analysis. After all, the dispute is typically over finances or the scope of some financial remedy, and expertise in assessing the appropriate means of cost accounting can be essential.

The Mediation Session

This is the heart of the process. It typically takes one to three days for the four essential ingredients to cook up success. The ultimate product must be a sauce acceptable to all. The cooking time is unpredictable and the flavor of the sauce along the way can range from rather tasteless to downright unsavory. It is the mediator's job to sell the aroma of success and somehow bring the taste in line with the smell.

It is essential to note that mediation is a dynamic process that is meant to be adapted to the particular problem at hand. Flexibility in the process allows for creative exploration, and a mediator is free, if he or she commands the respect of those involved, to facilitate designing this process with persistence, patience, and imagination. Yet there is a basic framework used by most mediators, at least at the outset.

The typical routine calls for an initial presentation by the parties' legal advisors, with the claimant proceeding first. It is beneficial to request the principal representatives to offer comments as well. To appreciate the values of the parties' representatives, it is highly effective to request each of them to deal with this issue: where do you think we as a group should focus our energies in order to resolve this matter? In other words, I ask, "what do you think is important to look at here?"

First off, this establishes the inclusionary aspect of mediation right from the outset of the discussion. The responses provided by the members of each party will immediately highlight or, at least, reveal if there are varying views of the priorities and issues within each camp.

Second, it will become apparent if the priorities of some people are less urgent than the priorities of other members of the group. More to the point, it helps the mediator and all other attendees begin to understand from an emotional, psychological, and commercial viewpoint (in other words, a non-legal viewpoint) what is important to that particular party.

For instance, in a recent $7 million construction dispute between a contractor and a government entity, I asked all attendees down to the clerical staff for their views. Strangely enough, a member of the clerical staff of each disputant said the taxpayer would be better served if the matter were resolved, though their reasoning was different. Hearing this commonality from ostensibly opposing sides led me to suggest that the very complicated engineering issue at the heart of the matter could be swept aside, and the matter might be decided by a jury relying solely on what was better for the taxpayer. The uncertainty of this kind of resolution evidently caused the parties to accelerate their desire to have the matter resolved. A resolution was agreed to on the second day of the mediation.

After the presentation by the parties, the mediator conducts caucuses with the parties' representatives. These caucuses typically take several hours each. During the course of my preparation for the mediation, it is my custom to jot down questions that I want to present to each party during the caucuses. The questions provide me with information and inspire reflection within the group on certain aspects of its positions. The form, order, and invited attendees for the caucuses should be flexible, and guided by the mediator's creativity or "gut feeling." The mediator makes judgments along the way regarding the best steps to take to move the group towards an agreement.

During the mediation process, I have used different means to facilitate the exchange of factual and expert information. I often place a chalkboard at the front of the main mediation room and develop a timeline of events with help from all sides. I encourage the parties' representatives to answer fundamental questions about the dispute in the interest of creating a unified picture of the events. Time and time again, I find that key dates or exact chronology have been presumed. Yet a truly accurate timeline is often of paramount importance for cause and effect analysis, particularly in the case of a construction dispute. Sticking to objective facts, the parties delineate incidents such as the dates of events or the number of days an activity was performed. They identify the number of people involved and the dates on which problems arose, as well as the dates on which efforts were made to resolve those problems.

Viewing this over the course of the parties' relationship creates a remarkably informative perspective. Moreover, this information is developed jointly, which accomplishes both the beginnings of a team effort as well as the fixing of mutual "stipulations" of fact, which heretofore have usually been too difficult to obtain through discussion or attorney exchanges. Typically, I leave this information on display in the mediation room so that the parties have the information in front of them for discussion purposes for the length of the mediation. More times than not, this is a stark portrayal of the origin of the dispute—developed step-by-step through participation by all.

Another methodology for exchange of information is for the mediator to discuss a narrow issue with the staff members of one or both parties to clarify what occurred. Again, the use of objective non-controversial, non-conclusory questions, at least initially, can establish a dialogue, and develop understanding and even agreement that did not exist before.

With regard to experts' disputes, the mediator can direct the conflicting experts to discuss their differences apart from the rest of the group, and be prepared to present their differences in front of the senior representatives for the parties.

About a year ago, in a $13 million dispute between a ship owner and a shipyard, I sensed that one expert had misused the customary ship-construction delay-assessment methodology that underlay his computation of damages. I had reviewed carefully the expert reports in advance of the mediation and confirmed my suspicions during the course of individual caucuses with the experts. Thereupon, I invited the experts and the senior representatives to sit with me for a discussion. Moments before the meeting, I told one senior representative in a private side conference that I suspected that his expert did not have a sound basis for his opinions. During the course of the conference, it became apparent that his expert was faltering and did not have valid explanations to support his opinions.

At the end of this discussion, the senior representative pulled me aside and said he recognized the weakness in his case. Shortly thereafter, the parties conducted a serious discussion of dollars, and the matter was resolved early in the afternoon of the second day of the mediation. This was an instance where the mediator's knowledge of the technical issues was helpful in the resolution of a dispute.

Another possible technique is to conduct meetings between the two senior executives. The risk with conducting executive meetings is that if it is done too early, the parties could be too far apart and/or too fixed in their positions, and pride may work against a change in those positions. A meeting between the executives should be conducted only in the very final stages, if at all. In the final stages, when the gap is small, and the decision for each to make is whether it is commercially prudent to continue the fight, then such a meeting can serve to close that gap.

In virtually every case that I have handled as a mediator, I have felt, at some point during the mediation sessions, that it was almost definite that the matter would not be resolved. However, the parties want help and direction and, eventually, they are driven to accept nothing less than resolution. It is almost as if they are demanding that the mediator provide a resolution for them. Once the level of commitment to the process and the desire for resolution reaches that level, the likelihood of success is exceedingly high. In fact, I have been involved with only one case in which I felt that one of the parties was not seriously interested in settling the dispute.

It has been CEDR's experience that where experienced international mediators are used, commercial mediation is successful over 80% of the time. In 1997, for 32 cases ranging in amounts from $160,000 to $80 million, settlements were reached 84% of the time in an average time of 1.5 days. Similarly, in 1998, in thirty-eight cases ranging from $48,000 to $1 billion, settlements were achieved in 85% of the cases in an average of 1.6 days.[3] One very reassuring aspect of mediation is that the more complicated and convoluted the legal and factual issues are, and the more parties and fora involved, the more suited the matter is for resolution by mediation, and no other means.

Limitations of Mediation

The truth is that some matters—or disputants—just won't settle. There could be a party involved who is not committed to the mediation process and is merely committed to "dancing" through the process with no intent to settle. For example, where a standard form contract calls for mediation as a condition to litigation, there is room for abuse of the process. However, I most enjoy and take great pride in resolving the dispute which starts with a party which is "convinced" that the mediation is a wasted effort. Watching the conversion of attitude is most rewarding.

Sometimes, there are instances where no mutually suitable resolution can be achieved. In one matter in which I served as a mediator, every rational settlement arrangement would likely have caused the contractor, in its dispute with the owner, to go into bankruptcy. The case did not settle, and the contractor filed for bankruptcy anyway. In the international realm, other impediments to reaching an agreement, such as cultural or language differences, could impair the ability to settle the matter through mediation.

---

[3] *Id.* at 29, 90-91.

Finality

Is final truly final? Trial courts render final decisions, but they are appealable. Arbitrations render final awards, but confirmation in court is frequently required to make the award enforceable. Successful mediations result in written settlement agreements. Are they final? By and large, when the parties have finished the mediation process and have worked together for a single resolution, there is little likelihood that they will not carry out the terms of the settlement agreement. However, if a party refuses to perform in accordance with the settlement agreement, the use of a continuing or second mediation to accomplish a new settlement may be out of the question.

While I have not had experience with this situation, my research on the subject led me to conclude that there are two ways in which to deal with the enforcement of a settlement agreement. First, if the mediation is conducted in the course of a pending arbitration, I would suggest that the settlement agreement be submitted to the arbitration panel to obtain an arbitration award on consent, thereby entitling it to enforceability beyond that of a contract right. An award on consent would be eligible for the protections to which any final arbitration award would be entitled.

If, however, a matter is the subject of a pending litigation, I would suggest that consideration be given to including a confession of judgment provision in the terms of the settlement agreement. Therefore, if the agreement were not performed, the confession of judgment could be filed with the court and a judgment would be obtainable for purposes of execution.

Conclusion

Mediation is not quite magic, but it has proven to be a highly economical means to resolve commercial disputes—big and small—with a high likelihood of success. Having recently served in the resolution of a $52 million dispute at a mediation conducted over three consecutive days, I can hardly express in words the sense of satisfaction that one feels in accomplishing such a result. The conversion of acrimonious emotions harbored by the parties to one of mutual satisfaction with the attainment of the sought-after goal—a resolution—is a delight to watch. The parties are typically filled with a sense of delight that the dispute is finally over and completely finished.

II. Tips for Better Mediation from the AAA

Mediator Wisdom from the Experts[†]

*by James Acret**

Everyone wants to hear tips from experts. At a recent American Arbitration Association training session in San Francisco, a team of experienced construction industry mediators held spirited discussions of techniques mediators can use to address assorted issues in mediation. Here are some of the tips offered by these experts.

Mediators serve a number of functions. One expert classified these functions as teaching, criticizing, supporting, probing and clarifying. Of the five functions (see sidebar below), some experts believe that criticizing and teaching are least appreciated by the parties and that mediators should concentrate their efforts on probing and clarifying.

Joint Sessions and Caucuses

Some mediators think joint sessions are a waste of time and may be dispensed with because they usually consist of exchanges, sometimes acrimonious, of information and arguments that the parties have already exchanged ad nauseam. Others, however, say that a joint session should be kept going as long as it is making some progress. When the joint session breaks down, that is the time to call for a caucus.

During caucuses, parties may throw out vague dollar figures. Many experts say the mediator should determine whether a particular number exposed by a party is a genuine offer. If it is, the mediator should evaluate whether the communication of that number to the other party will advance the purposes of the mediation. As a neutral who must not take sides, the mediator should avoid reacting negatively to the size of the offer, even if it might be considered outrageous. To finesse the situation, the mediator might attempt to obtain the party's agreement to

---

[†] This is an expansion of an article that previously appeared in the CALIFORNIA CONSTRUCTION LAW REPORTER (March 1998). Used with permission.

* The author is an arbitrator and mediator in Los Angeles. He serves on the American Arbitration Association's roster of neutrals and is a member of its National Construction Dispute Resolution Committee.

go a different way, rather than communicate an outrageous offer to the other party.

Experienced mediators caution against asking a party in a caucus for its bottom line. Once a party establishes its "top dollar" or "rock bottom" offer, its pride must be overcome if further movement is to be achieved in the mediation.

Should a mediator ever excuse lawyers and continue the mediation between the parties outside the presence of the lawyers? Some experts say it may be considered, but only if all parties and all lawyers agree. But others think that this procedure should be avoided, since it can jeopardize the mediation by giving one or more lawyers a vested interest in sabotaging the mediation.

One useful technique experts recommend using during the conduct of caucuses is for the mediator to ask one party to think about some aspect of the case that might generate some movement while the caucus with the other party is going on.

Insurance Coverage

The experts say it is imperative for the mediator to be aware, from the outset of the case, of the insurance issues. The mediator should ask the parties to include information about their liability insurance coverage in their mediation statements. Construction contracts usually require subcontractors to name the general contractor and the owner as additional insureds on their liability policies. This amounts to additional insurance coverage that may provide additional settlement money. In construction cases, the mediator should also ascertain whether the developer has made a claim on its builder's risk policy. If a claim has not been made on this policy, the mediator should encourage the developer to take advantage of this potential additional coverage.

By requiring both liability and builder's risk insurance information to be disclosed in the mediation statement, the mediator may call coverage issues to the attention of counsel ahead of time, rather than risk making counsel look bad at the mediation session by raising issues that counsel should have pursued earlier.

Once this information is obtained, the mediator should ensure that the insurance carriers are represented at the mediation. It is important to find out to whom the insurance adjusters report and to obtain the business and home phone numbers of the adjusters and their claims managers.

During the mediation, it may be productive to hold separate caucuses with the adjusters. One expert has suggested that, during these sessions, the mediator inquire whether the adjuster has given an opinion to the carrier about the claim, and what reserve the adjuster has recommended. This strategy may prevent the adjuster from making a lowball offer.

Experts

Many mediators feel that experts are more likely to obstruct than facilitate mediation and that mediators must develop techniques for neutralizing obstructive tactics. Some techniques suggested at the training session include the following.

Put all the experts in a room together and ask them to come up with a solution to the particular issue. Or hold a caucus session with the experts only—i.e., a "facilitated" expert meeting. An alternative is to consider recommending that the parties employ an "assistant" or "co-mediator" who is an expert in the disputed field.

The mediator should always avoid arguing with or trying to discredit an expert. If the expert seems to be way off base, experienced mediators recommend discussing the problem privately with the lawyer for the party who produced the expert.

Impasse

The experts consider an impasse to have occurred when both parties say they cannot reach an agreement, and not when only one party says so.

During impasses, mediators usually help the parties review their positions and explore their remaining options; they try to create doubt about the facts, the evidence, the availability of witnesses, the credibility of the party's position, and the soundness of the party's legal contentions; they ask the parties to consider whether a partial settlement of one or more issues is feasible; and they try to make the parties fulfill their commitment to work hard to settle the matter.

Other techniques have been suggested by expert mediators to deal with impasses. One possible approach is to obtain the approval of all counsel to a joint session of principals only, with or without the mediator, so that they can talk things out.

Another approach is to conduct "hardball" caucuses in which the mediator demands that each party determine its BATNA (best alternative to a negotiated agreement). A candid examination of its BATNA may persuade a party that its offer of settlement should be increased or that its demand for settlement should be reduced. The mediator should make sure that the BATNA includes, in addition to attorneys' fees, experts' fees and court costs, an estimate of the time that the party and its managers and employers will be required to devote to the dispute, and the impact of continuation of the dispute upon company morale and on the company's relations with its customers and vendors.

When all else fails, the mediator may even suggest that the parties reverse roles and pursue an exercise in role-playing. If the parties are enthusiastically committed to the success of the mediation, they may be willing to try anything, including putting themselves in each others' shoes.

Occasionally, a mediator will become convinced that one of the parties is not negotiating in good faith and does not really want the mediation to succeed. These are grounds for termination of the mediation. A party should not be permitted to abuse the mediation process by using it for discovery or delay or to impose expense on the other party.

Evaluation

Although the parties often ask for it, most expert mediators agree that it is not a good idea to make a monetary evaluation of the case or opine as to its settlement value. By venturing this kind of assessment, the mediator in a sense becomes a party to the process and likely will be perceived as defending his or her judgment about the case. This can lead to arguments with one or more of the parties and can doom the mediation to failure.

One number that the mediator can ask for during the mediation is an estimate of the parties' anticipated attorneys' fees if the case does not settle in mediation. The mediator can ask the parties' attorneys to provide detailed written estimates of the cost of resolving the dispute by arbitration or trial. Attorneys' estimates of their fees and the number of hearings that will be needed are usually optimistic. The detailed written estimate of attorneys' fees may therefore come as a surprise not only to a party but to the attorney. An attorney may be careful not to convey a low estimate of attorneys' fees to a knowledgeable mediator. The resulting figures can be a mighty motivator for settlement.

Settlement Agreement

Should the parties agree to a mediated settlement, the mediator should be cautious about drafting the settlement agreement, since it may create contention with a party. It is hard to mediate while defending one's own drafting. On the other hand, a mediator can act as a scrivener for the parties or their attorneys, and acting in that role, may make subtle improvements in language without appearing to become the author of the settlement agreement.

What Role Does the Mediator Play?

- Teaching—by explaining the mediator's understanding of the theories of liability, the parties' defenses and their damage claims.
- Criticizing—by raising doubt as to these matters.
- Supporting—by providing support to party positions that may induce settlement.
- Probing—by searching beneath bald statements of position to find out whether a party can really produce the evidence and sell its version of the facts and its legal theories to an arbitrator or a judge.
- Clarifying—by helping the parties understand the case and presenting clarified positions, if appropriate, to the other side.

Words of Wisdom for Mediators

- Don't create a negative image of anyone.
- Brainstorm.
- Create doubt.
- "Work the documents."
- Test the strength of the evidence.
- Test the computation of damages.
- Never use the word compromise. It has a negative connotation.
- Never take no for an answer.

III. Using Procedure for Effective Mediation

The Importance of Process Design to a Successful Mediation

*by Paul M. Lurie**

An article analyzing the 1991 American Bar Association dispute resolution database concludes that procedure was the key element that influenced successful outcomes of mediations.[†]

Construction parties who seek out the informality of mediation often overlook the importance of appropriate procedures to the success of mediation. Indeed, many users of the process give little thought to the design of the process until they appear at the first session. However, it is well before that time that the parties should be discussing and reaching agreement on such process issues as the mediator to be selected, the individuals whose attendance will be required, party representation, information exchange, use of experts, and scheduling, to mention only a few.

Mediation can take different forms depending upon the degree to which it is facilitative or evaluative. In a facilitative mediation, the mediator helps the parties overcome communication problems that have created an impasse. The mediator aids them to discover and explore multiple options for settlement without imposing any particular option on them. The evaluative mediator identifies the risks inherent in each party's position and suggests how a factfinder, such as an arbitrator, judge or jury, might rule on the issues, were the case to proceed to arbitration or trial.

The type of mediation can affect the procedures that are required. Developing the correct mediation procedures for the particular circumstances will significantly influence the likelihood of success of the process.

---

[*] Mr. Lurie chairs the construction group at Chicago's Schiff Hardin & Waite and serves on the American Arbitration Association's National Construction Dispute Resolution Committee. He is coauthor of ARBITRATION OF CONSTRUCTION DISPUTES.

[†] D. Henderson, *Mediation Success: An Empirical Analysis*, 11 OHIO STATE L. J. ON DISP. RESOL., No. 1 (1996).

Use of a Process Designer

The essential first step to a successful mediation, regardless of type, is the identification of a process designer. This person should be selected in advance of the first mediation session. It is preferable for the process designer not to be the eventual mediator because the selection of the neutral appropriate to the particular facts of the case is a key procedural choice. The designer may be a senior member of the American Arbitration Association's (AAA) regional office in your state or a neutral appointed by an AAA regional office. Senior AAA staff, having worked closely with various mediators in past mediations, may be particularly helpful in this regard. Too often the parties leave the design of the process to the mediator, who is given that role by default at the start of the mediation.

The major issues which may be decided by the parties in the design stage with the aid of the process designer follow.

Mediator Selection

Which mediator is best for the situation? For example, many former judges are known to be more evaluative than facilitative in style. The parties should consider whether a more evaluative mediator would be helpful or detrimental. Style is a trait that is often difficult to discern from written panel resumes. Parties can more successfully select the appropriate mediator by having a frank discussion of the issues with a knowledgeable process designer, such as a senior AAA staffperson, who understands the nature of the dispute, the personalities of the parties and their attorneys, and the style of the available neutrals. In addition, in cases in which large sums are at stake, the parties may wish to obtain additional information about the potential mediator by interviewing this person, provided they can agree on the methodology for doing so; they may also make inquiries of the AAA or others who may have useful information. The AAA makes available to parties comprehensive biographies of the neutrals who serve on its panel.

Attendees

Who are the stakeholders and who will represent their interests at the mediation? If the right people are not present at a mediation, the process can fail to settle the dispute. The right people include party representatives who have the ability to objectively evaluate the strengths and weaknesses of the parties' positions and see their true interests. They also have authority to make final decisions regarding settlement. Often, the parties' representatives at the mediation appear to have settlement authority by reason of their title, but in fact do not have that authority. Even if they have settlement authority, they may be too close to the problem or too tied to a particular solution to objectively evaluate their position. Sometimes the parties cannot agree on who should attend the mediation as a party representative. Helping the parties to identify and encourage the right party representatives is a function of the process designer. The process designer can also assist the parties in determining whether the presence of experts would be useful or detrimental to their positions. The proper experts can be extremely useful in explaining technical or scientific matters.

Information Exchange

How much information needs to be exchanged and how and when will that be accomplished? If a party does not understand the adversary, the party is less likely to respect the strength of the adversary's position. Sometimes the parties will come to a mediation session after a lawsuit has been commenced and formal discovery has taken place. However, if the mediation takes place prior to the commencement of litigation, the parties need to decide whether they will exchange documents or engage in other forms of discovery. While some may say that the purpose of mediation is to avoid litigation procedures, others may believe that having all of the facts on the table may facilitate a successful negotiation, leading to a mediated settlement. This is an issue that needs procedural process design.

One approach that can be used when information is not produced in advance of a mediation session is a mini-trial-type of presentation in which expert opinions and legal arguments are presented to the opposition in summary form. The parties will need to agree on who will make the presentations. Will they be experts, attorneys or the parties themselves? Will experts present graphics or reports? Will the opposing parties see this material prior to the session or have the right to ask questions? Decisions on these subjects will often affect the timing and dynamics of the mediation.

Scheduling

How much time will be set aside for the mediation and when will it be scheduled? The process designer can help the parties determine the amount of time the mediation may take, especially if significant information exchange is likely during the mediation. This situation may require a break between initial and subsequent sessions. This break allows a party to digest and respond to information first learned at the initial session.

The schedule is critical to ensure that the stakeholders' representatives can commit their attendance for the amount of time necessary to complete the mediation. Having key stakeholders prematurely leave the mediation is likely to cause the mediation to fail.

Role Change

What happens if the parties are at a true impasse? If the parties reach a true impasse in a mediation, they may always choose to have the mediator change from the role of mediator to that of a fact-finder or arbitrator. This issue may also be considered before the mediation, at the design stage. The parties should determine the conditions under which such a role change should occur and, if the mediator does change roles, whether the mediator's recommendations or rulings will be binding.

IV. Effective Advocacy in Mediation

Some Guidelines for Effective Advocacy in Mediation

by Howard D. Venzie Jr.*

Any meaningful discussion of advocacy in the mediation process should begin with a recognition of the fundamental tension that exists between the two concepts. Mediation involves negotiation, conciliation and compromise between parties who have become adverse because of a controversy or dispute. Advocacy, by contrast, seems to be the antithesis of resolution through compromise, insofar as it is premised on notions of "winning" the battle of persuasion between adversaries on important issues such as responsibility and entitlement.

The tension between mediation and advocacy can become a positive force in the evaluative phase of mediation if the parties and their counsel use effective advocacy techniques, mixed with common sense and good judgment, to focus the participants on the key issues, engender constructive dialogue and bring realistic expectations to the bargaining table. Mediation advocacy is "effective" when it raises the parties' awareness of the benefits of settlement and the risk and cost consequences of impasse and failure.

The evaluative phase of mediation usually occurs prior to the private caucus negotiation sessions. During this phase, the parties and the mediator typically consider issues relating to claimed entitlements, the risk and cost factors each side faces, as well as monetary issues pertaining to the worth of the case. The mediator assists the parties in

---

* Howard D. Venzie Jr. is a principal in Venzie, Phillips & Warshawer in Philadelphia. He is a member of the AAA's Board of Directors, its National Construction Dispute Resolution Committee and its Philadelphia Advisory Council for the Large, Complex Case Program and chairs its Philadelphia Regional Construction Advisory Committee. He also serves on the AAA's national roster of neutrals and on its President's Panel of Mediators. He is a member of the ABA Forum Committee on the Construction Industry and the ABA Construction Committee's Section of Litigation and the Section of Public Contract Law. He is also co-chair of the Pennsylvania Bar Association Arbitration and Mediation Committee. This article is adapted from a paper delivered by the author at the Union International Des Avocats, International Association of Lawyers XLI Congress in Philadelphia on Sept. 4, 1997.

assessing their respective positions, claims and demands (i.e., entitlements), and attempts to establish a realistic range for negotiation of the monetary issues and reasonable settlement goals. Party advocacy can play an important role in setting the proper tone for constructive evaluation of these issues.

While concepts of responsibility, liability, duty and obligation are terms of advocacy used to establish entitlements, an effective advocate develops, with the client, the legal and factual logic behind the client's demands. Together, lawyer and client should address the key "jugular" issues that drive the dispute, presenting the client's "best case" in the light most favorable to its position. This provides the mediator with an analysis of the case that can be used to work on the entitlement issues with the parties in private caucus sessions.

Mediation should be viewed as an opportunity for the parties to "test" the reasonableness of their settlement expectations and goals. An effective advocate causes the client to reconsider the cost and risk factors in the case and adjust expectations concerning monetary value before committing to the litigation process, where the risk/reward analysis can change dramatically as the uncertainties of the litigation unfold. By more accurately identifying legitimate items of cost and damages, eliminating speculation, more correctly gauging levels of direct and indirect financial impact, and preparing a more useful comparative risk/reward analysis, the parties are able to move through the mediation with a more accurate case valuation and more realistic financial goals.

All counsel should strive to improve their advocacy skills in the mediation context. Several pointers are set forth below.

Mediation is a process that produces results only if it is treated with the seriousness it deserves. The parties and their counsel must treat the mediation as serious business. The potential for a successful resolution through mediation will be enhanced if the parties and their counsel follow these advocacy guidelines.

Be Prepared

The need for serious preparation for mediation should never become lost in the informal and sometimes casual nature of the process. Poor preparation most often leads to either a poor settlement or no settlement at all. Serious preparation involves:

(a) Defining the "jugular" issues;
(b) Developing the logic and arguments to support the merits of the client's positions;
(c) Establishing the "value" of the client's case and what the settlement goals should be;
(d) Preparing a negotiation strategy to achieve settlement goals, including the identification of trade-offs and areas of concession;
(e) Establishing the client's needs in order of importance and anticipating the other parties' needs and interests;
(f) Selecting the best methods of communication during joint presentations, such as charts and other graphics, videotapes, or direct presentations by the client or its representative; and
(g) Identifying the right client representatives to bring to the mediation.

Be Credible

Credibility is the cornerstone of effective advocacy. If a party or its advocate loses credibility with the mediator or other parties, that party's case will lose value. Therefore, it is very important to the success of a mediation effort that the advocate and the client representative be believable, reliable and reasonably objective. Credibility is established by presenting comprehensive, unambiguous and well-reasoned positions, claims or defenses that are supported by facts in the record and by documents. Credibility in mediation advocacy also means "consistency" and evenhandedness. Speculation should be avoided, particularly in the computation of damages and the presentation of monetary demands.

Be Persuasive, But Brief

The goal of advocacy is to persuade. In mediation, as in litigation, a cogent presentation that is both brief and concise is the key to being persuasive. Persuasive mediation presentations generally include:

(a) Simplified presentations that avoid distractions and diversions into less important side issues;
(b) Graphics to communicate points;
(c) In cases involving technical issues important to the outcome (e.g., construction defects and the scope and cost of repairs),

presentations by technical experts to develop the parameters of those issues;
(d) Written summaries of claims or demands with dollar values where appropriate; and
(e) Client participation to provide positive emotional content.

Be Discreet

The language and tone of mediation advocacy are critical to its success. The advocate must avoid confrontation, be professional and courteous, and create a tone of compromise. Discretion and good judgment should be the dominant factors that mark the advocate's style and technique. An effective advocate:

(a) Will not ridicule or demean the opponent or its case;
(b) Will not be condescending or overly contentious toward opposing parties;
(c) Will not appear threatening;
(d) Will not file dispositive motions in pending litigation on the eve of mediation;
(e) Will recognize cultural differences and diversity;
(f) Will use language of persuasion;
(g) Will use the technique of apology with sincerity when appropriate;
(h) Will speak in terms of issues, transactional responsibilities, risks and likely outcomes, rather than in terms of blame or fault;
(i) Will use humor and avoid intemperate behavior;
(j) Will avoid the "good guy-bad guy" dichotomy; and
(k) Will keep emotions under control.

Be Conciliatory

Because settlement negotiations are inherently competitive in nature, adversarial behavior tends to take over the dialogue unless special efforts are taken to maintain a cooperative atmosphere in which problem-solving, conciliation and resolution are emphasized. Showing commitment to the mediation process and to the goal of settlement through conciliatory conduct goes a long way toward achieving a resolution satisfactory to all parties. There are numerous ways to communicate the message that finding common ground and a solution to impasse is the primary force behind a party's actions in the mediation. Some of these include:

(a) Being cooperative and avoiding conduct that will be perceived as rigid or intransigent;
(b) Setting a tone of compromise by talking to opposing parties and their counsel in a conciliatory manner;
(c) Demonstrating a willingness to compromise, such as by conceding on less important issues in order to gain momentum in the negotiation process;
(d) Avoiding extreme positions that unnecessarily restrict the other party's ability to maneuver, and leaving room for changes in position;
(e) Viewing the mediation process as an opportunity to create options; and
(f) Letting the opposing parties know you're listening.

V. Litigators and Mediation

Should Trial Counsel Represent the Client in Mediation?

by Robert Korn*

The virtues of mediation—a quick, cost-effective, confidential dispute resolution technique—are well known. Equally well known are the detriments of litigation—a protracted, expensive, often emotionally wrenching public airing of the dispute.

The litigated case wends its way slowly through the court system, once the complaint is filed. Typically, the defendant's counsel will file motions seeking dismissal of the complaint. Such motions are usually denied by the court. Following the court's order, discovery proceeds and depositions are taken, at which attorneys are often openly hostile to each other.

At the conclusion of discovery, it is the accepted practice for one or more of the parties to file summary judgment motions, which the court typically denies because of the fact-based nature of the dispute—leading to the setting of a trial date and eventually trial, if the case is not settled. This process is expensive and time-consuming, causing some clients to complain, "The lawyer made out better than I did."

Success in the court room is dependent upon an attorney's advocacy skills and not on the ability to negotiate. Yet this skill, which until recently was not taught in law school and is not easily learned through the practice of law, is central to successful representation of a client at a mediation. Having participated in many mediations, both as a mediator and as counsel for one of the parties, I have observed, all too frequently, the unequal negotiation skills of the parties' counsel. In my experience, attorneys with sharply honed negotiation skills invariably achieve the best results.

How can the client obtain the best result at a mediation? The premise of this article is that parties to a substantial dispute that lends itself to a mediated solution should retain, in addition to trial counsel, known, skilled negotiators for the limited purpose of orchestrating settlement

---

* Robert Korn is a principal in the law firm of Korn & Cohn, P.C., in Plymouth Meeting, Pennsylvania. He specializes in construction law and surety law. He serves on the American Arbitration Association's Regional Construction Advisory Committee and on the AAA's Large, Complex Case Panel.

discussions and participating in the mediation. Even a trial lawyer with negotiation skills may have a difficult time shifting from a litigation mode to a mediation mode. And even if this could be done easily, the other side may have a difficult time negotiating with someone who is vacillating between these two roles and is not perceived as a problem solver.

To be successful, mediation requires that the parties and their counsel explore, in an open and earnest fashion, the potential monetary and non-monetary solutions to the dispute. Many trial attorneys approach mediation with ambivalence—on the one hand wanting to reach a settlement, yet on the other hand not wanting to halt the litigation. Attorneys who represent parties in mediation must work diligently to bring about a solution of the dispute, unfettered by personal interest or ambivalence about the outcome of settlement discussions.

Good communication must exist among all participants. Posturing, positional bargaining, or hardball negotiations—all typical strategies employed by trial counsel—can strain the relationships between the parties at the mediation, making it difficult if not impossible for the mediator to open the channels of communication, let alone create an environment conducive to settlement. Having a skilled negotiator on the client's team—a person viewed as a problem solver, rather than a problem maker—can facilitate the communication between the parties.

What role do skilled negotiators play in the mediation? Skilled negotiators craft the opening argument. Often, the oral presentation is augmented by slides, photographs, videos, charts and other types of demonstrative evidence. This presentation is directed, for the most part, at the opponent's decision-maker and is intended to convince this person of the strength of the presenter's position and to create doubt as to the strength of the opponent's case. If not done properly, this opening argument can so alienate the opponent as to bring a mediation to a halt.

Skilled negotiators also try to enlist the mediator as an ally during the caucus sessions. They will have developed a carefully planned settlement strategy prior to the mediation. They will not allow their clients to walk into a mediation cold. Rather, they will have thoroughly acquainted their clients with the mechanics of the mediation and have worked out the settlement strategy to be used with the clients' cooperation.

Skilled negotiators demonstrate the utmost patience, knowing that mediation is a marathon, not a sprint. They do not play their cards too soon, a flaw exhibited by inexperienced negotiators.

Client Decision

What should the client do? Before engaging in mediation, the client should decide whether it is desirable to have trial counsel take the lead role. Factors to consider are the tenor of the dispute, what's at stake, trial counsel's skills as a negotiator, and whether there is another person with more finely honed negotiating skills who can achieve a better result than trial counsel. If the client decides to retain, in addition to trial counsel, a negotiation specialist who understands all of the nuances of mediation, the negotiator should work closely with the litigator in preparing for the mediation. I am not recommending that trial counsel be supplanted; rather, I suggest that the client's mediation team be augmented by adding a skilled negotiator to work closely with the litigator.

Large law firms have recognized the dichotomy and potential conflict between litigation and alternative dispute resolution by creating a separate ADR department, offering their clients the skills of both litigation and ADR specialists. And while there may be some conflicts between these departments, these conflicts should disappear as ADR becomes more widely used, and as litigators become more familiar with the role that ADR negotiators can play. Both litigators and ADR specialists serve the client's interest in resolving disputes. Together, they make a formidable team.

VI. Experts and Mediation

The Expert's Role in Construction Mediation

by Richard Lamb*

Recent changes in construction industry form documents have made mediation the ADR process of first resort. An essential factor in successful mediation is a high level of preparedness.[1] Only by gathering the relevant facts and by understanding the disputed issues, the pertinent contract provisions and specifications, the industry standards and practice in the community, and the foundation for calculating damages, can a party truly be in a position to rationally and objectively evaluate its position relative to the other parties, and convincingly articulate its positions on the issues in the mediation. While experts have long been used by construction parties in arbitration, their value in mediation is beginning to be appreciated.

There are two general approaches to using experts in mediation: separate retention and joint, shared retention. Under the former approach, the parties each retain their own expert to assemble information concerning the issues in dispute. The expert may also prepare various types of analyses to aid the retaining party in understanding the case, such as a "scheduling/delay" analysis, or an "accounting/damages" analysis. The expert's role at the mediation is up to the party. The expert may either present the party's claim or defense at the mediation, or act as an observer, advising the party in private sessions regarding the strengths

---

* The author is vice president of Hill International, Inc., an international construction consulting firm.

[1] The 1997 edition of the American Institute of Architects General Conditions of the Contract for Construction, AIA A201, provides in § 4.5: "Any Claim arising out of or related to the Contract, except Claims relating to aesthetic effect and except those waived as provided for in Subparagraphs 4.3.10, 9.10.4 and 9.10.5 [relating to claims for consequential damages, and to making and accepting Final Payment as a waiver of claims] shall, after initial decision by the Architect or 30 days after submission of the Claim to the Architect, be subject to mediation as a condition precedent to arbitration or the institution of legal or equitable proceedings by either party." The clause requires mediation under the American Arbitration Association Construction Mediation Rules. These rules were first published in 1980. In 1992 the Engineering Joint Council Documents Committee, in agreement No. 1910-1, adopted a clear preference for mediation.

and weaknesses of other parties' theories, supporting documentation, and demonstrative evidence.

Under the shared retention approach, the parties agree to jointly retain an expert to provide information and prepare graphics on agreed-upon subjects, which information and graphics both parties expect to rely upon during the negotiations.

Why Use an Expert?

To achieve the necessary degree of familiarity with the facts prior to the mediation, data collection and specialized analysis must take place in a relatively short period of time. This must include an understanding of the relationship between the alleged cause and the alleged damages, supported by calculations for each severable claim or issue. Using a construction claims expert to help the parties with these preparatory steps can be an extremely effective and efficient strategy—one that will enhance the mediation's chances for success. There are several reasons for using an expert in preparation for mediation. For one, it may be impractical to allocate a staff person to prepare for mediation while the construction project is ongoing. In addition, an expert is familiar with current developments in claims analysis in similar cases and can:

- Save valuable time by identifying critical issues and quantifying the resulting impacts;
- Provide an unbiased, objective view of the facts; and
- More easily organize pertinent information and depict it graphically to show comparative data.

In many cases, a single expert can provide the necessary information in a cost-effective way, so that the parties can negotiate from a fully informed position. When a single expert is retained, the parties are, in effect, working jointly toward defining and narrowing the issues in dispute or at least bringing them into clearer focus. The services which could be rendered to the parties by a single neutral construction claims expert include:

- Establishing an "as-planned" and an "as-built" schedule, which the parties could ratify and use as a standard measure to determine delay, if any;

- Establishing a chronology of critical events;
- Summarizing the progress of requests for information, change orders, and progress payment requests, from generation to response or approval;
- Summarizing important change orders or other events; and
- Preparing graphic illustrations. Examples include illustrating (1) the correlation between progress payments, work force, and percentage of work-in-place, or (2) progress specific to the issues in dispute, such as steel erection, concrete pours, delivery of electrical switchgear or elevators, installation of windows or other components of building "close-in."

The most valuable attribute of graphic presentation is the quick and concise delivery of summary information. Graphic comparisons may confirm or refute a party's contention that a specific event dramatically affected its performance. Often this will permit the parties to move beyond an impasse previously prohibiting settlement. Mediation can be successful when the parties are confident that they have complete and accurate information necessary for advocacy and negotiation. If the parties work from the same graphic depiction of project data, they may be able to progress more rapidly to resolution of the dispute.

Of course, the parties may not be able to agree on anything, let alone a chronology of critical events prepared by a single expert. In such a case, the parties may wish to retain separate experts.

Example

In this example, a construction consulting firm (Hill International) acted as an expert for a government agency in a $20 million dispute with a general contractor. The expert prepared the mediation brief and developed computer-projection graphics, summarizing the agency's position on twelve major issues.

Prior to the mediation, the expert presented its analysis and graphics to the agency's contracting officer and individuals with first-hand knowledge of the project. This produced dialogue and debate which served to hone the agency's arguments and identify areas for emphasis in a subsequent presentation by the expert to the agency's general counsel and top administrators. As a result of these pre-mediation presentations, by the time the mediation began, the agency's representatives and counsel were thoroughly prepared to negotiate.

Eventually, the expert's analysis and graphics were presented to the mediator, who requested that the presentation be made to the general contractor and its claims expert, as well as to representatives of the large subcontractors. The general contractor's expert also made a presentation illustrating its client's viewpoint.

After the initial presentations, the agency's expert continued to participate in group discussions with the client, in private caucuses with the mediator, and in joint sessions with the contractor, through the last day of mediation when a settlement was reached.

An Expert Can:

- Quickly identify critical issues;
- Provide an unbiased view of the issues;
- Analyze and quantify data and damages;
- Aid the retaining party in preparing for the mediation; and
- If desired, present the party's case at the mediation.

VII. Closure Issues

Closure Issues in Construction Mediation

by Howard D. Venzie Jr.*

Yogi Berra's prophetic statement—"It ain't over till it's over"—contains a lesson that is particularly pertinent to "closing" a negotiated settlement in mediation. Only at the point where all parties sign the settlement agreement is the mediation really over. The failure to resolve overlooked or inadequately addressed issues can undermine closure of a settlement just at the point when everyone thinks that complete agreement has been reached.

The importance of identifying and resolving all the closure issues is even more critical in construction mediation because of the many parties that are typically involved, the multiplicity of contractual obligations, and the technical complexity of the issues. Construction disputes often involve a mix of money, delay, performance and construction defect issues, each of which raise a series of closure issues.

Setting the stage to deal with the closure issues in an effective way begins much earlier than the eve of the parties' "handshake deal." It requires good preparation coming into the mediation, which means, among other things, knowing the facts, the issues in dispute, and the strengths and weaknesses of your case and that of the other parties.[1] It is also essential for all the parties with a financial or other significant interest in the outcome to willingly participate in the mediation process.

This article will identify some of the key closure issues that parties should address when mediating construction disputes involving work completion claims, time-related claims, and allegations of defective workmanship, and when negotiating financial settlements. It also suggests an effective approach to drafting the settlement documents.

---

* The author is a partner in Venzie, Phillips & Warshawer in Philadelphia. He serves on the board of directors of the American Arbitration Association and is a mediator and arbitrator on the Association's roster of neutrals.

[1] *See* Howard Venzie, *Some Guidelines for Effective Advocacy in Mediation,* PUNCH LIST, Fall (1997).

Work-Completion Claims

Many construction disputes involve claims that a contractor or subcontractor failed to perform work required by the construction agreements. Claims of this type raise numerous closure issues.

Future contract work and punch list items. If the mediation occurs at or near substantial completion of the project, the parties should focus on the nature and scope of the contract work and punch list items that remain to be performed by the contractor. Their determination might involve changes to the scope of work specified in the original contract documents.

Schedules. The parties should also address the schedule for completion of the remaining work and the timing of progress payments to be made.

Site access. To carry out its obligations under the settlement, the contractor will require access to the site. To prevent this issue from becoming the source of a later dispute, the parties should agree during the mediation on when access to the premises will be allowed so that the work can proceed without disruption or delay. This is often an issue in renovation projects where use and occupancy of the premises has been a cause of the dispute.

Retainage guarantees and warranties. Because work completion claims involve future performance they raise several closure issues of significance to the owner, including retainage and contract guarantees and warranties.

Retainage is a sum withheld from progress or other payments as "security" to ensure performance of the remaining work. If the owner raises the issue of retainage, the parties should focus on the extent of retainage and when the sums withheld will be paid.

The owner probably will be concerned about the contract guarantees and warranties, raising the issue of how long they will run and the extent to which the original construction agreements will govern future performance.

Surety consent. Owners typically require the contractor to obtain a performance bond protecting against the contractor's default and a payment bond protecting against the contractor's failure to pay subcontractors and suppliers. If a bond or the contract documents require the surety's consent to the settlement, that issue should be addressed in the mediation.

ADR. Since disputes could arise out of the settlement agreement, the parties should address the subject of dispute resolution. For example, will settlement-related disputes call for further mediation proceedings or another ADR procedure?

Time-Related Claims

Time-related claims may allege damages for delay on the part of the contractor, owner or design professional, acceleration of performance under the contract, or lost productivity. They may also involve claims for the cost and expense of additional administration.

Global v. individual settlements. A key issue in such cases is whether disputes between fewer than all parties must be resolved in a global settlement or can be resolved separately by the affected parties. For example, can the contractor separately settle a delay issue with its subcontractor, or must resolution of that issue be part of a global settlement? Can the owner resolve with the design professional a claim for extended administration service costs and expenses, or must this claim also be included in a global settlement? If so, what will be the outcome of delay claims of other contractors whose contracts have not yet been closed out? These issues are fundamental to reaching closure of the dispute.

Work-Defect Disputes

A key issue in work-defect disputes is determining who bears responsibility for the defective condition, and how that responsibility will be shared. Any settlement will determine how much of a financial contribution each party (or its insurer) will make toward the settlement and/or toward the costs of repair or remediation.

Responsibility for design and performance. The parties should focus on who will be responsible for the design, specifications and performance of the repair. It is usually more effective to separate the design aspects of the repair from the performance of the repair work itself. For example in the case of a defective roof, it is preferable for the scope of the repair to be designed and specified by a technically qualified person, working in conjunction with the roofing system manufacturer.

Schedule. The parties should agree on a schedule for completion of the remedial work and the conditions for its performance.

Site access. Access to the site must be arranged so that the repair work can be done. If the facility is occupied, the remedial work may have to be performed outside normal business hours. This issue should surface during the negotiations in order to lay the groundwork for a lasting settlement. Other similar issues that could be addressed are whether the owner will provide staging and storage areas for construction materials during the repair.

Withheld payments. Where construction defects are to be cured by future remediation work, the owner may wish to withhold some contract money which otherwise would be paid until the repairs are completed. This issue should be raised during the mediation, not after.

Additional guarantees and warranties. Another concern of the owner should be to obtain additional or extended guarantees and warranties with respect to the repair. For example, in the roof defect example, the owner may require the contractor to obtain a warranty of performance from the manufacturer of the roofing system.

In addition, there should be an agreement on who will be responsible for the defective condition should it fail to be cured.

Insurance. In a work-defect case, the owner may want the contractor to purchase "extended completed operations coverage" to protect the owner in the event the repair or remedial work causes property damage. This issue should be resolved in the mediation negotiations.

Surety consent. If a performance bond has been issued, the owner will probably wish the surety to extend the time for the owner to bring suit on the bond. This is also a factor in bringing closure to the settlement.

Inspection and certification. A negotiated settlement of a defective work claim can fall apart if there is a disagreement later about the individual who will inspect the remedial work and determine whether it has been perform-ed according to specifications. To avert this possibility, the parties should agree on the person who will serve as the owner's representative for this purpose. Will it be the architect or another design professional retained as a consultant? A related issue to be determined is who shall pay the fees for such services.

ADR. The parties should not ignore the possibility of a dispute arising out of the remediation work. Accordingly, they should address the method of dispute resolution to be used.

Monetary Settlements

Other issues must be addressed whenever a mediation settlement involves a monetary payment.

Treatment of payment. The parties should determine in the mediation how the settlement payment should be treated. Will it be a final payment under the contract, which has no further consequences? Or will it be a liquidated settlement, which has the effect of releasing all claims and extinguishing all further obligations under the contract, except to the extent reserved by the parties?

Disbursements. Another issue is the manner in which the settlement sum and any contract funds required to be paid will be disbursed. Will they be disbursed in a lump sum or in installments? Will disbursements be tied to completion of all or a portion of the work?

Collateral. If payments are to be made over time, the parties should determine whether any property will be provided as collateral to ensure that those payments will be made. They should also determine what waivers and releases will be given and how "payment act" obligations will be met. In addition, they should consider whether the settlement should include indemnification for future claims against the project.

Insurance. An issue that may need to be addressed when insurance coverage applies after payment of a deductible is whether the insured can afford to pay the deductible. If not, the parties may wish to deal in the mediation with the possibility that the insured will have to finance the deductible payment.

Default

Since default under a contract is always a possibility, the parties should address the consequences of default under the settlement agreement. Here are some questions to be resolved: Will the non-defaulting party have the right to be restored to its pre-settlement position at its election? Or will it be limited to the remedies under the settlement agreement? Will the non-defaulting party have the right to recover its costs and expenses, interest and attorneys' fees if it has to seek enforcement of the settlement agreement?

The Proactive Mediator

The mediator always hopes that the parties and their counsel will identify all of the closure issues that must be addressed in order to fully resolve the dispute. In a simple case, that usually occurs. But if the case is at all complex, and the parties have not focused on all the key issues, the mediator should assist the parties in the identification and resolution of these issues, always being careful not to compromise mediator neutrality. Offering suggestions for the resolution of an issue that will clear the path for final and complete settlement does not put the mediator in the position of being an advocate for a party. The parties usually will adopt the suggestion as their own if they like it, and will be thankful for the mediator's help in reaching a settlement.

Once a closure issue is raised, the mediator should push for its resolution, all the while expecting that new, related issues will emerge in the process.

The failure to anticipate and resolve closure issues as the mediation progresses may lead to unexpected complications later on, including impasse.

It is often necessary for the parties to focus on construction issues (such as determining who will design and "spec" repair of a defectively installed roof, and the scope and specifications of a roof repair) at the same time that financial issues are moving toward closure, so that the potential costs of future work can be factored into the negotiations, enabling the parties to adjust their financial expectations.

Settlement Documents

The devil is in the details when it comes to closing the settlement of a construction dispute. Thus, implementing the settlement through comprehensive settlement documents will involve further negotiations. This raises the risk that a settlement reached "in principal" might unravel because the parties (or their counsel) find that they disagree on one or more closure issues.

A sound approach is to draft the settlement documents immediately after the agreement in principal has been reached. With today's word-processing technology, immediate preparation and turnaround of comprehensive settlement documents can be easily accomplished as long as time is built into the mediation process for this purpose. Allotting this drafting time can eliminate many headaches later on.

At a minimum, a written Mediation Memorandum of Understanding should be prepared on the spot, before anyone leaves the mediation. It should be executed by the parties and the mediator. The MOU should set forth all of the principal terms of the settlement since it serves as a master checklist of the points and concepts the parties' attorneys are to include when they draft the final comprehensive settlement documents.

To ensure that the final settlement documents are prepared and signed, the mediator should hold the mediation open to monitor the closing of the settlement documents and intervene in the process the moment it looks like the parties may be going backwards.

Conclusion

Successful closure of construction mediation proceedings requires the mediator to think globally and take a proactive role in ferreting out the issues that, if ignored, can thwart the proceedings. Resolution of these issues is vital to achieving a lasting, final settlement. By implementing a strategy that allows the negotiations to incorporate these important issues, the mediator will put the parties on a path to a complete "contract close-out," which is the surest way to achieve a lasting settlement.

VIII. Mediators Not Giving Participants What They Want

Construction Attorneys' Mediation Preferences Surveyed Is There a Gap between Supply and Demand?

by Dean B. Thomson*

The results of a recent survey of construction attorneys suggest that there is a gap between what they want from mediators and what mediators are supplying. Mediator techniques valued highly by the respondents were not observed as frequently as their importance to respondents suggested they should be.

The survey was distributed to the members of the American Bar Association Forum on the Construction Industry, the largest organization of construction attorneys in the United States. The survey sought to identify the method and criteria used to select a mediator, preferred mediator styles, desirable mediator behaviors and how often mediators displayed them.

Six hundred-and-seventy-two attorneys representing owners, subcontractors, suppliers and design professionals responded to the survey questionnaire. All had mediation experience as an attorney; most had participated in more than ten mediations and more than 120 had participated in over forty mediations. Collectively they participated in 10,581-15,540 mediation proceedings.

Mediator Selection

Nearly three-quarters of the respondents (72%) reported selecting the mediator by mutual agreement. The remainder used an ADR provider (21%) or some other method (7%).

Respondents ranked eight factors that most influenced their decision to choose a mediator from another region of the country.[1] The results

---

* The author is a shareholder in Fabyanske, Westra & Hart, P.A., in Minneapolis. He conducted the survey through the ABA Forum on the Construction Industry. Helen Hawkinson and Michael Roller helped tabulate the survey results. This article is adapted from a longer article, which appeared in THE CONSTRUCTION LAWYER.

[1] In descending order of importance (1 being highest) the selection factors by average were ranked as follows: (1) 2.36-subject matter expertise; (2) 2.86-reputation; (3) 2.89-mediation experience; (4) 3.73-acceptability to all parties; (5) 3.94-mediation style; (6) 4.73-size of claim; (7) 4.88-legal expertise; (8) 5.71-mediator's expenses.

were contrary to the commonly held opinion that subject-matter expertise is less important than mediation experience.[2] In fact, subject-matter expertise received the highest rank while mediation expertise was ranked third. Legal expertise ran a distant seventh.

When asked to choose between having a lay mediator or an attorney mediator where both had equal experience in mediation and in the field in dispute, 94% of respondents opted for the attorney. When the assumption changed so that both only had experience in mediation, the results were almost identical. The results changed only when the lay person, but not the attorney, had experience in the field of the dispute. In that scenario the lay person was preferred by more than 2:1; 69% favored the lay mediator while 30% opted for an attorney mediator with no knowledge of the subject matter.

The overall preference for attorneys is not surprising, given the population surveyed. On the other hand, the fact that a lay person with subject matter knowledge was preferred at least 2:1 over an attorney without such knowledge is more consistent with the high rank given to the mediator's subject matter expertise as a selection criterion.

Claim size and mediator expenses were ranked low as selection criteria, confirming that selecting the appropriate mediator is more important than economics, whether examined from the point of view of case size or mediator cost. The average value of a case for which respondents might consider paying the costs of a non-local mediator, as determined by a bell curve, was around $1 million, a relatively low figure.

Well over a majority of respondents (62%) said that if the mediator was asked to confidentially evaluate a client's case and opine about the outcome in litigation, they would rather that evaluation be made by someone with whom they were not personally acquainted. The remaining respondents took the opposite view. This result shows that attorneys prefer the presumed objectivity of an unknown neutral over the possibility that a prior relationship with the mediator might influence the mediator's evaluation.

---

[2] *See* Fred D. Butler, *The Question of Race, Gender & Culture in Mediator Selection*, 55 DISP. RESOL. J. 36 (Jan. 2001); Jessica Pearson & Nancy Thoennes, *Divorce Mediation Research Results*, in JAY FOLBERG & ANN MILNE eds., DIVORCE MEDIATION: THEORY AND PRACTICE 429 (1988).

Mediation Procedures

Preparation for Mediation. Most respondents (92%) expressed a preference for a mediator who asks for mediation position papers from all counsel before the mediation. This finding indicates that respondents want the mediator to be prepared for the mediation and believe that pre-mediation statements facilitate preparation. A substantial number also want to have procedural and substantive discussions with the mediator before the mediation begins. More than 40% preferred a mediator who speaks to counsel before the mediation; and almost one-third (29%) favored a mediator who meets with each party and counsel before the session.

Opening Statements. Some mediators think opening statements identify issues and allow parties to approximate "having their day in court." Others believe that opening statements alienate the parties and ultimately make settlement more difficult.[3] Of the respondents who answered the question pertaining to the desirability of opening statements, 48% preferred the mediator who made opening remarks optional; 41% preferred the mediator who insisted on them; and 5% preferred the mediator who did not allow them.

Multiple Parties. Construction mediations often involve multiple parties. As a result, the parties often spend a lot of time waiting to meet privately with the mediator. Two hundred-and- eight respondents offered suggestions to improve the process. The suggestion made by the greatest number of respondents was for the mediator to undertake significant pre-mediation preparation and planning. Activities that could help educate the parties and/or the mediator about the dispute included exchanging pre-mediation statements, expert reports, key exhibits and other documents, and providing the mediator with confidential settlement positions. Also suggested was conducting pre-mediation meetings to establish ground rules.

Some respondents thought the mediator should conduct separate mediations with particular parties or groups of parties before convening all parties in one large mediation. Several suggested, in like vein, that the parties be divided into logical groups which would confer with the mediator together.

Using co-mediators was proposed as a means to increase the time that parties spend with a mediator. Specific issues could be assigned to

---

[3] *See* Marc Kalish, *Using Mediation to Settle Your Dispute*, 37 ARIZ. ATT'Y 22 (Jan. 2001).

each co-mediator, while a "master mediator" would control the entire enterprise. Few respondents suggested how to avoid the difficulties inherent in this approach. For example, how would information learned by multiple mediators be shared?

To address the time-consuming nature of multiparty mediation, some respondents emphasized the need for the mediator to schedule a sufficient number of days for the mediation and to establish a mediation schedule and stick to it.

Other suggestions seemed equally applicable to two-party mediations, such as ensuring that decision makers with authority to settle are present and using trained, skilled mediators.[4] One interesting suggestion had the mediator assign "homework" to a party before leaving them to meet with another party (e.g., estimating the probability of success on specific issues or calculating a detailed litigation budget).

Mediator Conduct

Countless articles have been written about the respective merits of facilitative versus evaluative mediation and the vast spectrum of options and alternatives between the two poles.[5] Respondents rated from 1-10 (10 being the highest rank) the desirability of nine common mediator behaviors (or attributes) starting with those considered to be the most "facilitative" and progressing to the most "evaluative," and indicated how often in their experience the mediator displayed the attribute.[6]

---

[4] Steve Nelson, a Fellow in the American College of Construction Lawyers, collected an interesting online discussion among various Fellows of the College regarding how to successfully manage multiparty mediations.

[5] Advocating a facilitative role: *See, e.g.*, Kimberlee K. Kovach & Lela P. Love, *Mapping Mediation: The Risks of Riskin's Grid*, 3 HARV. NEGOTIATION L. REV. 71, 79-81, 88-89, 92 (1998); Lela P. Love, *The Top Ten Reasons Why Mediators Should Not Evaluate*, 24 FLA. ST. U. L. REV. 937, 941 (Summer, 1997); Robert B. Moberly, *Mediator Gag Rules: Is it Ethical for Mediators to Evaluate or Advise?*, 38 S. TEX. L. REV. 669 (1997). Advocating an evaluative role: *See, e.g.*, John Forester & Lawrence Sussking, *Activist Mediation and Public Disputes*, in D.M. KOLB. ET. AL. EDS., WHEN TALKING WORKS: PROFILES OF MEDIATORS 323, 328, 331, 333 (1994); Maureen E. Laflin, *Preserving the Integrity of Mediation Through the Adoption of Ethical Rules for Lawyer-Mediators*, 14 NOTRE DAME J.L. ETHICS & PUB. POL'Y 479 (2000); Samuel J. Imperati, *Mediator Practice Models: The Intersection of Ethics and Stylistic Practices in Mediation*, 706 WILLAMETTE L. REV. 33:3 (Summer 1997).

[6] The behaviors were ranked as follows in order of preference (10 being highest):
8.9-Presents various settlement options or solutions to the various parties based on the mediator's understanding of the case;

In terms of desirability, respondents gave the highest rank to the mediator who "presents various settlement options or solutions to the various parties based on the mediator's understanding of the case." They gave the next highest rank to the mediator who "confidentially discusses with each party the merits and potential outcomes of the case." These findings suggest that attorneys want creative, evaluative discussions based on the mediator's informed understanding, experience and judgment. Despite the high rank these attributes received in terms of demand, respondents said they encountered mediators who presented settlement options only 60% of the time, and mediators who engaged in confidential discussions about the merits only 67% of the time.

Respondents valued communicating the parties' settlement positions and helping the parties avoid personality disputes, ranking this behavior third in desirability. Since being able to keep the lines of communication open is an essential skill for a mediator,[7] it is somewhat surprising that the respondents reported that the mediator engaged in this behavior only 69% of the time.

Rated fourth was a mediator who, "at an appropriate time during the mediation, encourages the parties to accept a settlement proposed by one of the parties or the mediator." Respondents reported observing this behavior only 62% of the time, perhaps because attempting to bring closure to the dispute in this way is discouraged by some mediation training programs.[8]

8.4-Confidentially discusses with each party the merits and potential outcomes of the case;

8.1-Communicates the parties' settlement positions and helps the parties avoid personality disputes;

7.3-At an appropriate time during the mediation, encourages the parties to accept a resolution proposed by one of the parties or the mediator;

7.1-At an appropriate time during the mediation, forcefully and vigorously reviews with each party in confidence the mediator's opinion of the likely outcome of the case;

6.5-Reviews with the parties the likely costs and expenses of proceeding and the uncertainty of the legal process;

6.3-At an appropriate time during the mediation, forcefully and vigorously recommends a resolution proposed by one of the parties or the mediator;

6.0-Will not let the parties leave the mediation unless the mediator, not one of the parties, declares an impasse;

4.5-Asks the parties themselves to confidentially evaluate their own cases, but does not suggest any evaluation of the merits.

[7] *See* Love, note 5 *supra*, at 941; Robert D. Benjamin, *Guerilla Mediation: The Use of Warfare Strategies in the Management of Conflict*, at www.mediate.com (1999).

[8] *See* TRAINING MANUAL FOR CONSTRUCTION INDUSTRY MEDIATORS 84 (AAA 1997); Love, note 5 *supra*, at 941.

Respondents ranked fifth reviewing with each party in confidence in a "forceful" and "vigorous" way the mediator's opinion of the likely outcome of the case. Respondents said they experienced this highly evaluative behavior from the mediator 51% of the time.

Respondents ranked sixth reviewing with the parties the costs saved as a result of settlement and the uncertainty of litigation. Respondents said they encountered mediators who reviewed these matters 72% of the time. These mediators were probably taught to emphasize costs and future risks in mediator training programs. They no doubt believe that mediation is a logical juncture at which to emphasize that future costs can be avoided by settling the case. The low score for this behavior in terms of desirability may reflect the fact that respondents usually discuss with the client the avoidance of costs and litigation risks when making the decision to mediate. It is also possible that they are uncomfortable with the idea of discussing potential legal fees and costs in great detail with the client.

Ranked seventh was the technique of forcefully and strongly recommending a resolution proposed by one of the parties or the mediator at an appropriate time during the mediation. Respondents reported seeing this overtly directive and evaluative behavior 51% of the time.

Respondents ranked eighth a mediator who would not let the parties leave the mediation until the mediator declares an impasse. Respondents indicated that mediators conducted their mediations in this way 42% of the time. The relative infrequency of this behavior may stem from a belief that the parties, not the mediator, should control the mediation.[9]

The behavior least favored by respondents (ranked ninth) was asking the parties to confidentially evaluate their own cases, without suggesting any evaluation of the merits. Respondents presumably believe that a good lawyer would have made this analysis before the mediation, so that this request would be considered completely unproductive. Nevertheless, respondents reported that mediators demonstrated this behavior 50% of the time. One could easily conclude from this that attorneys want more evaluation of the merits by the mediator.

---

[9] A good discussion of impasse-breaking strategies can be found in the AAA TRAINING MANUAL, note 8 *supra*, at 87.

Conclusions

The survey indicates that the respondents have a clear bias in favor of selecting attorneys as mediators. Given that the respondents were attorneys, this result may simply indicate a preference for individuals with similar backgrounds. On the other hand, the preference was so strong (94%) that it may indicate an assumption that attorney mediators have a skill set not possessed by lay mediators. Of course, many lay mediators vigorously argue that they are often effective precisely because they don't "think like lawyers." With training and experience, the skill set necessary to be an effective mediator can be possessed by attorney and lay mediators alike. The trick is finding out which individuals possess those skills.

The survey indicates that the highest ranked mediator behaviors were evaluative (up to a point) rather than facilitative. Moreover, mediators engaged in the more desirable behaviors less frequently than their desirability would suggest that they should. Indeed, none of the mediator behaviors (except discussing the costs of litigation) were reported to occur more than 70% of the time.

The survey suggests that mediators should be more aware of the preferences and expectations of the mediating parties and, when appropriate, should strive for greater congruence between these expectations and the techniques the mediators employ. To accomplish this, mediators will have to be more flexible about what works in practice and pay less attention to constraints imposed by certain theories of mediation.

Counsel for the disputing parties can improve the prospect of having their mediation expectations met by entering into an agreement concerning the type of mediator and the type of mediator conduct they desire. Then counsel can conduct a thorough search for a mediator who can satisfy their wishes. They should discuss their expectations with each prospective mediator that they interview and with the mediator they ultimately choose.

The survey indicates that mediators should be better trained in the conduct that construction attorneys and their clients find desirable. For example, if users highly value a mediator who encourages them to accept a particular settlement proposal, then training programs ought to teach mediators how to do this effectively. If overcoming an impasse is a valued skill, impasse-breaking options ought to be taught.

It is important periodically to discuss and evaluate whether mediation is meeting the needs of those using it. The empirical data derived from this survey may help stimulate that discussion.

IX. Mediator Confidentiality and Court Testimony

Danger Looms for Mediation—Mediators Likely to Testify under UMA Draft

by Mark Appel*

What will become of mediation—hailed by most users as the favored dispute resolution process—under the Uniform Mediation Act (UMA), a statute intended to replace the current patchwork of state laws on mediation confidentiality? Can it withstand the efforts by the drafting committee, whose December 2000 interim draft of the UMA virtually ensures that mediators will be required to testify in post-mediation proceedings?

Parties feel comfortable mediating because (1) they believe a neutral mediator will add value to their negotiation, and (2) their communications in the mediation will be considered confidential. Parties are willing to confide in the mediator, candidly revealing sensitive information and admissions. Would they continue to do this if they knew that the mediator could be required to testify against a party's interest in a post-mediation proceeding? Would counsel allow a client to participate freely in mediation proceedings in light of the risk that the mediator might testify? Is it more likely than not that parties will decide to avoid mediation altogether?

No Strong Statement

The December 2000 interim draft of the UMA practically invites courts, agencies and arbitrators to require mediators to testify about mediation communications. One way it does this is by omitting a strong statement that mediation communications are confidential.

The drafters have chosen to treat the confidentiality of mediation communications as a limited privilege (see UMA Section 5, Privilege Against Disclosure),[1] not as an exclusion. Previous drafts of the UMA

---

* The author is a senior vice president of the American Arbitration Association and the official observer for the Association at meetings of the UMA drafting committee. He is a member of the Colorado state bar.

[1] The privilege may be asserted only in proceedings before a court, administrative

also took the "privilege" approach. Like those earlier drafts, the December draft contains a statement in Section 6 (Admissibility; Discovery) that mediation communications are not subject to discovery or admissible in evidence in post-mediation proceedings if they are privileged and the privilege is not waived or precluded. That statement is helpful, but it does not go as far as it should in declaring as a general principle that mediation communications are confidential and that mediators should be required to disclose confidential communications only in extraordinary circumstances.

The only other statement referencing confidentiality in the December draft is a relatively weak rule of construction in Section 2 (Application and Construction). This provision says that "consideration must be given" to four items, the second of which is "the need to promote candor of parties and mediators through confidentiality...." Thus, Section 2 also fails to make a clear statement that mediation communications are confidential.

Numerous Exceptions

Another way in which the December draft invites mediator testimony is by providing, in Section 8, numerous exceptions to the confidentiality privilege. The breadth of one of these exceptions (Section 8 (b)(2)) is very troubling. It provides that there is "no privilege against disclosure" for a mediation communication "offered in a judicial, administrative or arbitration proceeding to prove a claim or defense recognized by law as sufficient to set aside, rescind or reform a contract."

The disclosure required by Section 8 (b)(2) repudiates any notion that mediator communications are privileged or confidential. Under this provision mediator testimony can be compelled, after an in camera hearing, in any case attacking the validity or enforceability of a settlement agreement.[2]

---

agency or arbitral tribunal. It has no application outside these venues, thereby allowing disclosures, absent a confidentiality agreement, to the press, interested parties or others.

[2] The *in camera* hearing requires the court, administrative agency or arbitral panel to find "that the party seeking discovery or the proponent of the evidence has shown that the evidence is not otherwise available, that there is a need for the evidence that substantially outweighs the importance of the policy favoring the protection of confidentiality under this [Act]," and that "the mediation communication is offered in a judicial, administrative or arbitration proceeding to prove a claim or defense recognized by law as sufficient to set aside, rescind, or reform a contract." Early drafts of the UMA included an "omnibus"

Thus, rather than limiting the circumstances in which mediators will be placed in an adverse position to a party, the drafters have taken an expansive approach. In *Olam v. Congress Mortgage Co.*,[3] a federal district court in California, after conducting a balancing test, required the mediator to testify in a post-mediation proceeding in which the plaintiff challenged the enforcement of the mediation settlement agreement on the grounds of undue influence and incapacity.[4] The drafters of the UMA not only adopted the holding in *Olam*, they went beyond it in allowing mediator disclosure in any post-mediation proceeding in which a party seeks to overturn a mediation settlement agreement.[5]

The approach taken by the drafters assumes that the mediator can provide the "best evidence." But this assumption does not withstand close examination. Mediation proceedings are not recorded. There is no written record to refresh the mediator's recollection. Any notes taken by the mediator are necessarily going to be incomplete, assuming they have not been destroyed to protect confidentiality, as good mediation practice teaches. Moreover, the mediator is focused on keeping the parties engaged in productive negotiation. It is unrealistic to expect the mediator to accurately recall all that occurred. It is worse to make her divulge that information.

Even if the mediator could provide valuable evidence, requiring mediator testimony that could be adverse to a party's interest assaults the policy of mediator neutrality. It can only undermine confidence and trust in the mediator and the mediation process. It should be an unalterable principle that mediators should not be compelled to testify except under extraordinary, clearly defined, easily understood circumstances. The overly broad exception to the confidentiality privilege in Section 8(b)(2) of the December draft does not meet this criterion.

---

exception to the confidentiality privilege "in the interest of justice." This exception was dropped due to criticism that it swallowed the rule of confidentiality for mediation communications. The exception in Section 8(b)(2) may be viewed as another way of framing this exception.

[3] Olam v. Congress Mortgage Co., 68 F. Supp. 2d 1110 (N.D. Cal. 1999). *See also* Foxgate Homeowners' Association v. Bramalea California, Inc., 78 Adv. Cal. App. 4th 653 (Cal. Ct. App. 2d Dist. 2000) (review by the California Supreme Court is pending).

[4] That decision is not without critics. *See James Madison, Is Mediation Confidential: A Critique of the Olam and Foxgate Decisions*, 5 No. 2 ADR CURRENTS 1 (June-Aug. 2000).

[5] Early last year the American Arbitration Association and the Society of Professionals in Dispute Resolution, in separate comments, urged the drafting committee to define limited, appropriate exceptions to a clearly stated confidentiality rule.

The lack of an unequivocal and sweeping statement of mediation confidentiality, taken together with an exceedingly broad exception to the confidentiality "privilege," pose a serious threat to the continued use of the mediation process. These flaws prompted Hanan Isaacs, president of the New Jersey Association of Professional Mediators, to say in a recent e-mail to concerned colleagues, "If adopted in its current form, the UMA would KILL OFF mediation 'as we know it.'" (Emphasis in original.) He suggested that unless these problems are remedied in the final draft, the act will not be worthy of support.

James Madison, president of the California Dispute Resolution Council (CDRC), a professional organization of ADR neutrals, told the Punch List, "If mediation is to remain more useful than a judicial settlement conference, everything that is said in or written for the mediation should be excluded from evidence in any proceeding between the parties or with a third party, and mediators should be precluded from giving testimony except when, as in the Rinaker case in California, constitutional due process rights are implicated." He predicted that the CDRC will oppose enactment of the UMA in California if it is approved in its present form.

How are parties, who have the most to lose if mediation becomes unattractive, reacting to these aspects of the UMA? P.D. Villarreal, counsel for litigation and legal policy at the General Electric Company, said, "There is no question but that a lack of mediation confidentiality will make mediation a less attractive alternative to litigation."

While there have been some positive changes in the December draft, they cannot overcome the fundamental flaws in the UMA that have been described here. Drafting any statute by committee unquestionably involves making many compromises. Here, the compromises that evidently have been forged threaten to stifle a very successful process. Less policing and more enabling would be in order.

CHAPTER SEVEN

LARGE AND COMPLEX CASE MANAGEMENT

I. Managing the Preliminary Hearing under Rule L-4

Management of the Preliminary Hearing Under Construction Rule L-4 for Large, Complex Cases

by Anthony E. Battelle*

The AAA recently revised its construction industry rules. This article takes a look at Rule L-4 which outlines, for the first time, a variety of case management techniques at the preliminary hearings stage in large, complex cases. Battelle shows how good management at this stage of the process is a key factor in reducing arbitration time, costs, and inconvenience.

Most would agree that the 1996 revisions to the American Arbitration Association's Construction Industry Arbitration Rules[1] (the "Rules") have modernized the construction arbitration process in many areas. The focus of this article is new Rule L-4 governing preliminary hearings in the "large, complex case."[2] Rule L-4, as outlined in the Association's 1999 revisions to the Rules, sets out for the first time a comprehensive array of case management techniques and compels inquiry into just what should be taking place, or being accomplished, at this early point in the arbitration process. Should Rule L-4 be applied literally in all cases, or does it represent merely a suggested means of proceeding? How should a panel implement the rule?

---

* The author is an attorney at Construction Law Services in Boston, has lectured extensively on ADR in the construction industry and produced several papers on the topic.
[1] Effective April 1, 1996, the AAA adopted substantially revised Construction Industry Arbitration Rules, the product of a two-year effort by a large and diversified task force of experts from throughout the industry. The rules were changed again, effective Oct. 15, 1997, and renamed the Construction Industry Dispute Resolution Procedures ("C.I.D.R.P." and the "Rules").
[2] A "large, complex case" is defined under the new rules as one that exceeds $1 million. *See* Rule L-1.

Regardless of how panels choose to adhere to the literal mandate of Rule L-4, its inclusion within the Rules elevates the preliminary hearing to a status of paramount importance in the large, complex case. Application of the Rule also substantially influences case presentation at the formal hearing stage.

For large cases, these case management measures were long overdue. In the past, far too many large cases were heard in the absence of any serious efforts by their panels to "manage" the hearing process or streamline the submission of information. As a result, these cases often became inordinately protracted and expensive to the point where serious questions were being raised concerning the suitability of arbitration for resolving them. Rule L-4 is good medicine for past ailments in the arbitration process.

The purpose of this article is to heighten awareness of the panel's enhanced management role under Rule L-4 and to offer some practical suggestions to panelists and attorneys alike as they adjust to a new and far more sophisticated preliminary hearing process. Participants in cases not large enough to fall within Rule L-4 may also benefit from becoming familiar with the implications of this rule, which encourages a far more proactive management approach with all sizes of construction arbitrations.

Rule L-4 (a) and (b)[3]

Rule L-43 is one among six new rules applicable to the large, complex case. Subparts (a) and (b) of the Rule[4] establish, for the first

---

[3] C.I.D.R.P. L-4 provides in part: "At the preliminary hearing the matters to be considered shall include, without limitation: (a) service of a detailed statement of claims, damages and defenses, a statement of the issues asserted by each party and positions with respect thereto and any legal authorities the parties may wish to bring to the attention of the arbitrators; (b) stipulations to uncontested facts; (c) the extent to which discovery shall be conducted; (d) exchange and premarking of those documents which each party believes may be offered at the hearing; (e) the identification and availability of witnesses, including experts, and such matters with respect to witnesses including their biographies and expected testimony as may be appropriate; (f) whether, and the extent to which, any sworn statements and/or depositions may be introduced; (g) the extent to which hearings will proceed on consecutive days; (h) whether a stenographic or other official record of the proceedings shall be maintained; and (i) the possibility of utilizing mediation or other nonadjudicative methods of dispute resolution."

[4] This article addresses primarily subparts (a) and (b) of Rule L-4. Other subparts, particularly subpart (c) providing for discovery, also are important but do not represent a significant change from prior practice. Discovery, moreover, has never been as significant a process in the resolution of construction disputes as in other areas of civil

time, a comprehensive preliminary hearing procedure that is designed to narrow the scope of a dispute and focus and expedite the hearing process through the use of several techniques of modern case management. Greater emphasis on active management by the panel resonates clearly from Rule L-4 and throughout the new Rules.

Implementation of Rule L-4, however, will require considerable skill, experience, judgment, and initiative on the part of large case panels. Identifying, sorting out, organizing, and analyzing information submittals[5] in complex cases is no small challenge, even for a seasoned panelist.

Rule L-4 (a) and (b) provide for the panel, at the prehearing stage, to implement and oversee an orderly exchange of factual information including detailed statements of claims, damage calculations, and defenses intended to be addressed at the formal hearings, the further exchange of fact statements underlying those claims and defenses, and the achievement of a stipulation of uncontested facts. Not mentioned expressly in the Rule, but extremely important to the effectiveness of prehearing case management, is the need to ensure that claims and defenses and the facts underlying them are well organized, so that formal hearings are time- and cost-efficient and final awards are not arrived at loosely.

The arbitration process is distinctly different from judicial litigation and should remain so, but the processes converge when Rule L-4 is considered in light of equivalent provisions of the Federal Rules of Civil Procedure, as well as a number of states' procedural rules. Fed. R. Civ. P. 16 and 26, for example, often in conjunction with local rules, call for many of the case management techniques that are prescribed by Rule L-4 of the Construction Industry Dispute Resolution Procedures (C.I.D.R.P.).

Despite the difficulties presented, the importance for large case panels to implement Rule L-4 cannot be understated. All construction disputes are notorious for their factual as well as legal complexities. Good prehearing management that identifies, organizes, and reduces the scope of a complex dispute allows for a smoother, more rapid, and clearer submission of information at the formal hearings. This in turn facilitates a more "correct" disposition of the dispute grounded upon

---

litigation, owing to the wide circulation of most relevant documents that characterizes all construction projects.

[5] The word "information" is used instead of the more familiar "evidence" to underscore that the new rules expressly exclude the rules of evidence as a criteria for the submission of information to or the receipt of information by the panel concerning a dispute. See C.I.D.R.P. Rules R-10 and R-31.

solid factual findings and the correct application of legal principles, not simply upon an "equitable" or "rough justice" assessment by the panel. Effective management at the preliminary hearing stage should also make the formal hearing process far less an ordeal for party representatives who must provide testimony.

Going About the Job

The Rule's operative requirement is for panels to "consider" the various management techniques. Its clear implication, however, is for panels to use them. The panel's new responsibilities—in particular to manage effectively the organization, distillation, and submission of large quantities of facts at the preliminary hearing stage—is formidable and likely to represent unfamiliar territory for most panelists. It is unlikely, for example, that most large, complex cases can be organized effectively in one preliminary hearing. In order to achieve the critical objectives of the preliminary hearing process, panels should anticipate that two or more preliminary hearings will be necessary.

Effective case management has always been an art form to some degree, and no one management technique works best in all situations. Hence, large case panels should not look for "lockstep" case management guidance. Rule L-4, for example, provides nine listed management techniques that are "without limitation" to the adoption of other techniques, thereby encouraging panels to be creative in developing case management plans and strategies that may best serve the peculiarities of their individual cases.[6]

All of the case management techniques listed in Rule L-4 should be familiar to litigating attorneys who must deal with similar techniques employed by judges. The first two subsets of the Rule, however, are truly significant within the context of a large construction arbitration. They contemplate a substantial management undertaking at the preliminary hearing stage, when a panel is newly formed and its members are not fully familiar with the dispute or acquainted with each other. At such time, the panel is expected to immediately arrange for the "(a) service of a detailed statement of claims, damages and defenses, a statement of the

---

[6] Rule L-4 is reinforced by Rule L-5, which requires arbitrators to "take such steps as they deem necessary or desirable to avoid delay and to achieve a just, speedy and cost efficient resolution....." It is important to note that this rule compels each panel to seek a "resolution," not merely a conclusion, to its case.

issues asserted by each party and positions with respect thereto, and any legal authorities the parties may wish to bring to the attention of the arbitrator(s); [and] (b) stipulations to uncontested facts..."

A Caveat

There may arise a temptation, born of past habit or a panel's inherent distaste for beginning a new case by issuing potentially unpopular instructions, to pass over the preliminary hearing process as contemplated by Rule L-4. After all, the inclination to begin formal hearings immediately can be justified by the notion that the panel will "get up to speed" by listening to live testimony and reading documents as the formal hearings proceed. In the past, however, it was the very absence of case management at the outset of arbitration proceedings that often doomed these large disputes to endless costly hearings with some cases ultimately being resolved solely on the basis of attrition.

Bypassing the preliminary hearing as a case management opportunity, moreover, disregards the mandate of Rule L-4 and may produce undesirable consequences. First, the panel foregoes an opportunity to take charge of and establish its own ground rules for the conduct of the formal hearings to follow. Second, it sows the seeds for protracted formal hearings, because: the dispute has not been pared or organized; the proof may not be distilled or well-organized prior to presentation; the claimant fears presenting too little; and the respondent believes it must match the quantum and repetition of information submitted by the claimant. Third, because all parties are entitled to the same "rights," it is much more difficult to streamline the formal hearing process partway through it.

The traditional approach of starting testimony without case management has been proven historically to be both inefficient and ineffective. The Arbitration Rules Task Force inserted new rules for large, complex cases specifically to address this deficiency. It would seem, therefore, that new panels must undertake to become familiar with and learn how to implement these special rules in complex cases.

A Management Plan

The large panel's first formal task occurs at the preliminary hearing stage. It must determine how to effect the service and exchange of detailed statements of claims, damages, and defenses in a manner that serves the next objective of achieving a stipulation of agreed facts, and it must otherwise facilitate an efficient resolution of the dispute. Prior to the first preliminary hearing, it is desirable for the panel to meet and discuss a suitable management plan for identifying and achieving the objectives of the preliminary hearing process. This also allows the panelists to become acquainted, to select a chairperson, and to develop some degree of bonding as a team before engaging with the parties.

The first objective should be to determine the nature and parameters of the dispute, often no small task. Neither the preliminary hearing nor the formal hearing process that follows can be managed effectively if the panel has an unclear picture of the dispute. The panel must comprehend the liability basis for each of possibly numerous (if not innumerable) individual claims, as well as the damage calculations that go with them. Attorneys at the outset of complex construction arbitrations are often not yet certain of the factual details or precise legal bases that underlie their claims and defenses. Time spent defining the nature and parameters of the dispute and the accounting of damages claimed, therefore, is likely to be time well-spent.

The large case panel's attention then shifts to the identification of material facts underlying the disputed claims and defenses, to organizing, isolating, and reducing the number of facts in dispute, to obtaining stipulations of agreed facts, and to arranging for an efficient information submittal at the formal hearings. This can be a tricky exercise because parties are often reluctant to agree to anything but the most inconsequential facts at the outset of an arbitration. If the nature and parameters of the dispute have already been well- defined, however, the parties may be more willing to agree to non-disputed facts, because each can see the significance of a given fact to a given claim or defense and be better able to judge whether it is "safe" to stipulate to such a fact. It is a primary objective of the preliminary hearing process to achieve agreement on as many material facts as possible, and not simply to go through the motions of a proposed fact exchange that essentially produces no agreed facts.

In situations where a very large number of issues or parties are involved, a panel might request the claimant first to identify and number each of its claims, giving the general basis in liability for the claim and a short statement as to how it would calculate the damages. Next, the panel might ask the claimant to set forth the principal facts that support each of its claims. Requiring specificity and placing limitations on the length of written submittals are techniques for bringing issues into focus. Limiting the fact exchanges to the largest and most important points of the claim may also be a suitable approach. Identifying key factual issues and planning to address them first in the formal hearings is yet another valid approach in some circumstances.

An effective panel will study and assess the number and types of claims confronting it and be creative in devising the most effective means to achieve organization, clarification, fact stipulations, and reduction of issues so that formal hearings are efficient. The preliminary hearing process, however, should not become so elaborate as to overwhelm or burden the parties. A key objective during this process is to develop a balanced and effective management plan. This may require time to accomplish, and multiple approaches may have to be tried within a single arbitration.

Milestone Objectives

There is probably no single process best suited to accomplishing the management objectives of every preliminary hearing, and to attempt to prescribe one may serve to discourage management plans designed creatively to suit the particular challenges of a given dispute. It is possible, however, to sketch a number of general "milestone objectives" within the preliminary hearing process on which a panel's initial management plan might be based. Working from these milestone objectives, a panel may be able to fashion its own management plan tailored to suit the peculiarities of its case.

The key milestone objectives of the preliminary hearing process in most cases are (a) to comprehend thoroughly the general nature and parameters of the dispute, (b) to effect the exchange of detailed statements of claims, damages, and defenses including legal authorities, (c) to manage the organization, exchange, and agreement on all possible factual information concerning the dispute, culminating in a written stipulation of agreed facts, (d) to reduce the scope of the dispute and eliminate minor or marginal claims and defenses if possible, (e) to prioritize the submission of information to the panel at the formal hearings, including focusing upon key issues first, and (f) to establish ground rules for the submission of information at the formal hearings.

Dealing with Difficulties

If extensive acrimony underlies the relationships among the parties or their attorneys, or if one or both parties appear substantially unprepared, all aspects of case management become more difficult. An unprepared party may choose to be uncooperative simply to delay the day of reckoning or to allow time to become prepared. Another party may believe that an obstructionist approach is in its best interest. A panel may not be able entirely to prevent these tactics or circumstance from occurring or to control them completely if they break out. Effective case management, nonetheless, must undertake to prevent or limit the extent of such conditions from disrupting the arbitration process. Proactive, rather than passive, management by the panel in such situations is almost always the more effective approach.[7]

There are numerous pure management techniques that may be considered to soften harsh attitudes exhibited by a party. One is to order an uncooperative party to submit factual summaries or direct testimony affidavits to support the facts underlying a palpably unreasonable position. The imposition of a more extensive writing requirement in place of live testimony may be sufficiently inconvenient to dissuade an unreasonable party from its uncooperative tactics. It also may shorten the hearings and provide more reliable and better organized submittal of information.

This technique, and others, to maintain control in difficult circumstances must be used carefully to ensure fairness and expedience. Probably more than in any other circumstance, a panel must be imaginative yet controlled in developing case management techniques where one or more of the parties is acting in an obstructive manner. It is often wise for a panel to caucus and discuss possible options before acting, but decisive management is called for in situations where one or both parties are acting unreasonably.

The skill of a panel in managing issue reduction and fact identification is perhaps the single most important factor in achieving effective case management, which in turn is the key to reducing arbitration time, costs, and inconvenience. A panel should not underestimate its own ability, with polite persistence, to achieve significant

---

[7] An arbitrator does not have the same powers of discipline or contempt held by a court but does possess considerable powers to control acrimony, lack of cooperativeness, and misconduct in the form of instructions concerning receipt of information about issues in dispute. Refer to C.I.D.R.P. Rules R-10, 25, 26, 29, 30, 31, 32, and L-5.

results during the preliminary hearing process, as well as throughout the formal hearings. Even if a panel is only marginally successful, good management will produce such collateral benefit as improved understanding of facts and issues being considered. Also, panelists will become, with the experience, more skilled case managers in the future.

Prototype Preliminary Hearing Schedule[8]

A. First Meeting of the Panel. Each panelist will have read the demand for arbitration and the response and will have a rudimentary understanding of the dispute. Prior to the first preliminary hearing, the panelists meet to discuss the principal elements of a prehearing management plan. The panel recognizes that its first objective is to learn in greater detail the nature and parameters of the dispute, which is the first objective of Rule L-4 (a). It decides to do the following before the first preliminary hearing:

- In a conference call with the parties, attempt to obtain a clear understanding of the claims and defenses;
- Instruct the claimant to submit in writing the liability basis of and damages resulting from each claim, together with any legal authorities it may wish to identify, by a certain date;
- Instruct the respondent to submit in writing each defense it will assert against each claim and damage assessment, together with any legal authorities the respondent may wish to identify, by a certain date; and
- Provide similar instructions for counterclaims.

The foregoing steps may require one or more months to accomplish, particularly if resubmittals are necessary. Bearing this in mind, a tentative date for the first preliminary hearing may be established.

B. First Preliminary Hearing. The agenda for the first preliminary hearing includes:

- A discussion of the parties' written statements of claims and defenses with the objective of converting these submittals into a

---

[8] The proposed number, timing, and subjects covered at each preliminary hearing is suggestive only and not intended as a rigid specification.

Joint Statement of claims and defenses that sets forth clearly the general nature and parameters of the dispute (this joint statement will not contain underlying facts);
- A discussion of Rule L-4 (b) and the best means to achieve a stipulation of uncontested facts;
- An instruction to the claimant to set forth each of the material facts on which it intends to rely to establish the liability and damages elements of each of its claims, by a certain date;
- An instruction to the respondent (a) to agree or disagree with each of the claimant's proposed facts and (b) to submit its own proposed facts in support of its defenses, by a second date; and
- An instruction to the claimant to agree or disagree with each of the respondent's proposed facts, by a third date.

C. Second Preliminary Hearing. The panel has reviewed, met, and discussed the fact submittals before the second preliminary hearing and decides to:

- Engage the parties in a thorough review of the fact submittals in an attempt to enlarge the number of agreed facts, reduce the number of outstanding issues, and arrive at a joint stipulation of facts;
- Instruct the claimant, by a certain date, to submit a proposed plan for the submission of factual information in support of its claims, i.e., the remaining or "disputed" facts, at formal hearings (the "claimant's proposed hearing plan"); and
- Instruct the respondent that its proposed hearing plan will be required no later than at the conclusion of the claimant's case.

D. Third Preliminary Hearing. The panel:

- Finalizes the joint statement of facts;
- Approves, or discusses possible improvements to, the claimant's proposed hearing plan, paying close attention to the organizational aspects of the plan, and searches for abbreviated methods for submittal of large quantities of detailed facts;
- Ensures that the hearing plan:
  (a) tracks the organizational format established in the joint statement of claims and defenses,

LARGE AND COMPLEX CASE MANAGEMENT

    (b) Is complete so that all information needed to establish claims and defenses is covered, and

    (c) Includes instructions for submittal of project documents, direct testimony affidavits, chalks and spreadsheets, and any other means for efficient transmission of necessary information to the panel.

- Reminds the parties that the rules of evidence do not apply in arbitration;
- Instructs the parties that direct testimony from live witnesses at the formal hearings will be permitted only at the conclusion of all other, more expeditious methods of information submittals;
- Receives relevant project documents, tables, spreadsheets, and chalks, all duly marked;
- Addresses the remaining requirements of Rule L-4; and
- Schedules the first two or three hearings.

II. Large-Case Management Techniques for Arbitrators

Now Is the Time to Control the Big Case

by Allen L. Overcash*

Large, complex construction cases require a considerable amount of management by arbitrators. The American Arbitration Association (AAA) recognized this when earlier this year, acting on recommendations of its National Construction ADR Task Force, it revised its construction arbitration rules to include a special "track" for large, complex construction cases involving claims in excess of $1 million.[1] While the AAA's new rules will vastly improve the process and increase the arbitrators' control over the large case, there are additional case management techniques discussed below that arbitrators can and should borrow from the judicial system that will aid in complex case management.

Normally the large, complex case deals with a construction project that has turned into a disaster and may even jeopardize the livelihood of one or more of the parties. This disaster spawns a major conflict in which virtually everything about the project is disputed. For example, a major defective specification claim may also involve a dispute over hundreds of changes by the owner or architect. The contractor, who faces a large loss on the project, is loath to compromise any of its claims. The owner and/or architect or engineer, both of whom face an uncertain potential liability, are concerned about establishing any precedent by acknowledging liability on even minor matters.

As a result of the primary disaster, there is a secondary disaster: a proliferation of issues to a degree that can overwhelm the trier-of-fact. This proliferation often spawns broad requests for document discovery and depositions and long lists of factual and expert witnesses.

With the parties unable to agree on or understand the nature of the major issues between them, they have little basis for any empathetic

---

* Allen L. Overcash is a partner at Woods & Aitken in Lincoln, Nebraska. He served as a member of the American Arbitration Association's Construction ADR Task Force.

[1] The revised rules established a three-track system which also includes a "fast track" for claims under $50,000 and a "regular track" for claims between $50,000 and $1 million.

exchanges over those issues. Therefore, the chance of settlement or using nonbinding ADR is unlikely. Consequently, the opportunity for an early settlement of the large case may be lost.

Revised AAA Construction Arbitration Rules

The AAA's new rules applicable to large, complex cases contain procedures that enable the arbitrator to better manage the large construction case. These procedures are mandatory for cases involving claims of more than $1 million, unless the parties agree otherwise. Parties may also elect to use these procedures for cases involving claims under $1 million or in non-monetary cases or in cases involving claims of undetermined amounts.[2]

An important management technique provided for in the new rules is an early preliminary conference after the selection of the arbitrators. At this conference the matters to be considered include, among other things: (1) service of a detailed statement of claims, damages and defenses, (2) a statement of the issues asserted by each party and positions with respect thereto, (3) the extent to which discovery will be conducted, (4) the exchange and pre-marking of documents each party believes may be offered at the hearing, (5) the identification and availability of witnesses, including experts, (6) the extent to which affidavits and depositions may be introduced, (7) the scheduling of the hearing, (8) whether there will be a stenographic or other record of the proceedings, and (9) the possibility of utilizing mediation or other methods of dispute resolution.

The new rules give the arbitrators more management authority. They allow the parties to agree to the extent of document discovery but also provide that the arbitrators may place limitations on that discovery if they deem it appropriate. Arbitrators also have the ability, upon good cause shown, to order depositions of persons with information necessary to resolve the case.

The new rules for large, complex cases are not intended to restrict the approaches arbitrators may use to administer cases. The rules expressly provide that arbitrators "shall take such steps as they deem necessary or desirable to avoid delay and to achieve a just, speedy and cost-effective resolution" of the case. Arbitrators, therefore, are

---

[2] They may also agree, prior to the appointment of the arbitrator, to eliminate, alter or modify any of the prescribed procedures. After appointment of the arbitrator, modifications to the procedures require the arbitrator's consent.

encouraged to adopt innovative procedures which are suited to expediting the particular case before them.

Pre-trial Judicial Management Techniques

Arbitrators should use their vast discretion to ensure that the large, complex case is handled as expeditiously and inexpensively as possible. There is no statutory or AAA rule that would prevent arbitrators from borrowing certain pretrial management techniques from the judiciary to more efficiently handle large, complex arbitration cases. Although much criticism of the court system has validity, that system has developed a number of techniques associated with the administration of large, complex cases that have merit and, in my view, have much to offer arbitration in the large case context.[3] Arbitrators can benefit from using these techniques and, in so doing, confine the hearing of the large case to manageable central issues. What are some of these techniques?

The Federal Judicial Center's Manual for Complex Litigation calls for an initial conference, which starts the process of identification, definition, and narrowing of the issues.[4] This is the "sine qua non of management of complex litigation." The Manual states, "unless the controverted issues have been identified and defined, the materiality of facts and the scope of discovery (and later of the trial) cannot be determined."[5] Furthermore, "early identification and clarification of issues is essential to meaningful and fair discovery control" enabling the court "to assess the materiality and relevance of proposed discovery."[6] The Manual advocates a discovery plan which is limited in time and quantity and is to take place according to a schedule.[7] It recommends additional conferences following the initial conference to monitor the progress of the case and address problems as

---

[3] *See Do We Need Special ADR Rules for Complex Construction Cases*, CONSTRUCTION LAWYER (Aug. 1991). This article was essentially a debate over arbitration rules among several prominent construction attorneys. While they differed over whether discovery in complex cases should be mandated, they all agreed that any limited discovery should follow a definition of the issues involved in the arbitration.

[4] MANUAL FOR COMPLEX LITIGATION, THIRD, § 21 (1995). Now in its third edition, the Manual devotes nearly 100 pages to pre-trial procedures. The initial conference generally is held within 30 to 60 days after the case is filed. § 21.11 at 37.

[5] *Id.*, § 21.31 at 47.
[6] *Id.*, § 21.41 at 55.
[7] *Id.*, § 21.422 at 57.

they arise.[8] It also allows for referral of issues to court-appointed experts or special masters as well as the use of magistrate judges.[9] The final pretrial conference requires detailed planning and disclosure of the evidence to be presented at the hearing.[10]

Another innovative technique is the concept of two-stage discovery.[11] It involves an initial conference at which the key issues in the case are identified and the amount of first-stage discovery (if, in fact, any discovery is necessary), is established. This is the minimal amount necessary before a realistic assessment of the strengths and weaknesses of the case can be made. Following completion of first-stage discovery, an ADR procedure best suited to the particular case is utilized in an effort to settle the case. If the case cannot be settled, it proceeds to the second-stage of discovery and trial.

The boards of contract appeals have also used extensive pre-trial orders to direct the parties toward limiting issues for trial. One such order is the so-called "Lacey Order."[12] Among other things, this order embraces the concept of bringing steady pressure to bear on the parties' counsel to reduce the contested issues in the case prior to trial. Each side is required to present detailed findings of fact to the board, with each side responding to the findings. Discovery is limited to the issues actually contested. Other pre-trial requirements include the identification of exhibits and witnesses, with the testimony of witnesses tied to the contested findings of fact.

These judicial approaches, which are by no means the only ones used to manage the complex case, embody certain common principles:

- There is an emphasis on active management. The judge is no longer a passive figure whose function is to observe the trial and issue rulings when called upon. That method of deciding cases has been abandoned. The judge must become involved in the case from its very start and manage all of the activities prior to the determination of the ultimate issues in the case. These

---

[8] *Id.*, § 21.22 at 45.
[9] *Id.*, § 21.5 at 109.
[10] *Id.*, § 21.6 at 116.
[11] Robert F. Pecham, *A Judicial Response to the Cost of Litigation: Case Management, Two-stage Discovery Planning and Alternative Dispute Resolution*, 37 RUTGERS L. REV. 253 (1985).
[12] *See* Steven L. Schooner, *The Lacey Order: Control of Complex Litigation Before the BCAs*, CONSTRUCTION LAW (Apr. 1989).

activities cannot be left to the attorneys. The judge must also become involved in the factual issues well before the trial.
- There is a focus on early definition of the issues through statements by the parties of the ultimate facts that they each expect to be found.
- There is a need to define the issues prior to discovery. There is a general recognition that mandatory discovery has not been an unmitigated blessing, particularly in large cases where legal budgets can support numerous depositions. Wide-ranging discovery is expensive. Unless it is confined to a particular purpose, discovery tends to take on a life of its own, which may not help the resolution of the case. Many decry the excesses of discovery, but few have proposed constructive solutions to the problem. One means of controlling discovery's excesses is to confine discovery to the real differences between the parties over ultimate facts. This necessitates the early involvement of the judge.
- There is a need to eliminate as many factual disputes as possible before the trial. Many factual disputes between parties to a complex construction case are simply not practical for the judge to hear for a number of reasons: They are not significant in size; they bear little, if any, relationship to the major dollar issues between the parties; and the time needed to devote to them far outweighs their importance to the ultimate decision of the case. The judge needs to be involved before the trial not only in the definition of the issues but in the elimination of issues which would encumber the trial. This effort to reduce the number of issues may also involve neutrals such as special masters who are familiar with the industry and can lead the parties by recommendation or decision (which, while not binding, will be reported to the judge or jury) to a resolution of certain of the issues between them.
- There is a recognition of the need to control the conduct of the trial itself. The trial should be limited to the evidence pertinent to the major issues reasonably disputed by the parties. While everyone would agree with this objective, it is important to understand that it cannot be attained solely through rulings made after the trial starts. Without early involvement of the judge in the issues in advance of the trial, efforts at controlling evidence become a patchwork affair.

Applicability to Arbitration

The applicability of these principles to arbitration proceedings involving large cases is obvious. For example, since initial arbitration demands contain even less definition of the issues than legal pleadings, there is a need to have these demands immediately supplemented by detailed statements of ultimate facts.

These statements should be analyzed in detail by the arbitrators. Only after they are satisfied that there are real factual issues between the parties that will be dispositive of the case, and the parties understand what those issues are, should discovery proceed. Discovery should be confined to the identified factual issues. In addition, the arbitrators should seek to bring the parties to mediation or another nonbinding ADR procedure following limited discovery early in the case.

If the case cannot be entirely settled, a strong effort should be made to settle issues which would encumber the hearing. The arbitrators should consider the use of other neutrals as factfinders or facilitators to support this effort. Minihearings might be held to dispose of issues not central to the proceeding.

The arbitration hearing should be the final step in a process of winnowing down the issues and the evidence. If the arbitrators aggressively follow these recommendations, there should be few surprises at the pre-hearing conference. The conference should be used to carefully structure a hearing whose parameters were set long ago. Arbitrators are concerned with the issue of evidence exclusion, one of the few grounds upon which an award can be overturned. If prior to the hearing the issues are well-defined and evidence is restricted to those issues, evidence exclusion should not become a legal problem.

There often has been a gross imbalance between the amount of time spent by arbitrators before and after the hearing. The first day of the hearing is too late to begin to control the large case. By that time, the parties will have spent their money and time on discovery, hearing preparation and selection of evidence. Time spent before the hearing in an effort to limit the issues, discovery efforts and proof will save time at the hearing as well as the total time spent on the case. The AAA's revised Construction Industry Arbitration Rules take a significant step in this direction, opening the door to arbitrators to effectively control the large construction case. These procedures and the others discussed above give arbitrators the needed tools to effectively and efficiently resolve complex construction cases.

III. Selecting a Mediator for a Complex Dispute

Choosing the Right Mediator for a Complex Construction Dispute

by Joseph C. Malpasuto*

In our private lives most of us would not use an internist to perform open-heart surgery, engage a general law practitioner to represent us in a complex tax matter, or retain an architect to perform engineering calculations. Instead, we would seek a highly skilled professional with specific knowledge of our problem and the ability to remedy it, and then only after considerable thought and research.

Yet, when faced with having to choose a mediator for a complex construction dispute, many attorneys and their clients either don't know (or underestimate) just how important it is for the mediator to have construction experience and knowledge of construction law. So they end up selecting a mediator based only on the candidate's mediation, litigation or judicial experience. When the mediator is chosen without regard to construction experience and knowledge of the relevant law, the odds are that the mediation will fail to achieve the desired result. This article explains why selecting a construction lawyer with experience in construction can enhance the likelihood of having a more efficient and successful mediation.

Why Construction Experience?

Complex construction disputes exist in a world of their own. They often involve technical construction matters, myriad parties (owners, contractors, subcontractors, sureties, design professionals and others) and a specialized body of law. To understand the dispute usually requires knowledge of construction industry practices, terminology and the law pertaining to construction matters. Thus, even though in mediation, the mediator does not make any dispositive decisions as to the merits, it is

---

[*] Mr. Malpasuto is of counsel with Monteleone & McCrory, LLP, in Los Angeles. He has been a construction attorney since 1975. He is also an arbitrator and mediator on the AAA's roster of construction neutrals. In addition, he has served on mediation panels of the Los Angeles County Bar Association and the state of California. Mr. Malpasuto has spent 16 years in the construction materials manufacturing business.

nonetheless desirable for the mediator to have this knowledge in order for the mediation to progress efficiently.

At its root, mediation is a process in which the parties, with the assistance of the mediator, assess the risk of the likely success or failure of their respective positions on the issues in dispute, coupled with the cost attendant to litigation if the dispute does not settle. Is it more likely than not that, as to the key issues and the case as a whole, the plaintiff (or one or more defendants) would prevail? What are the risks on each side? What is the extent of potential liability of each party? If the case were litigated, what would be the estimated costs each would incur, taking into account attorney's and expert's fees, the expense of conducting thorough discovery, and the time spent by that party's employees in preparing for and attending the trial? Finally, are any of these costs recoverable, such as expert witness fees or deposition transcript costs?

How can a mediator who is unfamiliar with construction practices and terminology assist parties to a construction dispute in assessing risk? Any risk assessment requires an understanding of the facts (which are often complicated as well as in dispute) and the practices of the industry. It is true that mediators usually ask parties for mediation statements before the mediation begins in order to prepare for the process. But these statements provide only a limited education. Parties should desire to have a mediator who already has knowledge of the context in which this dispute has arisen.

The mediation starts when the parties, their attorneys and the mediator meet in a joint session at the outset of the mediation. During this session, the mediator usually will make a statement describing how mediation works, explaining his or her role in the process, and summarizing in brief his or her credentials. Then the parties will hear, maybe for the first time, the other parties' version of the case. In complex cases these presentations often are made by counsel and not uncommonly by experts the parties have retained. The purpose of the joint session is not only to define the issues in dispute, but to provide each party with an opportunity to evaluate the opposition's position and its advocacy skills first hand.

The real risk assessment actually takes place in private caucuses. In these sessions the mediator meets separately with each side, shuttling back and forth between them. This is when the mediator discusses the issues raised in the joint session and explores their factual and legal basis. Because the matters the parties separately discuss in private caucuses with the mediator are considered confidential and generally may not be disclosed in a subsequent trial, the caucusing sessions provide the best opportunity for the parties to realistically evaluate the strengths and weaknesses of their respective positions. By playing the role of devil's advocate, the mediator probes the basis for these positions to assist the parties in assessing whether to alter their stance and identify potential solutions.

An effective mediator must have the ability to quickly grasp the facts and issues, and the parties must have confidence in the mediator's abilities. There is no doubt that a mediator who knows construction first hand will readily understand the facts and issues at stake, and appreciate their significance to the outcome of the dispute. This mediator will be better able to have effective discussions with the parties' attorneys, their experts and their sureties and insurers.

A mediator whose sole knowledge about construction derives from the parties' mediation statements will likely miss the significance of many technical issues. How can this mediator accurately convey each side's position to the other as he or she shuttles back and forth between them in an attempt to create movement in the mediation? How can the parties have confidence in this mediator's ability to act as a sounding board regarding the strengths or weaknesses of the parties' positions?

Why Construction Law Knowledge?

But the mediator should have more than just construction experience. The ability to mediate a complex construction case is greatly diminished without knowledge of the legal landscape pertaining to construction disputes. Thus, parties should not think that anyone with legal knowledge has the requisite credentials to mediate a complex construction dispute. A mediator with an excellent grasp of the law generally, but without an understanding of construction law as well as the technical aspects of construction is, in my view, not the right choice either. I believe the most potentially helpful mediator should be familiar with the legal issues involved in construction disputes and the law that governs them.

What Construction Mediators Must Know

Some of the subjects that successful construction mediators understand include: how extended job site and home office overhead costs are determined; the suitability and applicability of "total cost," "modified total cost," and "jury verdict" approaches to calculating damages; the propriety of using the "cardinal change "or "abandonment" theory to avoid strict adherence to contract terms and conditions; the legal effect of warranties relating to the correctness of plans and specifications; the effectiveness of a waiver of warranty in private and public construction projects; the legal effect of a change order containing "full and complete compensation" language; the legal authority to direct extra work or issue change orders in public versus private projects; the legal rights, obligations and liabilities of the contractor in design-build projects; the right to withdraw a subcontractor's or materialman's bid on public and private projects; how rights of indemnity work; methods of calculating delay damages; the use of "critical path" analyses to determine the cause of delays and the party at fault; theories of liquidated damages; and the rights, remedies and liabilities as between insurers, insureds and reinsurers. Without a working knowledge of these and other concepts a mediator cannot realistically assist the parties in their evaluation of the risks in the case.

Take an owner who seeks to recover liquidated damages for delays both in the completion of project milestones and the project as a whole. The prime contractor and its subcontractors claim the owner is responsible for the delays because the plans and specifications resulted in the contractor having to perform extra work, which took additional time. The prime contractor also is seeking indemnification from the subcontractors if any delays were the subcontractor's fault. At the mediation, each party's expert presents a "schedule analysis" and each one uses a different type of logic. For example, one takes the position that both the owner and contractor are responsible for a delay in a single item of work (concurrent delay), while the other assigns responsibility to the contractor for one item of work and to the owner for another (i.e., nonconcurrent delay).

It is the mediator's job to work with these issues in such a way as to encourage the parties to reach a resolution. If the dispute involves claims of delay damages, the mediator must understand "critical path" issues, the concept of "concurrency" in the assignment of responsibility for the delays and the logic behind the parties' respective schedule analyses. Only a mediator who understands this could help the parties see that one analysis is less likely to be accepted than the other.

In short, if the parties to a complex construction dispute are to maximize their opportunity to achieve a settlement, they should select a mediator with the greatest knowledge of construction procedures, practices and law.

IV. Effective Mediation Techniques for Complex Cases

Effective Mediation Techniques in Complex Multiparty Synthetic Stucco Cases

by C. Allen Gibson, Jr.*

Construction disputes have always been uniquely suited to resolution through ADR. Mediation has become an increasingly important tool to resolve disputes between parties who value their business relationships, appreciate the hidden costs of continuing the dispute, and desire to put the dispute behind them. Although individual homeowner plaintiffs may not be motivated by these incentives, mediation can work for them.

This article offers a proven technique for mediating a type of complex construction dispute, often involving home owners, that has surged in recent years. These cases involve the application of allegedly defective synthetic stucco to residential or commercial buildings. Like other complex disputes, the parties in the stucco cases often have differing interests. Because they are not usually bound by arbitration agreements, the dispute invariably ends up in litigation. I became involved as mediator when these cases were referred to mediation by the court.

The plaintiff is almost always the owner of the affected residence or building, which often appears to be problem-free based on a visual inspection of the exterior. However, forensic investigation frequently reveals that unseen water intrusion has occurred and that a myriad of problems exist within the walls of the structure.

The usual cast of defendants includes the architect, the general contractor, the manufacturer of the synthetic stucco and the subcontractor that applied it. Sometimes a stucco supplier also will be named. Because it is often difficult to tell whether the water intrusion is from some other source, a window manufacturer and roofer may also be parties to the lawsuit. The defendants typically assert claims, cross-claims and third-party claims, creating a complex web of pleadings.

---

* C. Allen Gibson Jr. is a partner in the Charleston, S.C., law firm of Buist, Moore, Smythe & McGee, P.A. He serves on the American Arbitration Association's roster of mediators and arbitrators. He is chair-elect of the ABA Forum on the Construction Industry.

A notable feature in some of the residential synthetic stucco cases is that a cluster of cases may involve the same group of defendants and attorneys, although each plaintiff's case may have some unique aspects. Typically, when insurance is available, the same insurance companies are involved in case after case. In some of these situations, the companies insuring the builder, the manufacturer and the subcontractor have prearranged a division of responsibility for all cases in a particular region. However, most of the time there is no agreement of this type.

When a case comes to the mediator, each party will have its own agenda. For example, the plaintiff may have preconceived ideas about who should pay the greatest share of any ultimate settlement. Meanwhile, the defendants have probably reached their own conclusions. For one thing, they almost always maintain that the plaintiff's problems can be corrected for much less than is claimed. If the defendants (or their insurers) have not already agreed to an allocation of responsibility for any settlement, one or more defendants might think or say, "I'm not willing to pay more than what X pays."

In traditional mediation, all parties know what each party is offering to contribute to the settlement. There is a tendency on the part of each defendant to evaluate its offer in relation to that of other defendants. This is often detrimental to a timely resolution of the dispute, since it requires two battles to be fought: one to determine how much to pay to satisfy the plaintiff, the other to resolve the dispute among the defendants as to their varying contributions. It distracts from the ultimate goal when the parties begin arguing "relative" positions. There are, of course, times when such peer pressure can be helpful, but for the most part it is not conducive to achieving an overall resolution.

My approach to mediating these cases addresses this specific problem. The key is to obtain each defendant's commitment to make a fair contribution towards a reasonable settlement, while keeping the plaintiff focused on the overall reasonableness of the settlement amount.

Methodology

The mediator's first goal is to obtain agreement from all defendants that the plaintiff's claim has merit and to place a settlement value on that claim. It is important to reach this point without discussing the allocation of responsibility with respect to any individual defendant. Once the defendants agree on a reasonable settlement value, and perhaps discuss whether they believe the plaintiff would actually accept that figure in settlement, the mediator meets privately with each defendant, encouraging each one to make a significant initial offer. Each of these offers is "blind" in that it is kept confidential from the other defendants and the plaintiff. Once all the defendants have made blind offers, they are told the aggregate amount, which becomes their "initial collective offer."

The mediator brings this offer to the plaintiff without disclosing how much each individual defendant has offered to contribute. At this point, the plaintiff must be encouraged to react by making a reasonable initial demand. If a demand was made going into the mediation, the plaintiff must be encouraged to move from that position. The plaintiff's demand in response to the defendants' initial collective offer must give the mediator the ability to maintain optimism that the case will settle.

The exchange of information about the initial collective offer and the plaintiff's demand allows the focus of the mediation to change from how large the offer and demand will be to the difference between them. This makes it possible to keep the defendants from becoming overly concerned with the plaintiff's demand, especially when the difference between the initial collective offer and the amount the plaintiff is asking for is smaller than the collective offer itself.

In the second round of private meetings, each defendant must react to the plaintiff's demand by increasing its offer. The mediator can usually identify some defendants who are approaching their maximum contributions. These are often the smaller defendants with less responsibility or involvement in the project, who have made more significant contributions relative to their exposure in the first round of private meetings with the mediator. It is helpful to try to obtain maximum offers from those parties. This allows the mediator more time to spend in later meetings with the parties who will contribute the larger portion of the overall settlement.

At this stage the mediator must work quickly with each of the parties, focusing completely on each defendant's offer. In multiparty mediation, one of the most detrimental factors to settlement is the long period of inactivity and inattention that results if the mediator is unable to return to each party within a reasonable period of time. It is also critical for the mediator to help the parties avoid the natural inclination to compete with each other, wondering how they are faring relative to one another. This is especially true when the same parties have been involved in other mediations and are still complaining about how one party did not pay its fair share in the last case.

Sometimes a defendant in the case has multiple years of insurance coverage with different insurers. Prior to the mediation, these insurers may or may not have agreed to an allocation of responsibility for the portion of the settlement to be paid by their insured. If they have not, at this point it is best to try to obtain their agreement to the amount of the contribution to be offered on the insured's behalf, leaving the allocation issue to be decided later. If they can agree on this, they can frequently agree to an allocation on their own, with minor assistance from the mediator. Alternatively, they can agree to mediate or arbitrate the allocation issue at a later time.

At the end of the second round of private meetings with the individual defendants, the mediator knows the revised offer of each defendant, the sum of which becomes the defendants' "second collective offer." This aggregate offer is, in a sense, "double blind" because the individual contributions that comprise it, and the collective offer itself, are not revealed to all the defendants.

Some defendants resist this approach at the beginning, but they usually go along with it because of the emphasis that is placed on whether each individual is willing to contribute a reasonable amount to resolving the case, without regard to what others are paying or the overall payment to the plaintiff.

After the mediator has transmitted the second collective offer, the plaintiff must respond with a revised demand that reduces the difference between them. To provoke movement in this direction, the mediator may discuss with the plaintiff the scope of needed repairs, the plaintiff's estimate of the cost of repairs compared with the defendants' estimates, and insurance coverage issues that might make collection of a judgment problematic. The mediator may also make the usual pro-settlement arguments, such as the desirability of avoiding the uncertainties of trial, the savings in time and expense, and the unique ability to resolve the matter on the parties' own terms.

Keeping the plaintiff's revised demand from the defendants avoids prompting judgmental evaluations of the plaintiff's position. Instead of disclosing this figure, the mediator discusses with the defendants separately and collectively the amount needed to settle the case. In these discussions, the mediator may compare the plaintiff's revised demand to the settlement value that the defendants earlier placed on the claim. By focusing on the small gap that should now divide the parties, and emphasizing the positive progress that has been made, the mediator can usually motivate the defendants to make their "top-dollar" offers. Resolution is achieved when the plaintiff is persuaded that there is no more money to be gained from further mediation efforts.

The settlement agreement is reduced to writing and signed by all of the parties. At that point the total settlement the plaintiff will receive is revealed to all of the defendants. However, the confidentiality of each defendant's contribution is still maintained. This is often important to defendants who thought they were paying too much and those who thought they got a "good deal."

I use separate settlement sheets for each defendant in which each signs off on the amount it will pay. There is one master agreement signed by everyone indicating the overall amount to be paid to the plaintiff. The defendants' settlement checks are made payable to a trust or escrow account maintained by the mediator, who writes one check to the plaintiff once all of the defendants' checks have cleared. As a result, neither the plaintiff nor the plaintiff's attorney knows how much each defendant contributed to the settlement.

I have used this approach in numerous synthetic stucco mediations and have found it to be a successful way to achieve a negotiated resolution. It may also be useful whenever a series of cases involve the same defendants, or in any multiparty case in which the defendants are sensitive about their respective contributions.

Chapter Eight

International Construction Dispute Resolution

I. Strengths and Weaknesses of the U.S. and English Systems

Comparing Dispute Review Boards and Adjudication

*by James P. Groton, Robert A. Rubin & Bettina Quintas**

The construction industry has always had a special need for effective mechanisms to promptly resolve disputes. Over 100 years ago the industry developed a two-step process for resolving disputes at the project site: Whenever a problem arose that the parties could not resolve themselves, the project architect or engineer (A/E) would make an objective nonbinding ruling. If that ruling did not resolve the problem, the parties could refer the issue to a relatively informal ad hoc arbitration process to obtain a binding decision.

This approach served the industry reasonably well when used to resolve single-issue disputes shortly after they arose. Over time, however, decisions by the A/E ceased to be given the weight that they had traditionally been accorded. Also, arbitration involving large construction projects tended to become more formal and complex, with the parties accumulating their disputes over the course of construction for a massive arbitration at the end of the project.

The desire for a quicker "real time" resolution of construction disputes led to the development of the dispute review board (DRB) in the United States and the adjudication process in England. This article looks at both processes and evaluates their relative strengths and weaknesses.

---

* Messrs. Groton and Rubin are, respectively, president and immediate past president of the American College of Construction Lawyers. Ms. Quintas is an attorney with the New York City Transit Authority. This article is adapted from lectures presented at the Forbes Infrastructure 2000 Conference, the DRB Foundation Annual Conference, and the International Construction Law 2000 Conference.

Development of DRBs

The U.S. construction industry has experimented with "standing neutrals" of various types, including project arbitrators, project mediators and DRBs. A project mediator facilitates negotiations while a project arbitrator makes final and binding decisions. A DRB, on the other hand, issues nonbinding recommendations or decisions.

The parties appoint the standing neutral or DRB members in the contract or at the commencement of construction. In each case, the person or persons selected are kept informed about the project and its progress, and are supposed to be available on relatively short notice to help resolve any disputes that arise. Of the three types of standing neutral, only DRBs have been frequently used because of their remarkable success in resolving disputes between the owner and contractor.

First used in the 1970s on tunneling projects, the DRB process also has been employed on other types of construction, including heavy civil engineering projects, industrial projects and conventional buildings. Virtually all DRBs have operated under procedures developed by the American Society of Civil Engineers' Guide Specification for DRBs.[1]

As of September 2000, DRBs were planned or used on 662 projects having a combined construction value of $35 billion. Some 841 disputes were settled after referral to DRBs and only twenty-five referred disputes were challenged. Virtually all of these were resolved shortly after litigation commenced.

Development of Adjudication

The construction industry in England also experimented with standing neutrals, but it favored making the neutral's decisions binding on the parties, subject to review, appeal or de novo hearing in litigation (or arbitration if authorized), usually after the project is completed. This process, named "adjudication," was introduced in the 1970s primarily to resolve subcontractor payment disputes in the building sector.

---

[1] MATYAS ET AL., CONSTRUCTION DISPUTE REVIEW BOARD MANUAL (McGraw-Hill 1996). The American Arbitration Association recently issued guide specifications and procedures for DRBs. *See* Robert Smith & Robert Rubin, *A New Look At DRBs: AAA Offers New DRB Roster And Protocol*, 5 ADR CURRENTS, No. 4 (Dec. 2000-Feb. 2001).

The concept was expanded to cover a wide range of construction projects and disputes when Parliament enacted the Housing Grants, Construction and Regeneration Act of 1996 (HGCRA). This Act, which applies to most commercial construction contracts entered into after May 1, 1998, gives any party to such a contract the right to use statutory adjudication.[2]

A contract that is subject to the HGCRA must comply with eight criteria.[3] These criteria require the contract to:

- Enable a party to give notice at any time of its intention to refer a dispute to adjudication;
- Provide a timetable with the aim of securing the appointment of, and referral of the dispute, to the adjudicator within seven days of such notice;
- Require the adjudicator to issue a decision within 28 days after the dispute has been referred;
- Allow the adjudicator to extend the 28-day period by up to 14 days with the claimant's consent;
- Impose a duty on the adjudicator to act impartially;
- Enable the adjudicator to take the initiative in ascertaining the facts and law;
- Provide that the adjudicator's decision is binding until the dispute is finally determined by legal proceedings or arbitration (if the contract provides for arbitration or the parties otherwise agree to arbitrate);
- Provide that the adjudicator is not liable for acts or omissions in the discharge of the adjudicator's functions unless done in bad faith, and that any employee or agent of the adjudicator is summarily protected from liability.

The HGCRA has brought about a dramatic escalation in the use of adjudication. Hundreds of disputes are resolved each year by adjudicators. Based on available data, less than 1% of these decisions have been appealed to litigation or arbitration.

---

[2] Exempted projects involve such industries as oil, gas, chemicals, pharmaceuticals and water.

[3] If the contract does not meet these criteria, then another detailed statutory scheme promulgated by government regulation applies.

Comparing the Processes

There are significant differences between the DRB process and adjudication. Some of these differences suggest that adjudication offers a speedier decision while the DRB offers a higher quality decision.

Timing of Decision. The fact that adjudicators are subject to strict time limits, having to decide a dispute relatively quickly (within 28 to 42 days), indicates that a quicker decision is more common in that process. DRBs have no required time limit to meet when it comes to rendering a decision, although in practice DRB decisions are usually issued within two months.

Selection Process. Factors that may influence the quality of the DRB decision are that DRB members are mutually selected by the parties, serve for the life of the project and are chosen for their construction expertise and integrity. These factors tends to generate party confidence in the DRB and motivate the parties to maintain the board member's respect.

By contrast, in adjudication a nominating body may select the adjudicator instead of the parties. The nominating body may be an association of construction professionals, such as "quantity surveyors," architects or engineers, or an association of lawyers. The nomination typically follows the profession of the nominating body. This method of selecting the adjudicator is used in small cases.[4] It is also used in large cases when the person the parties selected as adjudicator cannot serve. Since the adjudicator serves only for a single dispute, the parties lack motivation to stay in this person's good graces for the life of the project.

Relevant Construction Experience. The quality of a decision is likely to be higher if the neutral has experience in the type of construction at issue. Because of the way an adjudicator often is selected, that person may not have construction experience that meshes with the particular project or dispute. Compare that with DRB members who usually have the relevant type of construction expertise.

Knowledge of the Project. The neutral's familiarity with the project and the parties also may affect the quality of the decision. The adjudicator obtains all knowledge of the project and the parties after the matter is referred to adjudication. In the case of the DRB, board members are briefed at the beginning of the project, make site visits and receive

---

[4] In large cases, the parties typically appoint an experienced construction lawyer who has been trained and accredited as an adjudicator to serve in this role.

progress reports. They have the opportunity to observe the parties over a long period of time. As a result they have a global view of the project and its problems when called upon to decide a dispute; this gives them a definite "learning-curve" advantage over adjudicators.

Due Process. A DRB will hold a hearing on each dispute that comes before, it. A hearing is not required in adjudication, although the adjudicator must act fairly. Thus, the DRB process may afford the parties a greater opportunity to be heard.

Conclusion

The DRB and adjudication processes both achieve their principal objective, which is to resolve project disputes on a "real time" basis. Both processes also have the potential to deter disputes. There was concern early on that the ready availability of a DRB would attract disputes. In practice, just the opposite has occurred. Although "non-events" are difficult to measure, the existence of the DRB seems to have had a positive effect, giving the parties an incentive to resolve disputes themselves.

Because the DRB process offers a high quality decision by three selected experts, it seems better suited to the resolution of complex technical disputes between the owner and contractor. In practice, DRBs are only called upon to decide disputes between these parties and they rarely address payment disputes. Adjudicators often decide payment issues. Moreover, they can deal with contract disputes between any participants in the project, including consultants and subcontractors.

Although only a small percentage of adjudicator decisions have been appealed, surveys indicate that users of adjudication have had a mixed reaction to the process. The experience of some users suggests that because adjudication results in a binding decision that produces a winner and a loser, it increases "adversarialism." Also, in adjudication, there is the risk that a party can "ambush" the other by fully preparing its position and then demanding adjudication; or fearing ambush, prematurely precipitate the adjudication process. There is no evidence that a DRB has ever been so used. This is probably because, as noted above, the parties wish to maintain the respect of the expert DRB panel; that respect might lessen or even disappear if the parties used the DRB process for strategic purposes.

Based on anecdotal reports, since hard data are lacking, party satisfaction with DRBs is high. Parties who have used the process on one project tend to use it repeatedly. We attribute the high level of satisfaction to the nonbinding nature of the DRB's recommendation (compared to the adjudicator's decision, which is temporarily binding); the mutual selection of DRB members by the parties; the DRB members' experience in construction; and their familiarity with the project and the project participants.

Another factor potentially contributing to party satisfaction is that nonbinding DRB decisions deal mainly with issues of entitlement, not "quantum," so that there is no clear winner or loser. This gives the parties the opportunity to take charge of the dispute resolution process themselves and negotiate their own solution. This also tends to enhance the relationship between the parties.

We must acknowledge, however, that the success of the DRB may also be attributable to the fact that both participants voluntarily chose to use it. In adjudication, it takes only one party to initiate the process.

Certainly empirical data needs to be collected about both processes in order to develop more rigorous conclusions about their value.

Results Achieved from Dispute Review Boards and Adjudication

Dispute Review Board	Adjudication
DRB decisions are rarely challenged. Those that are challenged are usually resolved quickly.	Adjudication decisions are challenged less than 1% of the time.
A nonbinding DRB decision on entitlement, not "quantum," encourages the parties to negotiate a mutually satisfactory final resolution.	A temporarily binding decision usually resolves the dispute. There is no immediate relief from an "incorrect" decision.
Parties are generally satisfied with the results of the DRB process.	Studies indicate that users have had mixed reactions to the results of adjudication.
The DRB process tends to improve project relationships and reduce adversarial attitudes.	There is some evidence that the adjudication process accentuates "adversarialism."

II. Dispute Resolution Advisors in Hong Kong

The Dispute Resolution Adviser as an ADR Method in Hong Kong Construction Disputes[†]

by John W.K. Luk* & W.T. Wong**

In recent years, the Architectural Services Department (ASD) of the government of Hong Kong, through agreements made with some main contractors, introduced on a trial basis the practice of using a dispute resolution adviser (DRA) on construction projects for the purpose of reducing construction contract disputes. Initial indications are that the DRA system is useful in preventing and resolving disputes. The presence of the DRA has a significant impact upon the parties and their efforts at cooperation. As a result, the Hong Kong government is considering implementing the DRA in important construction projects involving contracts above a certain sum of money.

Rationale behind the DRA System

The DRA system was implemented by the ASD, first in the Queen Mary Hospital (QMH) refurbishment project in 1992 on a trial basis and was used again in the Queen Elizabeth Hospital (QEH) refurbishment project in 1993. According to ASD senior executives, the DRA system was implemented to respond to the changing characteristics of the construction industry in Hong Kong. Previously, Hong Kong contractors were not claim conscious. However, the Hong Kong construction industry gradually became more mature and internationalized and construction projects became more complicated and larger in scale. As a result, many construction disputes occurred in the public sector in the

---

[†] This article is adapted from an article published in ASIA ENGINEER.
* A chartered civil and structural engineer, and a barrister and arbitrator, Dr. John W.K. Luk is a senior executive and legal adviser with Sun Hung Kai Properties Ltd. in Hong Kong. He is a past president of the Hong Kong Institution of Engineers and currently serves on the panel of the Chartered Institute of Arbitrators (Hong Kong) and the AAA.
** W.T. Wong is a senior executive with Sun Hung Kai Properties Ltd. and a member of the Chartered Institute of Building. He is a former chairman of the Building Division of the Hong Kong Institute of Engineers.

late 1970s and continued to arise throughout the 1980s and 1990s. This trend has made construction projects in Hong Kong unnecessarily costly and time consuming.

As the biggest employer in the Hong Kong construction industry, the government tries to make the best use of its resources in public sector projects, which includes avoiding unnecessary disputes. It also tries to strike a fair balance between it, as the employer, and the contractors, seeking to avoid causing the contractors undue hardship. It is under these circumstances that the ASD tried out the DRA system.

By adopting the DRA system, it was hoped that the following goals could be achieved. First, site-level disputes could be prevented, reduced or resolved with the assistance of the DRA. Second, claims and valuation problems could be determined as early as possible. This would avoid the problems of missing records and the unavailability of persons familiar with the matter, which often occurs in protracted litigation. Furthermore, all parties concerned would know what the situation was. Third, budgetary and time control by the employer would be enhanced, since at every step the financial and time implications of valuations would be accurately known. Fourth, the staff of the parties would be encouraged to work in an atmosphere of good faith, minimizing unnecessary personal conflicts.

The DRA System

The following is a general description of the features and operation of the DRA system derived from the contract conditions in the hospital projects.

Appointment of the DRA. The DRA, who is an individual with general construction experience and knowledge and dispute resolution skills, is jointly selected and appointed by the government and the contractor at contract commencement. Selection of the DRA may be by agreement between the parties or through a ranking system. If the parties cannot agree on a suitable DRA within a specified period, then the DRA is chosen by the Hong Kong International Arbitration Centre, which maintains panels of mediators and arbitrators.

Familiarization and Monthly Site Meeting. At the beginning of the project, the DRA has to spend a sufficient amount of time on site to become familiar with the parties concerned, who include representatives from the project consultants, the contractor and some or all of the specialist subcontractors and the hospital management. The DRA also has to become familiar with the construction, design and program of the project.

The DRA has monthly meetings with the ASD and the contractor to attempt to resolve problems that arise before they become formal disputes and to foresee future problems. The DRA will meet more frequently if either the employer or the contractor request such a meeting in writing.

Notice of Dispute. The employer and the contractor are required to negotiate any dispute in the twenty-eight days that follow the architect's decision, order, direction or certificate, or the surveyor's certificate or valuation. If the site-level representatives cannot settle the dispute through negotiation, the aggrieved party may serve a written notice of dispute following the termination of negotiations but not later than the end of this 28-day period. If the notice is not timely served, the architect's decision, instruction, order, direction or certificate, or the surveyor's certificate or valuation, shall become final and binding. After the notice is served, the DRA and the site-level representatives have fourteen days to resolve the dispute.

DRA's Report to Senior Officers. If the dispute cannot be resolved at site level within fourteen days of the service of the notice of dispute, the DRA will send to the employer's and the contractor's non-site senior officers a written report containing an analysis of the dispute, the key issues and the DRA's perception as to the obstacles to settlement. The DRA will meet with the senior officers only at their written request.

Short-form Arbitration. If the dispute is still not settled within fourteen days of the date of service of the DRA's report, the DRA may recommend to the parties another form of dispute resolution. In the absence of settlement or of the adoption of another dispute resolution approach, a short-form arbitration will then have to be conducted. This is to take place within twenty-eight days of the date that senior officer settlement efforts have terminated.

The arbitrator will be selected by the parties to the dispute. The DRA assists the parties in choosing the arbitrator. If the parties cannot agree, the DRA will select an arbitrator from the list that the employer and the contractor were considering or from a list that the DRA developed.

Views of the Participants

There were more than 333 architect instructions in the QMH project and over 100 such instructions in the QEH project up to the date we interviewed the major participants to determine their views of the DRA system. Despite the complexity and difficulty of these projects, no formal notice of dispute had been given as of that time. Yet, this might not be regarded as conclusive of the success of the DRA system.

In general, all of the participants interviewed were quite positive about the system. ASD, the DRAs and the consultants all shared the opinion that the "time limits" for claims by the contractor and for valuation by the project team were very important for the system to be effective. The DRAs also remarked that these "time limits" and the provision for short-form arbitration formed the vital parts of the DRA system.

The DRAs thought the system was particularly effective in preventing disputes from arising. Although there had been no formal notice of dispute, there were a number of potential problems which were successfully resolved before they developed into formal disputes.

The contractors expressed the view that the DRA system could resolve disputes at an early stage and would make their work easier and more efficient.

Some of the consultants observed that the DRA acted like a monitor to a class or lubricant to machinery, making the different components work more smoothly. Some, however, opined that the mere adoption of the DRA system alone would not eliminate or even reduce construction disputes in a complicated construction project, and that due consideration would have to be given to other factors.

Impact of the DRA System upon Parties

ASD observed that project team members were under pressure to produce information and documents on time, partly because of the "time limit" provisions in the system. In addition, it found that the staff involved in decision-making tended to make a greater effort in their deliberations. ASD also noted that the contractor tended to discuss problems more openly with the project team, in and out of the presence of the DRA.

In general, it seemed that the professional project teams and the contractors' project teams cooperated in good faith and concentrated more on technical matters rather than on personal conflicts.

The DRAs observed that sometimes their mere presence in the negotiation meeting would cause an apparently unreasonable party to back down so that a compromise was achieved by the parties without the actual intervention of the DRA.

The contractors noted that when the DRA was present, the parties tried to behave themselves. The contractors were deterred from over-claiming, while the project consultant team was more reasonable in dealing with the contractor.

The consultants found that with the system, they were more cooperative and worked harder to produce necessary information and documents, placing a greater burden on staff resources. Also, the consultants were less defensive, particularly in the assessment of additional costs and time, as they could rely on the opinion of the DRA as an independent third party. They also observed that with the presence of the DRA, the contractor tended to refrain from making unrealistic claims. This, in turn, reduced the likelihood of unnecessary disputes.

Conclusions

In sum, the DRA system is a bundle of ADR methods, involving the DRA as a neutral advisor, followed by a meeting of the parties' senior executives in the event the DRA fails to resolve the dispute, and a subsequent short-form arbitration, if required. The role of the DRA is mainly advisory and facilitative, not adjudicative. The DRA's decision is not binding on the parties. The DRA's authority does not undermine that of the professional consultant on the project. The DRA helps build flexibility into the system and the various relationships, and relaxes some of the rigidities imposed by the legal system.

In the two projects in which the DRA was tried out by ASD, the contractors found the system made their lives easier; the professional consultants found the system was, at least, an additional resource, be it managerial or otherwise; and the DRAs found the system useful to prevent and resolve disputes.

The Hong Kong government's consideration of the DRA system for all important construction projects with contract amounts above a certain sum is a welcome development. However, the DRA system can be expected to be further developed and to be adopted in the wider construction community in Hong Kong.

III. Construction Arbitration in The Netherlands

Arbitration in the Building Industry in The Netherlands

*by Etienne van Bladel**

In the words of the U.S. Supreme Court, arbitration is "an agreement to arbitrate before a specified tribunal, in effect, a specialized kind of forum-selection clause that posits not only the situs of suit but also the procedure to be used in resolving the dispute."[1] But this is not the only definition of arbitration. There are many other definitions of this subject.[2]

The use of arbitration in trade and business has expanded substantially and has become the norm for resolving commercial disputes. There are a number of reasons for this. First, the enormous increase in world trade since the Second World War. The second reason is the desire of the inter-national business community to have neutral and competent tribunals to decide their disputes. The third reason, the ease of enforcement, is more an advantage of international arbitration. Finally, an advantage of using arbitration in the international context is thought to be the avoidance of uncertainties of foreign litigation.[3]

Arbitration in the Netherlands has a long history. For many centuries it has been widely used for the settlement of a variety of disputes between states, state entities and private parties, and between private parties.[4] The general statutory regulation of arbitration is codified in chapter four of the Netherlands Arbitration Act 1986.[5] Dutch arbitration

---

* The author is a research fellow on arbitration law at the University of Utrecht, and is a paralegal at the law firm Van Zelm in Utrecht, where he deals primarily with arbitration issues in the construction industry.

[1] Scherk v. Alberto-Culver Co., 417 U.S. 506, 519 (1974).

[2] See O. GLOSSNER, COMMERCIAL ARBITRATION IN THE FEDERAL REPUBLIC OF GERMANY (1984). An arbitration agreement is a contract between two or more parties for settlement of disputes over the interpretation of a contract; G. BORN, INTERNATIONAL COMMERCIAL ARBITRATION IN THE UNITED STATES (1995). Domestic arbitration is a means by which a dispute can be definitively resolved, pursuant to the parties voluntary agreement by a disinterested, non-governmental decision-maker.

[3] See BROWN AND MARRIOTT, ADR PRINCIPLES AND PRACTICE 50 (1993).

[4] Id.

[5] *Arbitration,* paragraphs 1020-1076 of the *Wetboek van Burgerlijke Rechtsvordering.*

law leaves the parties much autonomy. Only a few provisions cannot be waived by agreement.

Commercial arbitration is extensively practiced in the Netherlands. Utrecht constitutes the biggest arbitration center, with 800 construction arbitration cases per year. Other areas where trade and commodity associations and chambers of commerce operate, such as Rotterdam and Amsterdam, also have a well-developed arbitration practice. Most of these arbitration institutions have their own arbitration rules.

The Form of Agreement

There are two kinds of agreements in arbitration: those which refer an existing dispute to arbitration, and those which relate to disputes which may arise in the future.[6] Agreements which refer to existing disputes are called compromise or submission agreements. An agreement which refers to disputes which may arise in the future is called an arbitration clause.[7] Both forms of agreement must be proven in writing.[8] By virtue of Article 1021, it is possible that both parties are bound by an arbitration clause as a result of their acceptance of the conformation by the intermediary.[9] The definitions mentioned above contain the essential features of arbitration: it rests on an agreement between the parties. There can be no arbitration proper without an arbitration agreement.[10] The courts have limited jurisdiction if the parties have entered into a valid arbitration agreement.[11] Although the court has wide statutory powers, its instinct is to use them only to support the arbitration, not to interfere with it.[12]

Arbitration can be either institutional or *ad hoc*. The business world has long recognized the need to overcome delays and other impediments to the settlement of commercial disputes.[13] It has resorted to an organized

---

[6] *See* article NAI Arbitration Rules: The agreement by which parties bind themselves to submit to arbitration an existing dispute between them or disputes which may arise between them in the future out of a defined legal relationship.

[7] Old French and Belgian arbitration law only knew the arbitration agreement after a dispute had arisen.

[8] In Article 1020 of the Netherlands Arbitration Act you will find these two terms.

[9] *See*, for example, A.J. VAN DEN BERG AND R. VAN DELDEN., NETHERLANDS ARBITRATION LAW 35-38 (1993).

[10] Brown, *supra* note 3, at 56.

[11] *See* Article 1022 *Burgerlijke Rechtsvordering*.

[12] *See* M.J. MUSTILL & S.C. BOYD, COMMERCIAL ARBITRATION, 5.

[13] *See* M. DOMKE, DOMKE ON COMMERCIAL ARBITRATION, 13 (1993).

form of arbitration by creating arbitration facilities within many business organizations. Institutional arbitration is therefore arbitration conducted according to the rules of a specified institution which may, to a greater extent, exercise a supervisory and supportive role over an arbitration conducted pursuant to its rules.[14] The best-known arbitration institutions in the Netherlands are the court of arbitration for the building industry (the court) and the Netherlands Arbitration Institute.

These institutions have promulgated sets of procedural rules that apply where parties have agreed to arbitration pursuant to such rules.[15] Among other things, institutional rules set out the basic procedural framework and timetable for the arbitration process.[16] The institutions themselves do not consider the merits of the parties' dispute. This is the responsibility of the particular individuals selected by the parties or by the institutions as arbitrators. Both institutions charge an administrative fee for rendering various services. The advantage of arbitral institutions for private parties is that the institute can provide considerable practical assistance during the procedure, particularly if a person defaults or delays the conduct of the arbitration process. An important role of the institution is the supervision of the award with particular reference to enforceability. *Ad hoc* arbitration is non-institutional arbitration which may or may not apply institutional rules and procedures.[17] If institutional rules are used, it is without the supervision of any institution.[18]

Both above-mentioned forms of arbitration have their advantages, but also their disadvantages. Automatic incorporation of a set of rules is one of the principal advantages of institutional arbitration. Another advantage is that most arbitral institutions provide trained staff to conduct arbitration proceedings. Institutional arbitration is conducted according to a standing set of procedural rules and is supervised, to a greater or lesser extent, by professional staff.[19] The major disadvantage is

---

[14] Brown, *supra* note 3, at 76.
[15] *See* G. BORN, *supra* note 2, at 10.
[16] *See* Art. 10-19 of the Statutes of the Court, *and* Art. 1042 of the rules of the Netherlands Arbitration Institute.
[17] The exact phrasing of the arbitration clause is very important in this situation, especially with reference to such procedures as the appointment of arbitrators, the designation of place of the arbitration, and the applicable law.
[18] *See* G. BORN, *supra* note 2, at 11.
[19] *See* G. BORN, *supra* note 2, at 11. The growing size and sophistication of the international arbitration and the legal framework for international arbitration, has reduced somewhat the benefits of the international institutional arbitrations.

that institutional arbitration tends to be very expensive and that there are the inevitable delays because of the bureaucratic machinery.[20] One big advantage of *ad hoc* arbitration is that it may be adapted to meet the wishes of parties and the facts of any particular dispute. The disadvantage is that it depends for full effectiveness upon the spirit of cooperation between the parties and their lawyers, backed up by an adequate legal system.[21] It is therefore easy to delay arbitral proceedings by asking questions about procedural matters.[22]

Advantages of Arbitration

The reasons why arbitration is resorted to are manifold, and fall into seven categories. To get a better perception of the advantages it is important to outline the arbitration procedure.[23]

1. Speedy Settlement

A trial before a national court must be conducted in accordance with the rules of that court. These rules are usually detailed and will have been established over a long period, and therefore arbitration is quicker than litigation.[24] It takes months and sometimes years before the case can be brought before a court. It is obvious that this judicial delay is damaging for trade where quick access to money is required. In judicial proceedings it takes time before the court hearing can begin; a hearing is generally more quickly arranged in arbitration procedures.

2. Costs

The cost of arbitration is a frequent subject for discussion. A full outline of these discussions would be well beyond the scope of this work.

---

[20] *See* A. REDFERN AND M. HUNTER, LAW AND PRACTICE OF INTERNATIONAL COMMERCIAL ARBITRATION, 55 (1991).

[21] *See* for a further discussion about the advantages and disadvantages of the institutions and *ad hoc* arbitration, A. GOLDSTAJN, CHOICE OF INTERNATIONAL ARBITRATORS, ARBITRAL TRIBUNALS AND CENTRES: LEGAL AND SOCIOLOGICAL ASPECTS, 32-33.

[22] Redfern, *supra* note 20, at 57.

[23] *See*, for a more detailed schedule, D. Sharp, *Applying Management Principles to Arbitration*, 62 J.CHARTERED INST. ARB. No. 1, 8 (1996).

[24] *Id.* at 23.

Parties generally have to pay the arbitrators for their services, whereas court fees are at present merely nominal.[25] The costs of the judicial procedure are limited to the summons, the listing of the case, court fees, and registration costs.[26] But in many cases the arbitrator can substantially reduce the party-incurred costs because of his ability to control the preparations, by means of the variety of procedures open to him, and because he is likely to be experienced in arbitrations of this kind.[27] This makes arbitration much faster than litigation. Furthermore, arbitration will seldom result in an appeal since the costs could escalate, because more arbitrators would be involved.[28] Arbitration can be cheaper than litigation in several circumstances. For example, the arbitrator is technically qualified, and specialist lawyers are involved, and between them they can narrow down the issue and shorten both the preparation and the hearing time to such an extent that the overall costs are lower than if the matter had been taken to court.[29]

3. A More Competent Judge

Arbitrators may be chosen for their special skills and expertise in commercial law, civil engineering, or some other relevant discipline. The arbitrator verifies the situation by hearing the parties and witnesses and obtains a comprehensive overview of the situation by making inspections, controls, and calculations. In this way important factual elements are recorded while they are still fresh.[30] An experienced arbitral forum should be able to quickly grasp the salient issues of fact or law and thus save parties both time and money. If the arbitrator is a technical rather than a legal arbitrator and is an expert in the field in which the dispute has arisen, evidence before him should, and in most cases will, take a different form from the evidence given before a judge.[31] The wish to have disputes settled by professional experts explains the success of arbitration.

---

[25] *See, for a more detailed outline concerning the costs of an arbitration procedure*: M. O'REILLY, COSTS IN ARBITRATION PROCEEDINGS *and* RUSSELL, ON THE LAW OF ARBITRATION (1995).
[26] *See* H. VAN HOUTTE, THE LAW OF INTERNATIONAL TRADE, 412 (1995).
[27] Redfern, *supra* note 20, at 11.
[28] Article 23 of the statutes from the court gives each party the right to appeal.
[29] *See, e.g.* R. BERNSTEIN, HANDBOOK OF ARBITRATION PRACTICE, 11-12 (1993).
[30] *See* M. RUBINO-SAMMARTANO, INTERNATIONAL ARBITRATION LAW 10 (1990).
[31] Bernstein, *supra* note 29, at 10-11.

4. Confidential Settlement

A major advantage is that parties can arbitrate with full confidentiality. They are able to keep certain facts secret from competitors, customers, and the public in general, such as trade secrets and know-how, defects of goods and financial losses or difficulties of the enterprise.[32] The confidentiality of the arbitration is under threat when the award is later discussed in court for an enforcement procedure. Furthermore, the arbitration institute could be entitled to publish its findings.[33]

5. Informal Settlement

Arbitrations are less formal and more flexible than court proceedings. It is also less formal because both lawyers and arbitrators do not wear gowns. The justice system is based on a number of principles and rules which of course must be praised, but which may be objectionable under the circumstances of a particular case. Parties wish to develop their arguments using common language. Furthermore, parties are able to agree on how the matter should proceed.[34] Therefore, this informal atmosphere enhances the chance of an amicable settlement.

6. Amiable Composition

The power of amiable composition has been defined in a variety of ways: "Arbitrators are not bound by legal formalities," and "Arbitrators shall settle the dispute according to their knowledge and understanding."[35] This concept is originally French.[36] Most legal systems require that the parties confer the power to act as amiable compositeur by express agreement, or that the power must be inferred unequivocally from the parties' [37] submission. Absent such agreement, the parties are

---

[32] R. DAVID, ARBITRATION IN INTERNATIONAL TRADE 12 (1985).
[33] Article 18.4 from the statutes of the court.
[34] M. STEVENSON, JUDGES AND ARBITRATORS ARE THEY MEETING THE NEEDS OF COMMERCIAL MEN?, 115.
[35] Brown, *supra* note 3, at 64. *See also* HILL, REFERENCE AND FINDING TOOLS: "An arbitrator is authorized and required by the arbitration agreement to decide according to equity and good conscience, rather than the strict rule of law. He is distinguished from other arbitrators in that he is permitted to decide *ex acquo et bono*."
[36] This concept is unknown in common law systems.
[37] An amiable composition clause: "The arbitrator shall be entitled to act as amiable composition." Such clauses are called equity clauses.

presumed to have agreed to regular arbitration.[38] Court Article 18(1) states: "The arbitral tribunal shall decide *ex aequo et bono*, unless parties have agreed otherwise, and by a majority vote." Often amiable composition is chosen when parties feel that the international or technical character of the contractual relationship is too complicated for substantive laws to resolve. These amiable composition clauses are best reserved for transactions where the parties are contracting for a long relationship in which the maintenance of commercial trust between the parties is reasonably assured.[39]

7. A Binding Award

The arbitrator has the power to grant an award by consent. The arbitral award is final and the parties are deemed to have undertaken to carry out the resulting award without delay and to have waived their right to any form of appeal insofar as such waiver can be validly made.[40] Once the arbitrator has expressed a decision, he ceases to have further jurisdiction over that matter and is *functus officio*.[41]

The Court of Arbitration for the Building Industry in The Netherlands

This court, established in 1907, is an organization in the form of a foundation under Dutch law, and has its seat in Amsterdam. The purpose of the court is the settlement of disputes in the sphere of the building industry. The role of this court is to examine the merits of the case and render a final award. There exists a list with the names of the possible arbitrators. This list presently contains some seventy arbitrators.[42] Its governing board consists of representatives from the royal institute of engineers (K.I.V.I.), the royal society for the promotion of architecture, the confederation of Dutch architects (B.N.A.), and the association of the

---

[38] *See* Article 1045(3) which states: "The arbitral tribunal shall decide as amiable compositeur if parties have by agreement authorized it to do so.
[39] Brown, *supra*, note 12, at 77.
[40] *Id.* at chapter I G.
[41] *See* D. TURNER, BUILDING CONTRACT DISPUTES: THEIR AVOIDANCE AND RESOLUTION, 56 (1988).
[42] Article 4 states: "20 member-engineers shall be nominated by the executive committee of the K.I.V.I., 20 member architects by the executive committee of the B.N.A., and 20 member-builders by the executive committee of the A.V.B.B."

general confederation for the building industry (A.V.B.B.).[43] There are at least ten (and at most twenty) member lawyers on the above-mentioned list, called "extraordinary members."[44] The court must remain constantly alert to changes in the law and practice of arbitration worldwide and adapt its working methods to answer the various needs of the parties as well as those of the arbitrators. Therefore, the court is assisted by a permanent secretariat of some eleven lawyers for the day-to-day management of cases.[45]

To start the arbitral procedure parties must properly define their dispute and explain it in writing and send it to the court. Both parties will then receive a list with names of possible arbitrators. Each party has fourteen days to examine the list and submit in writing to the chairman the names of those favored for appointment as members of the arbitral tribunal.[46] Should the claim be exclusively for the payment of a sum of money amounting in total to more than Dfl. 65.000,00 the arbitral tribunal shall comprise three arbitrators.[47] When the court is requested to intermediate, the chairman shall call upon the petitioners to deposit a sum of money.[48] Each party shall have the power to demand that, of the three arbitrators, one is an extraordinary member. The lawyers mentioned in Article 9 of the statutes shall be attached *ex officio* to the arbitral tribunal and shall play an advisory role. An oral hearing is the usual procedure at this court. Besides this oral hearing, the arbitrator has the power to inspect the property at any time. The parties shall be given the opportunity to be present at the inspection.[49] Site visits are very helpful especially in complicated construction matters. Article 18 (2 & 3) of the statutes affords the arbitrator two significant varieties of settlement. First, there is the arbitral award and, second, the binding advice (*bindend advies*).[50] Article 23 of the statutes gives each party the

---

[43] *See* article 2 of the statutes of the court.
[44] *Id.* at article 3.
[45] *Id.* at article 9.
[46] *Id.* at article 10 (3).
[47] Unless both parties request adjudication by one arbitrator. *See* Article 10 (8) of the statutes.
[48] *Id.* at Article 15.
[49] The arbitral tribunal is empowered to do all that it deems necessary in order to achieve a good outcome to the proceedings. *See* Article 32 of the Arbitration Rules of the Netherlands Arbitration Institute.
[50] For discussions of these settlements *see* F. Knoopeler & P. Schweizer, *Making of Awards and the Termination of Proceedings*, *in* INT'L COMMERCIAL ARB., 160-177 (1989).

right to lodge an appeal against the award by the court. This possibility has existed since 1987 at the court.

At the court, parties can choose between three different procedures. First there is the "regular-track arbitration" described in Articles 10 to 19 of the statutes. Second, there is the "fast-track arbitration" described in Article 20 of the statutes. With this fast-track procedure, Articles 10 to 19 must also be taken in consideration. Third, parties may opt to request interim measures (summary arbitral procedure), in accordance with Article 20 (1) of the statutes and article 1051 of the Wetboek van Burgerlijke Rechtsvordering.[51] Summary arbitral proceedings are to be distinguished from fast-track arbitrations which are arbitrations conducted within short periods of time. Fast-track arbitration is like regular arbitration and takes a decision on the merits of a case.[52]

The Parties

All persons who have the capacity to conclude a settlement concerning the subject matter can enter into an arbitration agreement. The state, or state entities, may also resort to arbitration, both with nationals or with foreigners, under the same conditions as those that apply to private parties.

1. Clients

Conflicting parties often resort to arbitration in order, inter alia, to avoid in theory the headache of litigation.[53]

Construction clients all want the right building, at the right time, and for the right price. The response of the industry to clients as a whole shows first of all in a structure that has evolved over the decades. There are design consultants, cost consultants, contractors, subcontractors, and suppliers. Such a structure may make the flow of activities and

---

[51] Article 1051 of the *wetboek van Burgerlijke Rechtsvordering* states: "Parties may agree to empower the arbitral tribunal or its chairman to render an award in summary proceedings, within the limits imposed by article 289. Article 289 provides that summary proceedings are admissible if a case requires immediate injunctive relief.

[52] For further details about the Netherlands Arbitration Act 1986 *see* the article by P. Sanders and A.J. van den Berg, *The Netherlands Arbitration Act 1986, Text and Notes* (1986).

[53] *See* S.A. Hejailan, *The Prearbitral Phase: Matters Affecting the Arbitral Award*, INT'L COUNCIL FOR COMMERCIAL ARB., 53.

information more tortuous than a single operation might necessitate.[54] In construction practice, it frequently happens that the contracts between clients and contractors contain a reference to the standard conditions, called the U.A.V. (Uniform Administrative Conditions for the execution of works 1989). Article 49 of the U.A.V. states:

> Any dispute whatsoever which may arise between the employer and the contractor... shall be settled by arbitration with the rules defined in the regulation of the court of arbitration for the building industry in the Netherlands.[55]

The most important article according to Van den Berg is Article 1039 of the Wetboek van Burgerlijke Rechtsvordering.[56] This states: "Parties shall be treated with equality." The arbitrator should give each party an opportunity to deal with every relevant point. This does not require the arbitrator to listen to the endless speeches, but it does oblige him to act fairly and properly if he wishes to cut short the agreement.

2. Arbitrators

Justice must be seen to be beyond all suspicion as to the independence and impartiality of the judges.[57] This basic principle of justice in the courts is no less fundamental in the case of justice administered by an arbitral tribunal.[58] Any natural person of legal capacity can be appointed as an arbitrator.[59] In 1624, Rastell gave an excellent definition of an arbitrator: "An arbitrator is a disinterested person, to whose judgment and decision matters in dispute are referred."[60] It is often said that arbitration is only as good as the

---

[54] Turner, *supra*, note 41, at 3-5.
[55] For further details about U.A.V. in general see Slagter, *U.A.V., Bouwrecht,* 153-158 (1989).
[56] Article 1039 of the *Wetboek van Burgerlijke Rechtsvordering* states: "The parties shall be treated with equality. The arbitral tribunal shall give each party an opportunity to substantiate and to present his case."
[57] *See also* the IBA (International Bar Association) rules, and the AAA (the American Arbitration Association) and ABA (American Bar Association) rules of ethics for international arbitrators.
[58] This is sometimes referred to as "natural justice."
[59] David, *supra*, note 32, at 252.
[60] Brown, *supra*, note 3, at 56.

arbitrator. An arbitrator is neither more nor less than a private judge of a private court who gives a private judgment. He gives a decision in accordance with his duty to hold the scales fairly between the disputants in accordance with some recognized system of law and the rules of natural justice.[61] An arbitrator is the master of his own procedure.[62] Many arbitrators take the view that an arbitrator's function is to listen to the evidence and arguments and to intervene as little as possible, leaving the conducting of the case to the parties or their advocates. At the court there is a minimal requirement as to who may be an arbitrator.[63] The arbitrator must have some knowledge of the construction trade. The court also provides training facilities to assist arbitrators in fulfilling those qualifications.[64]

3. Secretary

The court shall arrange for the presence of a lawyer who acts as the secretary to the tribunal.[65] A secretary who may be engaged by an arbitral tribunal can be useful in larger cases in which the sole arbitrator or all arbitrators are not lawyers. As in practice, he may have great influence on proceedings and the drafting of the award, and he should be subject to the same requirement of impartiality and independence as applies to an arbitrator.[66] The secretary will assist the arbitrators in drawing up the award or awards made in the course of the arbitration.

4. Lawyers

What lawyers should be engaged in is problem-solving with a minimum of cost and trauma.[67] For most construction lawyers arbitration

---

[61] *See* above RUSSELL ON THE LAW OF ARBITRATION 106 (1995).
[62] Stated by Justice Goff in Carlisle Place Investments Ltd. v. Wimpey Construction (UK) Ltd., 15 Build L.R. 109 (1980).
[63] For a brief discussion of qualities and aptitudes see; A. Shilston, *Choosing an Arbitrator*, J. CHARTERED INST. ARB., vol. 61, no. 4, pp. 235-237.
[64] In England it is necessary to become a member of the Institute of Arbitrators, and to pass an examination under the control of the Institute.
[65] Article 13 of the statutes.
[66] Shilston, *supra* note 63.
[67] *See* Lord A. Weedon QC, *Training Lawyers–Healers or Hired Guns*, 61 J.CHARTERED INST. ARB. No. 4, 239 (1995).

is a consensual process. The construction lawyers are generally motivated to settle the dispute by negotiations. In the vast majority of cases, these negotiations eventually result in cases being settled by way of compromise, only a relatively small minority of cases actually proceed to trial and judgment. A construction lawyer must have, besides knowledge of the law and the U.A.V., some technical construction knowledge. In a complicated technical claim with substantial amounts of money at stake, with difficult points of law, and possibly difficult facts to collate and prove, the sooner the lawyers are involved in the process, the more efficient it will be.[68]

Conclusion

The growing enthusiasm for arbitration demonstrates that this is the direction that history is taking. The combined efforts of parties, the secretary, and arbitrators remain without any doubt the best ways to meet the challenges arising from arbitration proceedings. The advantages and disadvantages of arbitration must be taken seriously, if arbitration, proud of its progress in recent times, is not to suffer inevitable setbacks in the future.

---

[68] In England, the exclusion of lawyers from arbitration hearings is usually restricted to proceedings of certain trade associations. The issues before the tribunal in such arbitrations are mainly factual, frequently simply going to the quality or quantity of the commodity in question. Legal issues are few. Where factual issues have to be disposed of, the role of a lawyer is limited. There is a fear that lawyers add to the complexity, length, and expense of the arbitration.

INDEX

(*References are to page numbers*)

A

AAA CONSTRUCTION INDUSTRY ARBITRATION RULES
Postponement requests, arbitrator considerations, 41-42

AAA'S DISPUTE AVOIDANCE AND RESOLUTION TASK FORCE (DART)
Guide to partnering, 129-38

ADJUDICATION
Comparison to DRBs (dispute resolution boards), 290-92
Development of process in England, 288-89

ADR (ALTERNATIVE DISPUTE RESOLUTION) IN THE CONSTRUCTION INDUSTRY. *See* CONSTRUCTION DISPUTES AND ADR

ADVISORY DISPUTE REVIEW BOARDS
Boston Central Artery Tunnel Project (CA/T Project), 103-10

A/E FIRMS (ARCHITECT AND ENGINEER FIRMS)
Claims prevention, 54-61
Top claims preventers and starters, 62-64

AIA DOCUMENTS COMMITTEE
Arbitration, demands for, 21-22
Architect, submission of claims to, 19-20
Insurance, avoiding disputes, 23
Job site safety, avoiding disputes, 22
Mediation, demands for, 21-22
Payment for change orders, avoiding disputes, 23
Substitutions, avoiding disputes, 22
Termination for convenience, avoiding disputes, 23

AMERICAN INSTITUTE OF ARCHITECTS (AIA)
See also AIA DOCUMENTS COMMITTEE
Standard form A-201, 1997 revision, 19-24

ARBITRATION
Demands for under revised A-201, 21-22
Drafting clauses, dangers in, 171-73
Effective construction arbitration advocacy tips, 175-77
Explanatory awards, guidelines to writing, 187-94
  Editing, 193
  Parts of the award, 189
  Preparation and drafting, 190-93
  Reasoned award, definition, 188-89
  Stylistic tips, 193

Hybrid ADR, 35-36
Industry guidelines for avoiding and resolving disputes, 73
Pre-arbitration litigation, 183-85
Tips on avoiding, 185-86

ARBITRATORS
Duty to disclose, 39
Large, complex case management techniques for
   Applicability to arbitration proceedings, 276
   Pre-trial judicial management techniques, 273-75
   Revised AAA Rules, 272-73
Postponement requests, 41-42
Selection, 179-81

ARCHITECT
Architect and engineer firms. *See* A/E FIRMS
Claims submitted to, standard form A-201, 19-20
Design, role in merchant housing projects, 44
Neutral, use in merchant housing projects, 43-49

B

BUSINESS ROUNDTABLE
Construction cost influence curve, 2
Construction industry and ADR, 1

C

CLAIMS PREVENTION
Architects and engineers, top claims preventers and starters, 62-64

Full construction contract administration services, 60-61
Identifying and managing project risk, 51-64
Implementable contracts, 59-60
Lawyers, steps for, 61-62
Study of what precipitates construction claims
   Background, 52-53
   Factors important to a project's success, 55-59
   Findings, 54
   Firm stability, 57-58
   Owner's role, 56-57
Top claims preventers and starters, 62-64

CONSEQUENTIAL DAMAGES
Waivers of, 83-86

CONSTRUCTION DISPUTES AND ADR
Advisory arbitration, 14
   Submission of an existing dispute to, 14
American Subcontractors Association (ASA), guidelines for avoiding and resolving disputes, 71-74
Arbitration, 14-16
   Guidelines for avoiding and resolving disputes, 73
   Hybrid ADR, 35-36
   Standard pre-dispute arbitration clause, 16
   Submission of an exiting dispute to, 16
Associated General Contractors of America (AGC), guidelines for avoiding and resolving disputes, 71-74

INDEX

Associated Specialty Contractors (ASC), guidelines for avoiding and resolving disputes, 71-74
Claims prevention. *See* CLAIMS PREVENTION
Consequential damages, waiver of, 83-86
Construction contributions to ADR, 2-3
Construction industry, applicability, 1-49
Cost influence curve, 4
Design-build contracts. *See* DESIGN-BUILD CONTRACTS
Development of ADR systems, 3-5
Dispute avoidance, industry guidelines for, 71-74
Dispute resolution boards. *See* DISPUTE RESOLUTION BOARDS
Dispute resolution systems, 4
   Elements of, basic principles, 17-18
   Industry guidelines for avoiding and resolution of disputes, 71-74
Dispute review board, 9-11
   Sample agreement for AAA Dispute Review Board, 11
   Standing arbitration panel, 11
Duty to disclose, arbitrators, 39
Expert's advisory opinion, 13
Fact-based mediation, 13-14
Guideline on the Avoidance and Resolution of Construction Disputes, 71-74
Hybrid ADR, 25-38
   Arbitration, 35-36
   Mediated contract negotiation hybrid, 37-38
   Mediation, 33-35

Mediation/Umpire hybrid, 36
Partnering, 25-33
RegNeg, 25
Identifying risk to contain claims, 51-64
Industry guidelines for avoiding and resolving disputes, 71-74
Insurance, Form A-201, 23
International construction dispute resolution. *See* INTERNATIONAL CONSTRUCTION DISPUTE RESOLUTION
Job-site safety, A-201, 22
Management of disputes, 4
Managing risk to contain claims, 51-64
Mediated contract negotiation hybrid, 37-38
Mediation, 12
   Hybrid ADR, 33-35
Mediation/Umpire hybrid, 36
Mini-trails, 13
Negotiation, 5, 8-9
   Sample good faith negotiation specification, 8-9
   Sample step negotiation specification, 9
Negotiation-Mediation, 12
Negotiation-Mediation-Arbitration, 12
Partnering, 7
   See also PARTNERING
   Covenant of good faith and fair dealing, 7
   Hybrid ADR, 25-33
   Management of construction disputes and. *See* PARTNERING, Management of construction disputes and

Sample partnering specifications, 7
Voluntary partnership, 7
Payment for change orders, Form A-201, 23
Postponement requests, 41-42
Prevention strategies, 65-70
   ADR clauses, 69
   Assumptions, 68
   Contract disputes, reasons for, 65-66
   Drafting time, 67-68
   Fair contract, 69
   Low margin bids, avoidance, 67
   Preliminary project evaluation, preparation, 66
   Team approach, 67
   Transition from negotiation to execution, 70
Prevention techniques, 5
Principles for an effective construction dispute resolution system, 17-18
RegNeg, hybrid ADR, 25
Scope, 1-2
Spectrum of techniques, 5
   Lawyers, 6
   Mediation, 6, 12
   Mini-trials, 6, 13
   Negotiation, 5
   Outside consultants, 6
   Prevention techniques, 5
   Standing neutral concept, 5
   Third party binding decision, 6
Stair-step sequential model, 5
Substitutions, Form A-201, 22
Systems design, 4
Waivers of consequential damages, 83-86

CONSTRUCTION INDUSTRY INSTITUTE (CII)
Construction cost influence curve, 2
Construction industry and ADR, 1
"Continental Divide", 6

CIVIL ENGINEERS
ADR, use of, 2

CONTRACTORS
ADR, use of, 2

COSTS
"Continental Divide", 6
Escalating, 6

D

DESIGN-BUILD CONTRACTS
Tailoring agreements to avoid and resolve conflicts, 75-82
   Avoiding disputes within the design-build team, 81-82
   Avoiding owner-design-builder disputes, 78-81
   Dispute resolution, 76-77
   What is design-build? 75-76

DISPUTE RESOLUTION BOARDS (DRBs)
AAA Guide Specifications, 87
   Drafters, tips for, 92
AAA Protocol for, 87-94
Adjudication process, comparison to, 287-92
Advisory Dispute Review Boards, Boston Central Artery Tunnel Project (CA/T Project), 103-110
Anomalies and concerns, 98

Benefits of, 95
Comparison to adjudication process, 287-92
Characteristics of, 101-02
Description of process, 96-98
Development of, 288
Operations, 91
Panel and selection procedures, 89-90
Real time solutions, using for, 95-102
Recommendations, admissibility, 100
Resources provided by AAA, 87
  Guide Specifications, 87
  Roster of experienced panelists, 87
  Three-party agreement, 87
Role outside the construction industry, 100
Three-party agreement, 87, 91-92

DISPUTES, AVOIDANCE OF
See CONSTRUCTION DISPUTES AND ADR, Prevention strategies

DUTY TO DISCLOSE
Arbitrators, 39

E

ENGLAND, CONSTRUCTION DISPUTE RESOLUTION IN
Development of adjudication, 288-89
Development of DRBs (dispute resolution boards) in the U.S., 288
Differences between adjudication and DRBs, 290-92

Housing Grants, Construction and Regeneration Act of 1996 (HGCRA), 289

F

FACILITATION
Hybrid ADR, 25

G

GUIDELINES ON THE AVOIDANCE AND RESOLUTION OF CONSTRUCTION DISPUTES
Arbitration, 73
Nonbinding alternative dispute resolution methods, 72-73

H

HONG KONG, CONSTRUCTION DISPUTE RESOLUTION IN
DRA (Dispute Resolution Advisors) system, 293-98
  Features and operation of, 294-95
  Impact upon parties, 296-97
  Rationale behind, 293-294
  Views of participants, 296

HYBRID ADR
Use in construction disputes. *See* CONSTRUCTION DISPUTES AND ADR, Hybrid ADR

I

INTERNATIONAL CONSTRUCTION DISPUTE RESOLUTION

Hong Kong, DRA (Dispute Resolution Advisors) system, 293-98
   Features and operation of, 294-95
   Impact upon parties, 296-97
   Rationale behind, 293-294
   Views of participants, 296
Netherlands, construction arbitration in, 299-310
   Arbitration advantages, 302-05
      Amiable composition, 304-05
      Binding award, 305
      Confidential settlement, 304
      Costs, 302-03
      Informal settlement, 304
      More competent judge, 303
      Speedy settlement, 302
   Court of Arbitration for the Building Industry in the Netherlands, 305-07
   Forms of agreements, 300-02
   Parties
      Arbitrators, 308-09
      Clients, 307-08
      Lawyers, 308-10
      Secretary, 309
U.S. and English systems, 287-92
   Development of adjudication, 288-89
   Development of DRBs, 288
   Differences between adjudication and DRBs, 290-92

L

LARGE, COMPLEX CASE MANAGEMENT

AAA Rule L-4 governing preliminary hearings
   Overview, 259-60
   Rule L-4(a) and (b), 260-62
Arbitrators, techniques for
   Applicability to arbitration proceedings, 276
   Pre-trial judicial management techniques, 273-75
   Revised AAA Rules, 272-73
Case management techniques, use of, 262-63
For arbitrators, 271-76
Difficulties, arising of, 266-67
Management plan, creation of, 263-65
Mediation, effective techniques in complex multiparty synthetic stucco cases, 281-85
Mediator selection, necessary knowledge and experience, 277-80
Milestone objectives, 265
Prototype preliminary hearing schedule, 267-69

M

MEDIATION

Attendees, 222
Caucuses, 215-16
Closure issues, 239-45
   Default, 243
   Monetary settlements, 242-43
   Proactive mediator, 243-44
   Settlement documents, 244-45
   Time-related claims, 241
   Work-completion claims, 240-41

Work-defect disputes, 241
Complex disputes, effective techniques in, 281-85
Confidentiality, 255-58
Court testimony, mediators, 255-58
Decision to mediate, 202-04
Demands for, revised A-201, 21-22
Effective advocacy in, 225-29
    Conciliation, 228-29
    Credibility, 227
    Discretion, 228
    Preparation, 226-27
    Persuasiveness, 227
Elements of, 205, 207-10
Evaluation, 218
Expert tips from AAA, 215-20
Experts, 217, 235-38
Finality, 214
Hybrid ADR, 25
Impasse, 217-18
Information exchange, 223
Insurance coverage, 216-17
Joint sessions, 215-16
Limitations of, 213
Litigators and, 231-33
Mediation session, 210-13
Mediator conduct, 250-53
Mediator confidentiality, 255-58
Mediator role, 219, 224
Mediator selection, 204-05, 222, 247-49
    Large, complex cases, necessary knowledge and experience, 277-80
Memorandum of Understanding (MOU), 244
Preparation for, 206-07
Procedures, 249-50
Process designer, use of, 222
Scheduling, 224

Settlement agreement, 219
Uniform Mediation Act (UMA), mediator testimony, 255-58
What is mediation? 201-02

N

NETHERLANDS, CONSTRUCTION ARBITRATION IN
Arbitration advantages, 302-05
    Amiable composition, 304-05
    Binding award, 305
    Confidential settlement, 304
    Costs, 302-03
    Informal settlement, 304
    More competent judge, 303
    Speedy settlement, 302
Court of Arbitration for the Building Industry in the Netherlands, 305-07
Forms of agreements, 300-02
Parties
    Arbitrators, 308-09
    Clients, 307-08
    Lawyers, 308-10
    Secretary, 309

NONBINDING ADR
Industry guidelines for avoiding and resolving disputes, 72-73

P

PARTNERING
AAA Dispute Avoidance and Resolution Task Force Guide to Facilitator selection, 135-37
Partnering key components, 135

Partnering process, 131-35
What is partnering? 130-31
Benefits of, 139-46
Dispute management program,
  construction disputes and
  partnering, 148
  Establishing partnering as
    basis for working
    relationship, 148
  Implementing program, 149
  Techniques, 150-56
Effective, 157-60
  After the workshop, 157-58
  Life of the project, 158-59
  When problems arise, 159
  When project ends, 160
Limitations of, 165-70
  Combining with other ADR
    tools, 167-68
  Improving the process, 166-67
  Inconsistencies with legal
    instruments, 168-70
Management of construction
  disputes and, 147-56
  Establishing partnering as
    basis for working
    relationship, 148
  Implementing a dispute
    management program, 149
  Techniques, 150-56
    Arbitration, 156
    Change-order management
      programs, 152-54
    Improved people skills, 151
    Mediation, 156
    Partnering, 151-52
    Standing neutrals, 155-56
    Total Quality project
      management, 150-51
    Win/win negotiation, 152
Partnering workshops, 142-44

Strategic risk plans, 145
  Follow-up sessions, 146
  Partnering during concept
    phase, 145
  Partnering during construction
    phase, 146
  Partnering during design
    phase, 145-46
Subcontracting, jurisdictional
  labor disputes and, 195-97
Team players as result of, 161-63
Tren Urbano project, San Juan,
  Puerto Rico, 140-42
Trust issues
  Barriers specific to
    construction industry
    Contract obligations and
      hierarchy, 120
    Time constraints, 121
  Barriers to building trust, 119
    Generalizations and role
      models, 120
    Interaction history, 119
    Social categorization, 120
  Benefits of trust, 113-14
  Building and restoring trust,
    121
    Action plans
      Active listening, 124-25
      Clear communication,
        124
      Consistent and
        predictable behavior,
        123
      For top management, 125
      Honesty, 123-24
      Share information, 125
    First steps, 121-23
  Decision whether to trust, 116
    Category-based trust, 117-18
    Dispositional trust, 116
    History-based trust, 117

INDEX

Role-based trust, 118-19
Third parties as conduits of trust, 117
Direct application method, 126
Enhanced strategies of partnering, 125-26
Executive/sponsor involvement, 126-27
Fairness and good faith, 115-16
Intervention partnering, 127
Trust dilemma, 113
Trust in the partnering process, 114-15
What is trust? 112

R

REGNEG
Hybrid ADR, 25

RISK MANAGEMENT
Managing project risk to contain claims. *See* CLAIMS PREVENTION

S

STANDARD FORM CONTRACTS
A-201 General Conditions of the Contract of Construction, 19-24

SUBCONTRACTING
Jurisdictional labor disputes and, 195-97

U

UNIFORM MEDIATION ACT (UMA)
Mediator testimony under, 255-58

UNITED STATES ARMY CORPS OF ENGINEERS
ADR, use of, 2

NOTE ON SOURCES

LISTED BELOW ARE THE AAA PUBLICATIONS FROM WHICH THE MATERIALS IN THIS WORK ORGIANALLY APPEARED.

Chapter One: ADR in the Construction Industry

I. The Broadened Scope of ADR in Construction Disputes

Alternative Dispute Resolution in the Construction Industry
By James P. Groton

(*Dispute Resolution Journal,* Summer, 1997 – Vol. 52:3)

II. American Institute of Architects (AIA) Expands the Use of ADR

Construction ADR at Its Best: The New AIA A-201 Document
By Howard G. Goldberg

(*ADR Currents,* March 1998 – Vol. 3:1)

III. Using Hybrid ADR Techniques in Construction Disputes

"Hybrid ADR" in the Construction Industry
By James H. Keil

(*Dispute Resolution Journal,* August 1999 – Vol. 54:3)

IV. The Duty to Disclose

Neutral Corner—The Duty to Disclose
By Neil Carmichael

(*Punch List,* Spring 1997 – Vol. 20:1)

V. Postponement Requests

Neutral Corner—Dealing with Postponement Requests
By Neil Carmichael

(*Punch List,* Summer 1997 – Vol. 20:2)

VI. Using a Neutral Architect
Dispute Resolution Using a Neutral Architect
By Jack Kemp

(*Punch List,* Winter 1997/98 – Vol. 20:4)

Chapter Two: Managing Risk and Avoiding Disputes

I. Identify and Manage Project Risk to Contain Claims
The Key to Claims-Free Projects—
Identifying and Managing Construction Project Risk
By Ava J. Abramowitz

(*ADR Currents,* September 1999 – Vol. 4:3)

II. Preventing Contract Disputes
Strategies to Prevent Construction Contract Disputes
By Luc Picard

(*Punch List,* February 2001 – Vol. 23:4)

III. Industry Guidelines for Avoiding and Resolving Construction Disputes
ASA/AGC/ASC Joint Guideline on the
Avoidance and Resolution of Construction Disputes
ASA/AGC/ASC

(*Punch List,* May 2000 – Vol. 23:1)

IV. Tailoring Design-Build Agreements to Avoid and Resolve Conflicts
Avoiding Disputes in the Design-Build Environment
By Michael C. Loulakis

(*Punch List,* August 2000 – Vol. 23:2)

V. Waivers of Consequential Damages
Negotiating Consequential Damages Waivers
By Charles M. Sink

(*Punch List,* August 2000 – Vol. 23:2)

NOTE ON SOURCES

Chapter Three: Dispute Resolution Boards

I. New AAA Protocol for Dispute Resolution Boards

A New Look at DRBs—AAA Offers New DRB Roster and Protocol
By Robert J. Smith & Robert A. Rubin

(*ADR Currents*, Dec. 2000 – Vol. 5:4)

II. Using Dispute Resolution Boards for Real Time Solutions

Dispute Review Boards: Resolving Construction Disputes in Real Time
By Robert J. Smith

(*ADR Currents*, Spring 1997 – Vol. 2:2)

III. Experience with Advisory Dispute Review Boards

Expanding the DRB's Role—The Boston Central Artery Tunnel Project's Experience with Advisory Dispute Review Boards
By Brison S. Shipley

(*Punch List*, August 1999 – Vol. 22:2)

Chapter Four: Partnering

I. The Importance of Trust in the Partnering Process

I Don't Trust You, But Why Don't You Trust Me? Recognizing the Fragility of Trust and Its Importance in the Partnering Process
By Jeffrey S. Busch & Nicole Hantusch

(*Dispute Resolution Journal*, August-October 2000 – Vol. 55:3)

II. AAA Task Force Guide to Partnering

Building Success for the 21st Century: A Guide to Partnering in the Construction Industry
Report of the Dispute Avoidance and Resolution Task Force of the American Arbitration Association

(*Dispute Resolution Journal*, January 1997 – Vol. 52:1)

III. The Benefits of Partnering
The Benefits of Partnering
By James H. Keil

(*Dispute Resolution Journal,* February 1999 – Vol. 54:1)

IV. Using Partnering to Manage Construction Disputes
Partnering and the Management of Construction Disputes
By Steve Pinnell

(*Dispute Resolution Journal,* February 1999 – Vol. 54:1)

V. Effective Partnering
Practical Tips for Effective Partnering
By Bruce Johnsen

Dispute Resolution Journal, February 1999 – Vol. 54:1)

VI. "Beware of Partnering"
Team Players-Not "Partners"!
"Partnering" Does Not Create "Partners"
By Robert S. Peckar

(*Punch List,* Summer 1997 – Vol. 20, #2

VII. The Limitations of Partnering
The Truth about Partnering—Limitations and Solutions
By Allen L. Overcash

(*Punch List,* August 1998 – Vol. 21:2)

Chapter Five: Arbitration
I. Drafting Arbitration Clauses
Dangers in Drafting the Arbitration Clause
By Stanley P. Sklar

(*Punch List,* August-October 2000 – Vol. 23:2)

NOTE ON SOURCES

   II. **Effective Construction Arbitration Advocacy**
Tips on Advocacy in Arbitration Before an Industry Arbitrator
By Jorge R. Cibran

(*Punch List*, May-July 2001 – Vol. 24:1)

  III. **Selecting an Arbitrator**
Unilateral Selection of the Arbitrator
By Robert J. MacPherson & Sarah B. Biser

(*Punch List*, August 1998 – Vol. 21:2)

  IV. **Avoiding Litigation over Arbitrability**
Removing Roadblocks to Arbitration
By Paul M. Lurie

(*Punch List*, May 1999 – Vol. 22:1)

   V. **Guidelines to Writing Explanatory Awards**
The ABCs of Writing a "Reasoned Award"
By James R. Holbrook

(*Punch List*, August-October 2002 – Vol. 25:2)

  VI. **Jurisdictional Labor Disputes and Subcontracting**
Between the Devil and the Deep Blue Sea—Subcontracting and Jurisdictional Labor Disputes
By Gregory R. Begg

(*Punch List*, February 2000 – Vol. 22:4)

Chapter Six: Mediation

    I. **Successful Mediation**
Recipe for Success in Construction Mediation
By John P. Madden

(*Dispute Resolution Journal*, May-July 2001 – Vol. 56:2)

II. **Tips for Better Mediation from the AAA**
Mediator Wisdom from the Experts
By James Acret
(*Punch List,* May 1998 – Vol. 21, #1)

III. **Using Procedure for Effective Mediation**
The Importance of Process Design to a Successful Mediation
By Paul M. Lurie
(*Punch List,* Winter 1996/97 – Vol. 19:4)

IV. **Effective Advocacy in Mediation**
Some Guidelines for Effective Advocacy in Mediation
By Howard D. Venzie, Jr.
(*Punch List,* Fall 1997 – Vol. 20:3)

V. **Litigators and Mediation**
Should Trial Counsel Represent the Client in Mediation?
By Robert Korn
(*Punch List,* Spring 1997 – Vol. 20:1)

VI. **Experts and Mediation**
The Expert's Role in Construction Mediation
By Richard Lamb
(*Punch List,* November 1998 – Vol. 21:3)

VII. **Closure Issues**
Closure Issues in Construction Mediation
By Howard D. Venzie, Jr.
(*Punch List,* November 2000-January 2001 – Vol. 23:3)

NOTE ON SOURCES

VIII. **Mediators Not Giving Participants What They Want**

Construction Attorneys' Mediation Preferences Surveyed—Is There a Gap between Supply and Demand?
By Dean B. Thomson

(*Punch List,* August-October 2001 – Vol. 24:2)

IX. **Mediator Confidentiality and Court Testimony**

Danger Looms for Mediation—Mediators Likely to Testify under UMA Draft
By Mark Appel

(*Punch List,* February-April 2001 – Vol. 23:4)

Chapter Seven: Large and Complex Case Management

I. **Managing the Preliminary Hearing under Rule L-4**

Management of the Preliminary Hearing under Construction Rule L-4 for Large, Complex Cases
By Anthony E. Battelle

(*Dispute Resolution Journal,* February 1999 – Vol. 54:1)

II. **Large-Case Management Techniques for Arbitrators**

Now Is the Time to Control the Big Case
By Allen L. Overcash

(*Punch List,* Fall 1996 – Vol. 19:3)

III. **Selecting a Mediator for a Complex Dispute**

Choosing the Right Mediator for a Complex Construction Dispute
By Joseph C. Malpasuto

(*Punch List,* May-July 2002 – Vol. 25:1)

IV. **Effective Mediation Techniques for Complex Cases**
Effective Mediation Techniques in Complex Multiparty Synthetic Stucco Cases
By C. Allen Gibson, Jr.
(*ADR Currents,* June-August 2000 – Vol. 5:2)

Chapter Eight: International Construction Dispute Resolution

I. **Strengths and Weaknesses of the U.S. and English Systems**
Comparing Dispute Review Boards and Adjudication
By James P. Groton, Robert A. Rubin & Bettina Quintas
(*Punch List,* May-July 2001 – Vol. 24:1)

II. **Dispute Resolution Advisors in Hong Kong**
The Dispute Resolution Advisor as an ADR Method in Hong Kong Construction Disputes
By John W.K. Luk & W.T. Wong
(*Punch List,* Fall 1996 – Vol. 19:3)

III. **Construction Arbitration in The Netherlands**
Arbitration in the Building Industry in The Netherlands
By Etienne van Bladel
(*Dispute Resolution Journal,* May 1999 – Vol. 54:2)